SOE's
BALLS OF
STEEL

SOE's BALLS OF STEEL

OPERATION RUBBLE, 147 WILLING VOLUNTEERS AND 25,000 TONS OF BALL BEARINGS

SOPHIE JACKSON

The History Press

Front cover illustrations supplied by iStockphoto. Back cover: Narvik
during the Second World War. (Wikimedia Commons)

First published 2013

The History Press
The Mill, Brimscombe Port
Stroud, Gloucestershire, GL5 2QG
www.thehistorypress.co.uk

British Library Cataloguing in Publication Data.
A catalogue record for this book is available from the British Library.

ISBN 978 0 7524 8756 4

Typesetting and origination by The History Press
Printed in Great Britain

CONTENTS

ACKNOWLEDGEMENTS

When I began this book I was aware that finding sources for information would be tricky, particularly as the men involved were largely merchant seamen and Norwegian. For that reason I have to thank Siri Holm Lawson, whose website warsailors.com has been an invaluable source for the Norwegian side of this story. Lawson's comprehensive work on the men and ships involved in Operation Performance, taken from Norwegian sources otherwise inaccessible to a British writer, has enabled me, for the first time, to present the story of the non-British volunteers who made George Binney's operations possible. Lawson has also kindly provided me with a number of images of the ships involved.

Newly released files from the National Archives have also been instrumental in forming a picture of those daring Scandinavian adventures. The perspectives of the British seamen involved came through in detailed reports and have helped to flesh out the human side of this story. In addition, the books by Marcus Binney and Peter Tennant have been invaluable in filling in the gaps and confirming the technical and legal details of the adventures. Lastly, a writer is always indebted to many sources, and my thanks go to those responsible for the many archives and books I scoured for odd references and personal stories during the writing of this story.

I

THROUGH SNOW AND ICE

The Swedish coast in winter can be a barren and bitterly cold place. It was January 1941 and the Bro Fjord, just off the Skagerrak strait, was thick with 6 inches of ice. The skies had been particularly clear and the scene was almost picturesque as crewmen from the various ships anchored in the fjord took the opportunity to stroll across the ice to neighbouring ships or to shore. If only the Nazi presence had not been such a constant worry in Swedish minds it could have been a peaceful situation.

The arrival of dozens of Norwegian merchant sailors in Sweden over the last few months had been an unpleasant reminder that Hitler was not opposed to invading a neutral country. Norway had been in Nazi clutches for under a year, but its people looked harassed and nervous, their morale broken. Few civilians onshore paid much heed to the sight of the depressed-looking Norwegians moving about the cargo ships, nor to the loading of those same vessels. Any curiosity they showed fell instead on the British crews who milled among the Swedish and Norwegian sailors. For many months now there had been an embargo on allowing any ship bound for Britain to leave the fjord. Hitler was anxious his enemies did not receive the vital iron cargo they had bought from Swedish mines and factories.

It was intended for use in the manufacture of weapons and armaments to fight the Nazi war machine. Sweden, caught in an unhappy position between the Allies it favoured and the Nazis it feared, had banned the export of the iron despite it already being paid for by British coin. Not wishing to use force on the British, the Swedish authorities had spun a web of legal complications as to why the cargo ships could not leave. A web Britain was busily trying to unravel.

All seemed quiet and usual as it began to snow at Bro Fjord. The restrictions were still – apparently – soundly in place. The few Swedes outdoors hurried home in the dark and cold, looking forward to their warm fires. A stillness fell over the port.

A short time before 3 p.m. an engine rumbled into life. The snow was falling heavily now and no one was watching as the slow and heavy cargo ship *Ranja* manoeuvred her way carefully, out of the ice and slowly inched into the Skagerrak. Even if she had been noticed ashore few would have been concerned; *Ranja* was carrying only salt water ballast.

A few minutes later more engines were rumbling into life. The cargo ship *John Bakke* pulled free from the ice and followed the *Ranja*; then the *Taurus*, piloted by her First Officer Carl Jensen, joined the convoy. Next was the *Elisabeth Bakke*, pulling from her icy berth to join the grand departure, and last to come was the *Tai Shan* commanded by her enthusiastic Swedish First Mate, H.A. Fallberg, who had been left in charge while her master was away. All were Norwegian vessels, but the Swedes would have been worried to know that three of them were being sailed by British captains, their Norwegian captains having been roughly removed for being 'uncooperative'.

They would have been even more disturbed to know that aboard the *Tai Shan* stood the representative to Sweden of the UK Ministry of Supply (Iron and Steel Control), Mr George Binney. Binney had been working tirelessly behind the scenes to convince the Swedish authorities to release the valuable iron cargo due for Britain. His presence on a Norwegian ship mysteriously vanishing into the gloom of a wintry afternoon would have raised warning flags for any Swedish authority who noticed him.

Binney had been working for months trying to find a way to secretly remove the embargoed iron from under the Swedish and, ultimately, German noses. Political, legal and even moral arguments had been presented both for and against the operation in British circles, but finally the pressing need for the supplies and the dogmatic refusal of help from the Swedish Government tipped the scales in Binney's favour. The 40-year-old Royal Naval Reserve commander and former Arctic explorer was only too elated to finally get some action. Diplomacy had been tiresome and unproductive; now Binney was heading an expedition to release what rightfully belonged to the British.

He knew the backlash from the Swedes and, even worse, from the Nazis would be dreadful. The possible reprisals had been weighed in the balance during the planning process and ultimately the gains had been considered to outrank the potential risks. Yet as Binney stood on deck of the *Tai Shan*, freshly shaved and wearing a clean shirt and his best blue suit, he knew that slipping out of the Bro Fjord was the easiest part of his operation. Soon they would be in the open Skagerrak strait and the Germans would endeavour to stop them.

OPERATION RUBBLE

At 5.45 p.m. the *Tai Shan* dropped off her pilot and Chief of the Gothenburg Harbour Police, Captain Ivar Blücker, at Lysekil. Blücker had been instrumental in the scheme and had earned Binney's respect and trust. Operating under his instructions from the Swedish Government to ensure their waters remained truly neutral, he had kept a close eye on proceedings and ensured no attempts at sabotage were made while the five Norwegian vessels were being loaded.

Blücker was painfully aware that every move Binney was making was being monitored by German agents and that the scale of the operation would prevent it ever being truly secret. Even so, he was determined to help the British as much as he could, volunteering to travel on the *Tai Shan* through Swedish waters to ensure she was not hampered by any opposition. When he stepped off at Lysekil it was dusk and visibility was barely 1½ miles. He watched the *Tai Shan* vanish into a new shower of snow, wondering if her crew and his new friend Binney would survive the coming German blockade.

The Nazis were inherently suspicious of Swedish neutrality and with good cause; they knew they were not terribly popular among the Scandinavian nations. Norway had already proved itself faulty when it came to honouring its neutrality equally among the warring nations – an excuse Hitler had used for invasion. Sweden was a slightly different prospect. Overrunning Sweden, like Hitler had done in Denmark and Norway, was never really on the cards after the invasion of France and Hitler's expansions across Europe had stretched Nazi manpower. But there were still the worries over Britain's iron supplies. Sweden was so far honouring its embargo, but there was nothing those dastardly British wouldn't try to get what they wanted. As an extra line of defence the Germans had created a blockade just outside neutral Swedish waters and regularly patrolled it to prevent just the sort of escapade Binney was masterminding.

Aboard the *Tai Shan* visibility had reduced to just ½ mile. The other ships in the flotilla from Bro Fjord were impossible to sight and, without any wireless communication, Binney could only assume they had left the Swedish coast successfully. Everyone (aside from the engineers on watch) was wearing life-jackets, anticipating the worst. If the Germans made a successful attack on them they had orders to scuttle the ship rather than let her cargo fall into Nazi hands. The night was dark and no one could sleep; instead, those who weren't needed below decks stood on deck scanning the waters for potential signs of danger. The night was perfect for German motor torpedo boats (MTBs) and at any moment it was expected the ships would come under attack.

There had been endless problems finding loyal crews for the five blockade-running vessels. Many of their original men had refused to sail due to German pressures and a general attitude among some of the Norwegians that it wasn't worth their while to help the British – this was a left-over grudge from the seeming lack of help the British had given during the Nazi invasion of Norway. Almost as fast as Binney and the few Norwegians loyal to him recruited crewmen they would leave and refuse to work on the ships. In desperation Binney had put together a reserve crew of British sailors who had been trapped in Sweden when the embargo was dropped and the Germans began the blockade. The ultimate result was that the engineers operating the *Tai Shan*'s engines were unfamiliar with the craft, and her Norwegian captain, Einar Isachsen, made the decision that there was no point trying to force extra speed from her when the men below were so unprepared. Instead they crept along at 13½ knots (*Tai Shan*'s top speed was 14 knots). In a short time the *Tai Shan* passed close enough to the *John Bakke* and *Ranja* to sight them through the darkness and snow, but they were unobserved. The Scandinavian night was so thick that it was impossible to see anyone until they were almost upon them. Just such a night had been chosen on purpose for the advantage it gave the British as they tried to evade the German blockade undetected, but it also meant a Nazi MTB could approach them without being spotted until it was too late.

As the night began to fade away the weather lifted, and by 4 a.m. the flash of two Norwegian lighthouses could be observed indicating, as the crews of the ships had hoped, that they were on course to sail down the Norwegian coastline. They were 28 miles south of the coast and awaiting the arrival of the aircraft of British Coastal Command to provide them with an escort for their daytime journey. But with each passing minute, with no planes in sight, it became clearer and clearer that an airborne escort was not coming. Captain Isachsen found Binney on deck and complained bitterly about the missing aircraft. Using all his guile, Binney laughed off the matter. He told him: 'They [are] doubtless overhead, but at such a height as to be both invisible and inaudible, and … British submarines [are] probably in our vicinity keeping guard over us, though we [can]not see them.' Isachsen was, unsurprisingly, rather unimpressed. Binney only later learned that snow storms over England had prevented Coastal Command from launching its planes. Similar snow storms inland over Norway were also hampering German air operations. Fate does tend to have a sense of humour.

It was now full daylight and it was possible to see for 30 miles across the icy waters. The loss of darkness and the clearing of the weather meant the small convoy was a prime target for any watchful Germans. The lack of an air escort made Binney anxious. The five rugged little ships were no match for the Luftwaffe or a German patrol craft and there was still around 55 miles to sail before the convoy could meet up with their naval escort.

On the stern horizon Binney could see one of the slower ships in the group silhouetted against the bright sky. Perhaps it was the *Ranja* or *John Bakke*. Several miles ahead he could make out the *Taurus* ploughing through the waters. They were now so obvious in the bright sunlight that Binney anticipated a serious attack from the Luftwaffe at any moment. Without the aircraft of Coastal Command to ward them off, the little ships would be easy prey. 'It was Mediterranean weather with blue sky and clear seas,' Binney later reported. 'Our salvation lay in the fact that it was snowing on the Norwegian coast and that no air patrols were active.'

The last leg of their journey before rendezvous with the Royal Navy put them in constant range of the Nazi-occupied airfields at Egersund or Stavanger. That no Luftwaffe challenged them at that moment – when the weather was so clear they could be seen for miles and there was no hope of being defended by the distant Navy escort – was due more to luck than anything else.

That wasn't to mean that there would be no Luftwaffe activity at all. Late in the morning a solitary German aircraft appeared in the sky. Everyone braced themselves for the worst, but it was over the *John Bakke* that the aircraft hovered. The *John Bakke* was flying her Norwegian flags, as were all the ships in the tiny fleet. As they waited in horror for the ship to be struck, nothing happened. The German plane maintained its position above the *John Bakke* for another 2 hours, acting as an escort. Binney could only suppose that the pilot had wrongly assumed that the cargo ships were in fact operating in the service of the Nazi occupiers of Norway. As the fleet was currently on a north-westerly course along the coast of Norway this was a logical assumption, but Binney knew it would not last. Eventually the ships had to turn westwards to cross the North Sea and it was then that the Luftwaffe pilot realised his mistake. He turned his attention on the slow *Ranja* as his best target.

The *Ranja*'s fate had always been precarious. The slowest vessel in the fleet, she had the unenviable role of being a decoy for the other ships. As she slogged along at her trembling 11½ knots at the back of the convoy her crew realised it was only a matter of time before the Luftwaffe picked on her as the weakest member of the group. From the start the *Ranja* had been deemed expendable: filled only with salt water ballast it would not matter if she sank to the bottom and her demise would buy valuable time for the remaining vessels carrying genuine war supplies. But that was cold comfort to her civilian crew who now saw the German plane circling above them.

The Luftwaffe aircraft dropped its bombs, but they proved wildly inaccurate – not uncommon in aerial attacks against shipping – and they appeared to fall harmlessly into the sea. Resorting to his machine guns the German pilot began strafing the *Ranja* with a deadly hail of bullets. Against the unarmed *Ranja* it was a horrific attack. Bullets pierced the flimsy hull and there was nowhere for the crew to hide. On the bridge First Officer Nils Rydberg, a Swede from Gothenburg, was trying to keep the *Ranja* on course when fragments from a bomb that exploded away from the actual ship flew through the walls of the cabin and caught him in the abdomen. He collapsed in agony, his blood rapidly pooling on the floor.

Thankfully at that moment some British planes finally arrived, the weather having cleared enough for Coastal Command to restart its operations. Outnumbered, the Luftwaffe craft was driven away, shamefaced at the dramatic error it had made over the identity of the ships, knowing that the British were endeavouring to make a daring escape.

Binney felt he could relax. Unaware of the dying Rydberg, it seemed at first sight that the mission had been an unprecedented success. Around noon he followed Captain Isachsen below decks for some food. They had barely begun their meal when a crewman scrambled down to them.

'A man o'war in sight!'

Binney could have laughed with delight. He was certain, so near were they to the rendezvous point, that this had to be one of the British escort. Isachsen rushed on deck but Binney continued eating his meal, content that he had outrun the Nazi threat and was close to victory. It was 12.20 p.m. when the British destroyer challenged the *Tai Shan*. Captain Isachsen hastily flew their identification flags, a startling white sheet with the big letters 'GB' emblazoned on it. As Binney later pointed out, these could have stood for many things, but he chose to believe they stood for George Binney. This was his proudest moment; from being trapped at the start of the war in a fruitless desk job he had jumped to being commander of his own little fleet and defying the Germans. As several more of the escort vessels sent by the Navy hove into sight he couldn't help but contemplate that this was *his* fleet joining with his *country's* fleet: 'It became apparent to us how thoroughly the Royal Navy were redeeming their promise to protect us once we were out of the Skagerrak.'

The worst seemed over; the tense voyage unescorted through Nazi territory had passed uneventfully and now they were in open waters and surrounded by an impressive escort of Navy vessels. But the apparent negligence of the Germans in stopping the escaping convoy would not last forever. Only moments after the *Tai Shan* crept into the sheltered protection of the British destroyers and cruisers a submarine alert was sounded. One of the cruisers was under attack and retaliated with its own heavy fire: '… it was grand to see all its guns blazing off simultaneously, their flames belching red and orange through clouds of smoke. I do not know the result, but the cruiser was not hit.'

Almost as soon as the attack had begun it was over. The submarines perhaps thought better than to take on the large flotilla of heavily armed warships, especially as the British were now perfecting their ASDIC (anti-submarine detection) strategies and were better able to target U-boats. In any case, Binney was relieved that they had encountered such faint opposition, and the rest of the journey home proved surprisingly peaceful.

A SURPRISE PACKAGE

At 6.30 a.m. on 25 January 1941, Binney could look on the shores of Kirkwall, Orkney. His audacious voyage had surpassed all expectations and every ship had arrived in one piece with her precious cargo intact. As the *Tai Shan* moored in friendly waters she was joined by the *Taurus*. Two hours later the *Elisabeth Bakke*, the *John Bakke* and the forlorn *Ranja* appeared in Scottish waters. The *Elisabeth Bakke* had in fact made such good time that she had reached the Orkneys the previous evening and had waited offshore throughout the night for the rest of the convoy.

Binney was naturally elated. In the cargo holds of the ships were 24,800 tons of Swedish pig iron, special steels, ball bearings and machine tools – effectively a year's worth of supplies from Sweden that were desperately needed for the war effort. The cargo was valued at £1 million and the worth of the ships that had been removed from the grasp of the Nazis was £2.5 million;

147 men (fifty-eight British, fifty-seven Norwegians, thirty-one Swedes and one Latvian) and one woman (the wife of the Chief Engineer of the *John Bakke*) had taken part in the mission.

It was a huge coup for the British and particularly for the fledgling SOE (Special Operations Executive) that had helped to organise the mission. Binney, quickly moving for another mission on similar lines, viewed the lack of German interference less as a fluke and more as an indication of how choosing the right weather to operate in could be fundamental to his success. He was pressing for a second mission as early as March. However, his superiors were more inclined to count their blessings at obtaining one shipment with so little human loss and were not as convinced that it had been anything but fate that had spared the convoy from more serious harm.

The Germans were naturally furious about the escape. Their Foreign Minister, Joachim von Ribbentrop, was outraged. He confronted a member of the Swedish Government unfortunate enough to be in Germany at the time, conducting negotiations on behalf of his country. Lashed verbally by Ribbentrop at the laxity of Sweden at allowing five ships to escape their embargo and sail to Britain, the Swedish minister promised a full explanation once he was able to return home and talk to his colleagues.

When, a short time later, Ribbentrop received the full report from the Swedes on the matter his fury was whipped to new peaks – the Swedes explained that the German Government had been fully aware of the British attempt and had told the Swedish Government about it. They added that though they had hoped the British would not succeed in setting sail, they had believed it was the German Navy's responsibility to deal with them when they did. Therefore, concluded the Swedes, it was all the German Navy's fault that Binney's mission had succeeded.

The enjoyment the British took at fuelling German tempers was almost as great as the elation of capturing such valuable supplies. Binney was still considering the possibility of another attempt, and was due back in Sweden where he would return to his role as UK Minister of Supply, but the idea of further iron ore missions kept turning over in his mind. 'Hope springs eternal,' he remarked to SOE before boarding his aircraft for Sweden. 'But don't forget that though you use the same pack, the cards fall differently every deal.'

Meanwhile the unfortunate Nils Rydberg lingered in a hospital at Kirkwall, his wounds serious and life-threatening. He asked that his relatives in Sweden should remain ignorant of his condition, though there was no option but for Binney to inform the Swedish minister in Stockholm. On 7 February, when Rydberg took a turn for the worse and perished, a telegram was issued to Stockholm from the Foreign Office asking that Rydberg's family be informed and that any of his dependants should be provided for within the limitations of his mission contract. Nils Rydberg was the first and only casualty of Operation Rubble, but his sacrifice had not been in vain.

2

THE HEART OF THE ISSUE

George Binney's mission was a response to an issue that plagued both the Allies and Axis governments throughout the war: the urgent need for steel to maintain production of military weapons and vehicles.

Britain and Germany both relied heavily on Scandinavian sources for their iron ore and steel, and both quickly saw the potential for outflanking the other by severing these supplies.

Prior to the war, Sweden exported thousands of tons of iron ore. In 1938 alone, a total of 11,976,000 tons was shipped, of which 8,441,000 tons, about 70 per cent, was sent to Germany, while Britain received 1,603,000 tons, just over 13 per cent. During January 1939, Germany took receipt of 487,890 tons of Swedish iron ore and, in February 1939, received 475,482 tons. (In comparison, Britain received 67,730 and 70,234 tons respectively.) In the 1930s, 10 per cent of all British imports came from Scandinavia in the form of food (bacon, butter, eggs and fish) or raw materials including iron ore and timber. If these supplies were ever cut off it was believed that the fighting forces would suffer.

At the same time, as can be seen from the figures above, Germany's situation was far graver as its reliance on iron ore imports was on the rise, soaring from 14 million tons in 1935 to

22 million in 1939, with high-grade Swedish ore accounting for 9 million tons of the total. The ore was mined from the Kiruna-Gällivare district of Lapland, north of the Arctic Circle. Railway lines enabled the mined ore to be transported through Luleå in the Gulf of Bothnia or Narvik in Norway. Narvik was vitally important as during the long Scandinavian winter the Gulf of Bothnia froze over, making Luleå ice-bound from November to April. Narvik became the sole route for supply ships. During the winter of 1938–39, 6.5 million tons of Swedish ore were shipped via Narvik, 4.5 million of which was destined for Germany. After the outbreak of war a steady pressure was applied to Norway to cease, or at least limit, the amount of Swedish iron ore it allowed to be shipped via Narvik to the Germans. Norway was endeavouring to remain neutral, but with a discreet bias towards the British.

In September 1939, First Lord of the Admiralty Winston Churchill began considering the possibility of blockading steel to the Germans. Norway, as a transport route for goods, started to look rather enticing as a potential zone for scuppering or at least delaying the delivery of iron. Sir Cecil Dormer, British minister at Oslo, did his best to assure the British Government that Norway's sympathies, though technically neutral, rested firmly on the side of the Allies. He reported, 'They favour the British cause, to a greater extent perhaps than in any other neutral country.' The only real concern was whether the Norwegians would be prepared to break their neutrality and join a blockade of Germany.

Churchill was not keen to take a chance on Norwegian politics. Upon his arrival at the Admiralty it became clear in his mind that the 'thousand-mile-long peninsula stretching from the mouth of the Baltic to the Arctic Circle had an immense strategic significance'. He wanted to sever Germany's iron ore imports, in particular those coming through Narvik.

It was the constant diplomatic wrangles of the situation that caused him problems. Some of his senior staff favoured offensive action, even going as far as suggesting a division of destroyers be sent to Vestfjorden 'as a convenient tool'. The political fury this would have caused the Norwegians would have been immense; they would have seen it as a direct challenge to their authority and neutrality. Understandably Churchill wavered at such 'drastic operations'. He also turned down the idea of laying large-scale minefields, though he would consider the option of severing the Scandinavian Leads by placing mines there, 'at some lonely spots on the coast, as far north as convenient', basically at some place where the Norwegians might not notice them.

On 19 September, he set the matter before the War Cabinet, making it clear that heavy diplomatic pressure should be placed on Norway's Government to prevent German iron ore traffic from traversing the Norwegian Leads. He added, almost threateningly, that if this could not be done he would be forced into taking serious counter-actions, such as mining Norwegian territorial waters to force German ships outside the zone of neutrality, making them fair game for British destroyers.

The Cabinet refused to give its permission for anything other than diplomatic measures and told Churchill it had information that the shipping of iron ore via Narvik by the Germans had virtually ceased since the outbreak of war and 'that in view of Norway's economic importance to Germany Berlin was unlikely to violate Norwegian neutrality, unless provoked by an Allied Intervention or an interference with the iron-ore supplies'. It was also reluctant to incur the wrath of other neutral countries and the USA, should it be seen to violate Norway's rights.

Churchill was outraged:

My views on the naval strategic situation were already largely formed when I went to the Admiralty. The command of the Baltic was vital to the enemy. Scandinavian supplies, Swedish ore, and above all protection against Russian descents on the long, undefended coastline of Germany – in one place little more than a hundred miles from Berlin – made it imperative for the German Navy to dominate the Baltic.

Unfortunately various failures within the intelligence services, diplomatic services and among politicians meant the Cabinet did not realise just how much Hitler was coveting Norway and full control of the Swedish iron ore supplies – crippling his enemies just as Churchill wished to cripple him – as the war slipped quietly into its first year. Britain was still playing a gentleman's game in the winter of 1939 and had failed to realise that Hitler was a cheat.

Churchill refused to be defeated by the Cabinet's reluctance. By November the Royal Navy had drawn up plans of action to control the entrance to Narvik and force any German iron ore imports to Britain. It was a modern form of piracy. Churchill returned to the War Cabinet on 30 November with a report from the Ministry of Economic Warfare that stated that the war could be ended in a matter of months if the complete halt of Swedish iron ore to Germany was achieved. This would mean blockading more than just the imports through Narvik, but Churchill was positive that the coming winter would mean the Baltic would be closed with ice, forcing all German supply ships through the Leads. Strategic placing of minefields would force these ships out into international waters and the clutches of the Royal Navy.

Chief of the Imperial General Staff General Edmund Ironside was captivated by the idea, but he didn't want to see just minefields being laid. He advocated a partial invasion of Norway. Of course this would upset the Germans, but they couldn't do much about it until May when the icy waters unlocked. By which time, Ironside pointed out, the British could have developed a substantial defence as in 'such a remote and forbidding country a very small force could hold up a large one'.

The War Cabinet remained unconvinced, but its utter refusal to consider blockades against the Germans was no longer so fixed. They didn't know it, but it was now a race to see which force – German or British – would make its mind up first and seize Norway.

CHURCHILL'S BIG MISTAKE

The term 'quisling' has become synonymous with a traitor, but the original Vidkun Quisling saw himself as anything but when he approached Hitler in December 1939 to discuss what would occur should Britain invade neutral Norway. The former intelligence officer and defence minister had Nazi sympathies and hoped that a pro-German coup within Norway would enable him and his party, Nasjonal Samling (NS), which had always been on the fringes of Norwegian politics, to finally take centre stage. Quisling was ambitious, ruthless and narrow-minded. He impressed Hitler, who vowed that should Britain attempt to invade Norway the German response would be swift and brutal – even, he added sinisterly, if that meant a pre-emptive invasion. Other ministers in Hitler's party were less convinced by Quisling. Much of the information he gave for the German invasion plans would later prove faulty or totally wrong. Quisling had an over-inflated sense of his own importance and abilities, but despite criticism from German ministers in Norway, he was accepted by the higher echelons of the Nazi regime.

When he spoke with Hitler in December and made subtle pushes for a Nazi invasion, Quisling had his own motives for gaining power in Norway and casting out his enemies in the government, who he saw as holding back his party. He said all the right things to spark the Führer's anger. He stated that the Norwegian population was largely pro-British and would side with the Allies in the event of Norway being dragged into the war. He also said that it was his opinion that Britain had no intention of respecting Norwegian neutrality; in fact there was evidence (he claimed) that the Norwegian Government had secretly agreed to allow the Allies to occupy parts of southern Norway and threaten Germany's northern flank. In contrast, the NS was prepared to work with Germany; they agreed with Hitler's policies and had key people in the civil administration and the armed forces. Should the worst happen, Quisling was prepared to lead a coup which would open Norwegian doors for Germany before the British could get a foothold.

Quisling was exaggerating, but he appealed to Hitler's strong sense of paranoia. While other German ministers were scowling and writing Quisling off as a braggart, Hitler was captivated. Even so, he made no direct moves, though plans were drawn up for the hypothetical invasion of Norway. It would be a clumsy move by Churchill that would prove the catalyst for the real invasion and Hitler developing a firm belief in Quisling's views and opinions. This would prove fatal to many German soldiers and sailors.

In the early stages of the war, when Germany had been making decisive attacks against British merchant shipping with considerable success, Churchill's attention had been drawn to a German ship named the *Altmark*. The *Altmark* was a tanker (auxiliary to the ill-fated *Graf Spee*) which had been serving as a prison ship for captured sailors from sunk British merchant ships. There was solid information to suggest as many as 300 British sailors were being held on the *Altmark*, arousing British fury and instigating a hunt for the elusive tanker. Knowing he would be unable to defend his vessel if he was engaged in a sea battle, the captain of the *Altmark* sailed out into the south Atlantic and hid there for two months in the hope the British would eventually give up.

In February 1940 this appeared to be just the case to Captain Langsdorff as he stood on the bridge of the *Altmark*. It had been a long two months hiding from the enemy, and his crew were more than ready to sail back to Germany with their prize of British sailors. Everything looked to be in their favour as they altered course and headed for home. The weather was with them as they sailed unmolested between Iceland and the Faroes and found themselves in Norwegian territorial waters on 14 February. That was when Captain Langsdorff's luck evaporated. British aircraft spotted the ship they had been fruitlessly hunting for and word was rapidly sent back to Britain. Langsdorff was not entirely concerned. He was in neutral waters and any attack on his ship would require the British to break their pact of neutrality with

Norway. He doubted even the pig-headed British would risk such a political catastrophe to recapture a few civilian sailors.

Langsdorff was woefully mistaken. Churchill had the bit between his teeth when it came to securing the prisoners from the *Altmark* and he saw Norwegian neutrality as no obstacle. 'This ship is violating neutrality in carrying British prisoners of war to Germany,' he told the First Sea Lord. 'The *Altmark* must be regarded as an invaluable trophy.'

Just before midnight on 16 February 1940, the British destroyer *Cossack*, under orders from Churchill, sailed into Norwegian waters. Local naval vessels protested at the infringement, but Captain Philip Vian had his instructions and his sights were set on the German tanker. The *Altmark* slipped into Jösing Fjord, its retreat being guarded by two Norwegian gunboats trying to defend their country's right to neutrality. They insisted that the tanker had been boarded for inspection and there had been no armaments or prisoners. Vian was unimpressed, but he quietly withdrew and sent this new information to Britain.

Churchill was irate when he heard the news. He intervened directly and sent a new order to Vian: 'Unless Norwegian torpedo-boat undertakes to convoy *Altmark* to Bergen with a joint Anglo-Norwegian guard on board, and a joint escort, you should board *Altmark*, liberate the prisoners, and take possession of the ship pending further instructions.'

Vian needed no further prompting. He first boarded one of the torpedo ships to give his ultimatum, but again the Norwegians insisted that the *Altmark* had been properly searched and there was no call for any further action. Meanwhile Captain Langsdorff realised his time in the safety of the fjord was rapidly drawing to a close. In a desperate bid to escape the fjord he set the *Altmark* on a course to ram Vian's ship. The attack was an utter disaster: the *Altmark* missed her target and grounded herself, giving Vian a prime opportunity to come alongside her and send across a boarding party. Langsdorff's men resorted to hand-to-hand fighting to try to repel the British, but their hearts were not in it. In only a matter of moments four Germans were killed and another five wounded; those that remained either fled ashore or surrendered.

The *Altmark* came under British control and, with the Norwegians watching on anxiously, Vian ordered a search. He held no illusions about the thoroughness of the Norwegians' previous searches and was not surprised when it was reported to him that his crew had found two pom-pom guns and two machine guns. So much for the Norwegian claims that she was unarmed.

The British prisoners were even easier to find. The *Altmark* was not designed to hold prisoners and the British had been stowed wherever there was an inch of space. They now emerged from the ship's storerooms and even an unused oil-tank with the cry, 'The Navy's here!'

The attack made headline news across the world and Hitler was beside himself over the story. He was furious that there had been such poor resistance from both the Germans and the Norwegians. The British had sailed in with barely a challenge. The Germans had been humiliated and Hitler was now convinced that the Norwegians either couldn't or wouldn't defend their neutrality. Ironically the attack on the *Altmark* confirmed the phoney allegations Quisling had made, even if it was not the alleged precursor to invasion but a rescue operation.

Head of the Nazi Party Foreign Policy Office and Propaganda Section, Reichsleiter Alfred Rosenberg later wrote, 'Downright stupid of Churchill. This confirms Quisling was right. I saw the Führer today and … there is nothing left of his determination to preserve Nordic neutrality.'

The day after the assault on the *Altmark* Hitler ordered the planning of Operation Weserübung, the invasion of Norway, to be stepped up a gear. As part of the reasoning for the attack, which would seriously reduce manpower for other operations, the need to protect the supply of Swedish iron ore to Germany was put forward. Under no circumstances could Britain be allowed to get into Norway first.

Britain stood by its decision to take the *Altmark*. *The Times* protested that the government had been right to board her considering the perfunctory searches the Norwegians had conducted. Lord Halifax confronted the Norwegian minister and argued that his countrymen had failed in their duty to preserve neutrality in Norwegian waters. In return the Norwegian minister handed a note to the Secretary of State protesting the assault and demanding that the prisoners be given back.

Norway was caught between two dangerous powers, both with an incentive to invade the Scandinavian country. Germany was making a huge fuss over the matter, the Nazi papers calling the rescue operation 'an unexampled act of piracy' on 'a peaceful German merchantman'. They deplored the 'brutal murder' of German seamen and said it would leave a lasting stain on the British Navy. The *Deutsche Allgemeine Zeitung* told its readers furiously, 'We shall present the bill. As the British no longer command the sea they fall back on the territorial waters of a neutral country, and there attack a German merchantman, not like soldiers but like pirates.' The *Berliner Börsen-Zeitung* added its own spin on the matter. 'The shameful and cowardly way in which the British Government has behaved incorporates the spirit of the man who gave out as his motto on the first day of the war; "I hope I shall live to see Hitler suppressed."'

While the British ranted over the misleading newsprint and the deplorable suppression of facts by the Nazi journalists, Hitler was wondering how lucky he could get. Churchill had played straight into his hand, giving him a prime reason for invading Norway and to justify Operation Weserübung. Not that he would have delayed the operation if he had not had such a good excuse, but it enabled him to do the thing he loved best – presenting the Nazis as the heroes, standing up to the oppression and devil-may-care attitude of the British. He couldn't have been happier, especially knowing that Britain was firmly on the back foot despite its triumph over the *Altmark*. Churchill had no idea that he was about to be trumped when it came to occupying Norway.

OPERATION WILFRED

Life in neutral Norway was proceeding much as it had done before the war, with few civilians aware that their country was at the centre of a power play between two great warring nations. Even the government failed to truly understand how significant Norway was in the minds of the Allies and the Axis powers.

There had been warning signs; the German invasion of Poland had worried many Norwegians and had left an almost unanimous feeling of anger towards the Nazis. Quisling's talk of having many supporters who would gladly side with the Germans in the conflict was all lies. Norway's sympathies were firmly with the beleaguered Poland, but that didn't mean it was going to do anything about the occupation. The prevailing feeling among the government and the Norwegian people was that this wasn't *their* war and the best thing they could do was to stay neutral. This dogged determination for neutrality was so strong within the population and among the fighting forces that it would severely hamper Norway's efforts to repel the Germans when they did finally invade.

More than one soldier when told to shoot at advancing German troops felt the need to remind his commanding officer that he had live bullets in his gun and could kill someone! Many admitted after the war to aiming over the German soldiers' heads at first, unwilling to harm them, until it became apparent that neutrality was no defence against invasion.

Norway was blind to its future fate in those early days of the phoney war. After the invasion of Poland the government issued a declaration of neutrality, which was extended two days later to cover the war that France and Britain had just declared on Germany. There was an immediate freeze on all prices. Petrol, coal and certain imported goods were rationed. The public were reminded not to hoard, and advised that all would be well as long as they led cautious lifestyles. For a time the use of motorised vehicles was limited to preserve the petrol ration;

people returned to using horses and there was a new popularity for bicycles.

Yet, for the most part, life continued as normal and few Norwegians gave much thought to the war happening in another part of Europe. In the first seven months of the war Norwegian newspapers carried stories of the loss of fifty-five Norwegian merchant vessels, resulting in the deaths of 393 sailors, almost all due to German attacks. But the incidents had occurred outside Norwegian neutral waters and the belief still prevailed that Norway had raised an impenetrable wall of neutrality around itself.

Even the government was lulled into this false sense of security. Mobilisation of troops to maintain the neutral borders and deter infringements was limited and largely pointless. The Royal Norwegian Navy (RNN) was supposed to be patrolling the waters and preventing problems, but it was not taken seriously by either the British or Germans. More symbolic than functional, the RNN had been reduced to insignificance between the wars and in 1939 a massive recommissioning operation had to take place just to have enough ships in service, many from the naval reserve. By April 1940, the RNN had 121 vessels in service, fifty-three of which were chartered auxiliaries consisting of requisitioned fishing vessels, whale-boats and small freighters. The auxiliaries were hastily armed with either a 76mm gun or a pair of machine guns and were intended purely for patrol or guard duties. They were not expected to engage an enemy in combat and certainly were not fit to do so. Another nine vessels were simply unarmed support ships.

More alarmingly, out of the fifty-nine actual Navy vessels nineteen had been launched just after the First World War and seventeen had been built before 1900; they were woefully inadequate for modern warfare. To serve on them the RNN had to draft staff officers from the coastguard stations, naval airbases and communication centres. A total of 5,200 men were ready for service by early 1940, but out of these only 1,398 had any pre-war experience.

From his vantage point in Britain, Churchill could see that Norway stood little chance should Germany decide to ignore its neutrality. He knew this because he was already planning something similar – Operation Wilfred.

Since September 1939, Churchill had been pestering the government to do something about Norway – his *something* was laying mines around the Norwegian Leads and landing troops in the country as a 'prevention' against German retaliation. 'I called the actual mining operation "Wilfred", because by itself it was so small and innocent,' Churchill explained in reference to a popular *Daily Mirror* comic strip featuring the characters Pip, Squeak and Wilfred. Wilfred was a young rabbit who acted as the 'child' in the series, Pip the dog and Squeak the penguin being his adoptive parents. The long-running characters were favourites among the military; the three medals issued after the First World War to most British serviceman were nicknamed Pip, Squeak and Wilfred, and the RAF nicknamed its three post-First World War training craft after the characters. It is not surprising that Churchill, with his own brand of humour, enjoyed the idea of naming his mission after a small baby rabbit who could not even talk properly.

Operation Wilfred was touted by Churchill to his more cautious colleagues as a modest escalation of tension between the two nations. He did not consider that it might be too tentative, or even too late. Wilfred's goal was to send two minelaying groups to the Norwegian coast, one to mine the approach to Narvik and scupper, at least until it could be cleared, the route for Swedish iron ore. The second minelaying group would block the Norwegian Leads off Stadlandet.

Concurrently with 'Wilfred' it was hoped an operation could be launched to release fluvial mines into the Rhine. The theory was that if enough could be released and allowed to drift they would catch a variety of shipping and also cause fear and confusion until the Germans could conclusively clear them. This operation was another favourite idea of Churchill's, but the

French were unenthusiastic as they believed it would lead to repercussions on their own aircraft industry, which was far from protected from attack.

However, it was repercussions that Churchill wanted. The twilight war had tired him and strained his nerves yet without conclusive action or results. Worse, he noted that morale in the French Army was faltering as the waiting increased. Churchill had deemed the French troops at their best just before the winter of 1939; after that the lack of any positive action had allowed infiltrations by Communist, and more troublingly, Fascist propaganda that had weakened the French fighting spirit. Churchill wanted action to spur his Allies back into a war mindset, but his tentative prods at the Germans to provoke a response were like prodding a rather unpleasant bear.

On 28 March, Churchill sat with the War Cabinet feeling a touch of satisfaction. He was about to brief it on the final arrangements of 'Wilfred' but was also determined to finalise details on what would occur when the German reprisals began. He was hopeful that German reactions would give the British a legitimate reason to land troops in Norway with the consent of the country's government. He would not get the result he wanted that day, but on 1 April the War Cabinet endorsed a plan that became simply known as R4 and was viewed as the key to securing Norway.

OPERATION WESERÜBUNG

Hitler had two goals in mind with his Operation Weserübung plans: Weserübung Sud was the designation for the invasion of Denmark with the primary goal of capturing Copenhagen, while Weserübung Nord was the name for the invasion of Norway. The goals for the latter were to land large numbers of troops from warships at Narvik, Trondheim, Bergen and Kristiansand under the pretence that they were coming to help defend Norway against British infringements of their neutrality. Single companies of troops would be sent to capture the wireless stations at Egersund and Arendal, while the equivalent of two regiments would head for Oslo, securing Horten en route.

In the meantime air operations, including the first use of paratroopers in the conflict, would be conducted at Fornebu and Sola airports. The result would be the encirclement of southern Norway and the control of the country's administration and military forces. Hitler expected the invasion to be a walk-over after the stagnant resistance given to the British when they seized the *Altmark*, and it was hoped that Weserübung Nord would be a peaceful occupation. Commanders were given orders to approach the population in a non-aggressive manner, and to give the appearance of being friends rather than enemies. Others among his staff were more convinced the Norwegians would eventually resist, but in the end it would be left up to the commander of each invasion group to decide when to hold back and when to shoot. This would result in some confusion and at times put the Germans at an unexpected disadvantage.

On 9 April 1940, the Norwegians had been distracted by the tragedy of Finland's invasion by the Soviets and the resulting Moscow Peace Treaty signed in early March. Britain and France had also been anxious as the attack had scuppered their own plans to send troops to Finland as part of their operations to prevent the export of Swedish iron ore to Germany. But sympathies for Finland should not have prevented either Norway or Britain from spotting the growing warning signs coming from Germany. The US minister to Norway, Florence Harriman, wrote in 1941, 'Hindsight is all we seem to have. But it is fantastic that none of the things which happened in the week preceding the fatal daybreak of April 9th awakened us to danger. A hundred incidents should have prepared us. Instead we were transfixed, still watching the war in Finland.'

Blame for this blindness has since been laid heavily on the heads of Norwegian Intelligence, and while they played a significant part in the failure, criticism must also fall on the various military leaders and ministers who failed to share information and thus had only a fragment of the whole picture. Foreign Minister Koht in particular was prone to isolating himself, having over-confidence in his own opinions and lacking faith in others. In the end this combined negligence and lack of co-operation, affected by a prevailing idea in certain influential minds that Norwegian neutrality would remain inviolate, left the country open and utterly unprepared for invasion.

Britain was also lax in reading the warning signs – and there were enough of them. On 3 April, the War Cabinet was made aware that German troops had been seen in Rostock and there were troopships loaded and ready for a presumed intervention in Scandinavia. At the same time Churchill was informed that it appeared the Germans were preparing for imminent operations in south Scandinavia, but the prevailing belief was that this was a response to perceived British threats and that the Germans would do nothing until the Allies acted.

On 5 April, more news arrived that the Germans were massing troops and the likely targets seemed to be Stavanger and Kristiansand, because of their airfields, yet still no one realised the real danger. The following day, the British Vice-Consul in Copenhagen sent information he had learned from the US minister, who had a well-placed source in Germany, that Hitler had given firm orders for ten ships to land at Narvik on 8 April and occupy Jutland, leaving Sweden alone. A further telegram from Copenhagen said troops had embarked on 4 April, but as there was disagreement among the military as to the value of the attack there were high hopes that Hitler's orders would be rescinded.

Perhaps we should blame those longs months of the twilight war for Britain's caution and hesitation in believing such news and acting, even though the warning signs were becoming obvious. On 7 April, the Government Code and Cypher School (GC&CS) told the Admiralty it had noticed an increase in

German naval signal traffic, suggesting a number of ships were now at sea around the Baltic and west of Denmark. Unaware of the other warnings coming in, the report was treated in isolation and the significance not realised.

Meanwhile the RAF had noticed increased Luftwaffe activity, seeming to be reconnaissance over the North Sea and Skagerrak. Coincidentally the first aerial photographs of Kiel harbour were taken on 7 April and, had there been earlier photographs from the site for comparison, they would have shown an increase in the number of ships berthed there and the activity surrounding them. Instead the RAF analysts could see nothing urgent. As far as they were aware, the great destroyers *Scharnhorst* and *Gneisenau* were still at Wilhelmshaven, so whatever was happening at Kiel did not seem significant. How wrong they all were.

Also on 7 April, Operation Wilfred was in action and British ships were laying mines in the Leads. The crews of these ships would be some of the first to spot the German Navy heading towards Narvik, though they too failed to realise the significance. The destroyer *Glowworm* had signalled she was in action against a superior force; then her communications stopped. This was because *Glowworm* had sunk to the bottom of the ocean, the first victim of Operation Weserübung. Again this was not realised in Britain and it was assumed *Glowworm* had stumbled upon a German ship patrolling the waters near Narvik in case the British moved to invade!

On 9 April, Operation Weserübung swung into action. The German Navy had sailed discreetly into position, for the most part avoiding the British in the heavy, fog-bound seas. The great ships were carrying a cargo of seasick soldiers, many from the Austrian mountain divisions. Now all they needed was the signal to rush to their various targets and deposit their dangerous loads. Vizeadmiral Lütjens, acting C-in-C of the Western Fleet, recorded in his diary, 'weser-day is 9 April'.

However, Britain had finally realised the threat, albeit rather late in the day, and Blenheims flew over and attacked heavy

German forces in the Bight late on 7 April. Britain had sent out its own fleet, and a number of cruisers, destroyers and other ships were on their way to intercept. The Germans were not going to have the operation all their own way.

Norway still seemed mildly oblivious to its fate, or perhaps worse, disbelieved that there was any real danger. Early on the morning of 8 April, the Norwegian fishing vessel *Jenny* and coaster *Lindebo* stumbled across the Polish submarine *Orzel* (*Eagle*) (an escapee from the invasion of Poland now working for the British) launching torpedoes into the heavily laden German liner *Rio de Janeiro*. The *Rio de Janeiro* was loaded with supplies for the invasion, including four 10.5cm guns, six 20mm AA guns, seventy-three horses, seventy-one vehicles, 292 tons of provisions and 313 uniformed passengers.

The liner was under orders to avoid being boarded and risking the exposure of the entire operation at all costs. So she turned away and tried to flee when the *Orzel* challenged her. Commander Jan Grudziński of the *Orzel* issued a warning to abandon ship to signify he was about to open fire but there was no response. Below her decks the *Rio de Janeiro*'s military passengers had no idea what was going on and no knowledge of the impending danger. Banned from going above deck in case they were spotted in their uniforms they had spent all their time in the miserable cramped quarters, racked by claustrophobia and seasickness. It was therefore complete panic when the *Orzel*'s torpedo struck at 11.45 a.m. As the Polish submarine slipped back underwater, men in grey uniforms could be seen emerging in disorderly chaos onto the deck of the liner. Many instantly jumped over the side into the icy water. Lifebelts and bits of wood were thrown to the men, many of whom had no idea how to swim. No effort appeared to be made to lower the lifeboats.

The *Lindebo* and *Jenny*, astonished by the scene, moved in to help survivors. The *Rio de Janeiro* had listed starboard but was not sinking, so the *Orzel* circled underwater and launched another torpedo striking the damaged liner at 12.15 p.m. and breaking off her bow. Splinters of wreckage flew over the deck of the *Lindebo*, wounding or killing some of the men the Norwegian coaster had just saved. Within minutes the *Rio de Janeiro* sank below the surface, leaving the remaining survivors on board struggling for their lives in the icy water. As the *Orzel* slunk away to report, the sea was full of frightened men, surrounded by their drowned comrades and the horses (now all dead) that had been housed below. The Norwegian destroyer *Odin* was on its way to investigate, Justøy coastguard having raised the alert to the tragedy. Arriving at 12.45 p.m. in rough seas, the *Odin* managed to help rescue 150 men from the water, but 180 perished, most of them soldiers who had been trapped below decks and could not swim. All the invasion equipment had now sunk to the bottom of the sea. A later cross-reference of co-ordinates revealed that the *Rio de Janeiro* had been exceptionally unlucky (or the *Orzel* extremely lucky) as she had been caught just outside the Norwegian neutral 3-mile limit.

The sinking of and subsequent rescue of men from the *Rio de Janeiro* should have been the final piece in the puzzle for the Norwegians. The presence of dozens of soldiers on a liner was suspicious for a start, and the fact they were armed and that an officer was trying to maintain order among them with shouts of 'Wehrmacht hier! Marine hier!' should have rung alarm bells. But only Chief of Police Nils Onsrud, who arrived at Kristiansand where the survivors had been taken, realised the importance. Soldiers he questioned openly admitted they were heading for Bergen to assist the Norwegian Army against an Allied invasion! But the German officer denied everything and maintained that the *Rio de Janeiro* was just a merchantman bringing ordinary provisions.

Onsrud tried to make his concerns known to the authorities but only Undersecretary of State Rognlien believed him. He called the General Staff and Admiral Staff to inform them, only to discover that they already knew – the *Odin* had transmitted the same message – but were not really interested. They were more perturbed by the British mining of Operation Wilfred. How ironic that an attempt to cripple Germany was now helping it to return the favour to Britain.

3

NORWAY'S SWAN SONG

Operation Wilfred and Plan R4 had been designed to force Germany's hand, spring it into aggressive action and thus justify Britain occupying Norway. Instead it had horribly backfired and Germany was using the British mining as an excuse for the invasion it had already begun. Plan R4 was to involve the landing of 18,000 Allied troops at Narvik and sealing off the railway lines to Sweden. Some historians have argued that the sudden advance of German plans made R4 no longer feasible. This was the view taken by Churchill, but others have made convincing arguments that in fact the German assault only further justified R4 and the plan should have gone ahead.

If Plan R4 had proceeded, a much greater overland Allied response would have occurred in Norway. This might have tilted the balance enough to prevent a successful occupation. Throughout the German attack the Norwegians believed that the British were coming and would swiftly retaliate. If only British troops had been seen as a presence in the country it might have prevented the abrupt surrender of several towns and defensive positions, including Oslo. The initial forces the Germans were able to land were small compared with what they had hoped for, and it was Nazi bluff and bravado that saw vast numbers of Norwegians giving up to a handful of enemy soldiers.

Hindsight is wonderful, however, and as information fed into Britain, Churchill foresaw a largely naval-based battle and gave orders to disembark the troops from the cruisers, and for these ships to join the fleet. Perhaps keeping all their soldiers below decks had not been such a bad move on the Germans' part. Churchill misread the signs and he made a decision that would damage Norway irreparably and also his Prime Minister, Chamberlain. Churchill made the decision alone, but its consequences would be shared.

At the Cabinet meeting on 8 April, Chamberlain asked how far the cruisers had sailed and when they would be able to land troops, only to be told by Churchill that the troops had already disembarked and the cruisers were on their way to join the fleet. Chamberlain was both surprised and unhappy at the development. He looked 'decidedly sheepish' and followed the answer with a heavy, and pointed, silence.

In his book *The German Invasion of Norway: April 1940*, Geirr H. Haarr argues:

> The British soldiers would not have been in place before the German landings, but had they been at sea in fast cruisers, they could have made a significant difference in Stavanger, Bergen or Trondheim. By chasing a tactical, naval victory the Admiralty lost the strategic overview and initiative. This was to cost many lives, eventually topple the Chamberlain government and make way for Churchill in Downing Street.

He has a point, but would the result have shortened or lengthened the war? Norway brought down Chamberlain who was an unhappy war-maker and gave his place to Churchill and his fighting spirit. Could Chamberlain have won us the war? Would Plan R4 have really saved Norway or depleted British troops soon to be needed elsewhere? It is impossible to say, but the decision was made and, ultimately, Churchill's error would change him from First Lord of the Admiralty into Prime Minister.

Meanwhile the Norwegians were in a quandary. They had awoken on 8 April to the news that the British were laying mine-fields in Norwegian waters. Why would they do a thing like that? People were stunned and also scared; they knew Hitler would not fail to react. The Norwegian Government gathered to plan its next move. It would quickly issue a formal protest to London and Paris, making it clear to the Germans that Norway had not even tacitly agreed to this action. There was still a naive hope that Hitler might act rationally.

As soon as the British ships left, the RNN would be sent in to sweep the mines and open the waters again. Transports to Norway would continue as usual, but what was imperative above all else was that nothing should force the Norwegians to enter the war *against* Britain. Whatever happened, there was simply no way the Norwegians could side with the Nazis.

That night virtually all Norwegians listened to their radios and the latest update on the situation. There was a last bulletin at 10 p.m., but it gave little comfort. Still, few really believed there was any threat to Norway. They expected conflicts between the British and Germans in Norwegian waters and that the country's neutrality might be breached, but it would all resolve itself eventually. The blanket of non-involvement was once again drawn over Norwegian heads. The Nazi demons would be bound to be gone by morning.

Minister Dormer, at the British Embassy in Oslo, looked out on a strangely quiet city. It was only midnight, but the cinemas and concert halls were empty; no one was in the mood for light entertainment. As the cold, stormy night closed in, people were home thinking about the news. The only souls still awake in this new, dark world were the newspapermen preparing the morning editions and the duty rosters for round-the-clock reporting. Despite it all Dormer felt unconcerned. Even he had been overwhelmed by the idea of infallible Norwegian neutrality. He decided on an early night and, for the last time for a while, he slept soundly.

BLÜCHER'S DEMISE

Considering the limited Norwegian defences, the air of calm that now descended on Norway was surprising. For the commander-in-chief of 1st Sea Defence (SSD1), Kontreadmiral Johannes Smith-Johannsen, the situation was more depressing as he prepared for the defence of the Oslofjord, the direct sea route to Oslo and Fornebu airfield, and a key German target. At his disposal Smith-Johannsen had three obsolete submarines and lightly armed minesweepers, minelayers and auxiliaries, not the sort of vessels to be used in combat against an attacking German force. His hopes had to rest in the coastal forts for defending the city. However, not all of these were manned and those that were,often found themselves short-staffed.

Smith-Johannsen was living in hope that the forts would be enough to deter the Nazis when news reached him that the Germans were attempting to run the narrows at Oslofjord at 1.30 p.m. on 8 April. An order was issued for the minelayers to begin laying a barrage between the forts at Bolaerne and Rauoy. This order was soon delayed when news filtered in that the British were moving to intercept the German ships: no mines were to be laid until an express order from the Ministry of Defence was issued. Smith-Johannsen must have groaned as his hands were tied and the Oslofjord waters were left wide open. The Norwegians would never get the chance to lay any massive minefields, only token efforts being made once it was already too late.

At 11.10 p.m. RNN auxiliary *Pol III* launched signal rockets to alert everyone that the Germans were approaching. The guns at Rauoy were reported ready 18 minutes later. A thick fog had started to descend as Rauoy tried to scour the waters for enemy vessels with its 110cm searchlights. The searchers could barely see anything, yet within minutes the faint outlines of two ships were spotted. Two warning shots were quickly fired – one a dummy, one live – followed by four more rounds when the ships did not stop. They did not appear to hit anything and the vessels were rapidly moving out of range. At 11.43 p.m., 15 minutes after they had reported their guns ready, Rauoy had already failed and had let the Germans pass.

At Bolaerne the situation was depressingly similar. The thick fog was causing difficulties and while three ships were spotted and the order given to shoot, only one blank round was fired. This was due largely to the lack of experience of the gun crews, who faltered at the last moment, but it was not helped by the near blackout conditions imposed by the increasing fog that left Bolaerne shrouded and out of action until the following day.

Aboard the German vessels issues were also being caused by the dense fog. Sailors on the heavy cruisers *Blücher* and *Lützow* saw the shots of the fort at Rauoy and heard the splashes as they hit the water, but concluded that they were merely warning shots. They remained puzzled, though relieved, by the feeble efforts of the forts and sailed onwards with new hope for the ease of the invasion.

Smith-Johannsen, meanwhile, was in a quandary as to who exactly was sailing in the waters of Oslofjord. The forts had not been able to make a positive identification and as the ships had not fired back when challenged, it was possible that they were the British ships he had heard were coming to intercept the German forces. It is unfortunate that this erroneous piece of information had ever been accepted and repeated as it caused the Norwegians to hesitate. The British were nowhere near. Smith-Johannsen sent out a minesweeper to make a positive identification and finally received the news he had dreaded – the Kriegsmarine had made its move and was already in Norwegian territory.

The Drøbak Narrows were now the last line of defence for Oslo. At Oscarsborg there was a key coastal fort, but like the rest of the military in Norway, it had suffered from governmental neglect. It was undermanned and underpowered; worse still, the minefields supposed to have been laid to make the Narrows impassable had never been installed. One ray of hope was Oscarsborg's torpedo battery, built directly into the rock and with underwater launch tubes. Despite the difficulties ahead, the Norwegians were determined to make a fight of it and their best chance rested on 50-year-old torpedoes in their ammunition store.

The Germans were about to discover that the Norwegians were not complete push-overs. The *Blücher* was preparing to run the Narrows at 3.30 a.m. This was an unpopular decision as the pre-dawn light would silhouette the ships and leave the forts in darkness, and several objections were raised to sending the flagship of the group into highly dangerous waters. For whatever reason, Konteradmiral Kummetz of the *Blücher* was uninterested in warnings. Speculation remains as to why he chose to risk his flagship in waters that were rumoured to be mined and contained formidable torpedo batteries. On board his ship were the majority of the administrative and command personnel intended to take control of Oslo. They alone were a priceless cargo and should not have been risked unnecessarily. Kummetz had intended to use two auxiliary vessels, *Rau VII* and *Rau VIII*, as scouts to check the waters for mines ahead of the *Blücher*, but they had failed to arrive in time and Kummetz did not choose to switch the duty to another vessel. Instead the *Blücher* faced the waters alone, an easy target for Oscarsborg. Was Kummetz over-confident? Fooled by the feeble attack of the previous forts? Or was he just after the glory of first entry into Oslo himself? We shall never know his reasons, and significantly he never clarified them to the officers around him. He was soon to discover that the Norwegians were more than prepared to defend themselves.

At 4.21 a.m. the *Blücher* was inside the Drøbak Narrows and the Norwegians opened fire. Their first shots were meant more as warnings than a real attempt to harm, but one 28cm high-explosive shell sailed just past the heavy cruiser's bridge and crashed into the command tower, destroying the main flak fire-control platform. Most of the personnel were killed. Almost immediately a second shell hit the port side, killing a large number of soldiers still waiting below decks. The cruiser's aircraft hangar was severely hit; the two planes inside burst into flames and the hangar was ravaged by fire. Few who were in the hangar at the time made it out alive.

Further below deck, the boiler and engine rooms became engulfed in asbestos-filled smoke and the lights went out. When the emergency lighting kicked in, the fans that were supposed to bring fresh air down into the rooms could be seen to be drawing smoke, and, at times, flames licked out of them. It was a hellish pit as the men were given orders to force the cruiser up to full power. Several of the boilers had not been lit prior to the attempt at the Narrows and now the men scrambled to bring them to life. Tentatively the *Blücher* increased her speed.

At *Blucher*'s guns men worked hard to try to pinpoint a target, but as had been predicted, the early dawn light prevented them seeing anything. Those at the secondary guns fired randomly at anything that came into sight, including trees, telegraph poles and the odd shed. It was a pointless exercise and the gunners failed to inflict any Norwegian casualties.

Now the Norwegian batteries at Kopas and Husvik joined the assault, striking the *Blücher* with 15cm and 57cm shells. The batteries fired around fifty shells during the onslaught and the cruiser was too close for more than a handful to miss. Kopas was firing straight down onto her deck and many of the shells penetrated the hull before exploding. Seventy to seventy-five metres of the *Blücher*'s port centre section turned into an inferno of burning debris. Fires tore through the ship igniting the army supplies stored below, so burning pools of petrol and exploding ammunition added to the chaos. Then the majority of the ship's electricity gave out.

Oscarsborg now opened fired with its torpedoes. Two hit boiler room K1 and turbine room T2/3, killing virtually every-one inside. The turbines and pumps stopped working and the ship rapidly took on water from holes in her bulkheads. Slowly the *Blücher* listed to port.

On the bridge the dire situation below decks was not realised and even the loss of communications with the engine rooms did not alert the officers to the imminent demise of the ship. Orders were sent out to drop anchor to prevent the *Blücher* running ashore and the cruiser suddenly came to a halt, burning fiercely and turning miserably in the current.

Just behind the *Blücher* the heavy cruiser *Lützow* was sailing. She now came under fire, her captain rapidly making the decision to retreat and ordering the rest of the naval group following him to do the same. He was manoeuvring away as more torpedoes struck the *Blücher* and he watched the blazing flagship vanish behind Oscarsborg. Wrongly assuming that the heavy cruiser had run into mines, he later reported that the passage to Oslo was blocked due to Norwegian minefields. The *Lützow* fled and left the *Blücher* to her fate.

It was finally realised by everyone that the *Blücher* was not going to be saved. As the proud flagship rocked further over, below decks the surviving men were faced by a forbidding landscape of explosive fires, flaming wreckage and smoke-filled corridors. The torpedo workshop was now nothing more than a gaping hole and nearby stored ammunition and grenades were constantly exploding. Travelling between fore and aft of the ship was nearly impossible. Inexperienced fire crews made pathetic attempts to control the blaze. Hoses were damaged by flying splinters from the numerous Norwegian hits and many could not be used. In utter desperation some crewmen even tried to put out raging fires with hand-held extinguishers.

The *Blücher* was flooding; her pumps had failed. Hatches and companionways were blocked by wreckage or water. Communication had ceased between the sections of the cruiser and the men worked alone in isolated groups. Most fought the fires and flooding now not for the sake of the flagship but just so they could survive. The death-toll was quickly rising and the medical personnel could not cope. By the time the last of the *Blücher*'s own torpedoes were either ejected or disarmed to prevent further explosions and much of the stored ammunition dumped overboard, it was all too late. Evacuation procedures began.

The wounded were moved to the least threatened section of the ship, and the one boat that had survived the onslaught – the starboard cutter – was launched and ordered to take the seriously wounded ashore. The cutter managed only two trips before striking a rock and putting itself out of action. Only a handful of the wounded had been rescued. The remaining men on the *Blücher* had the agonising choice of burning to death or trying to swim to shore – a 10- to 15-minute trip, assuming they could swim – through icy waters.

From shore the Norwegians watched as more explosions racked the stricken cruiser and the fuel tanks finally ruptured, spilling flaming oil into the sea and making any escape even more perilous. Orders were at last given to abandon the *Blücher* and inadequate attempts were made to destroy important papers and codes. The signal to leave was spread by word of mouth and the German soldiers – who, remarkably, had remained below – now hurried onto the deck. They had never been drilled in fire evacuation procedures and left hatches open in their haste, allowing smoke and flames to burst onto the deck. To their horror many of the kapok life-jackets had been destroyed by fire and they had to plunge into the water unaided. German reports later stated the final moments of the *Blücher* were dignified by German discipline: sailors gave their own life-jackets to soldiers and threw anything remotely buoyant to men already flailing in the water.

The Norwegians on the shore saw only panic: men screaming and crying for help, running backwards and forwards in utter confusion and helplessness. Most of the soldiers had jumped overboard before the final order was given. Mark floats, which would inflate and provide a surface men could at least cling to, were thrown after them. These took 10 minutes to inflate and several soldiers perished trying to climb into them too early and sliding back beneath the icy water. It was the cold that would kill many of them. The unbearable temperature of the water pushed men into a stupor, froze their limbs and left them to drown, if hyperthermia did not catch them first.

The last to leave the stricken *Blücher* were the senior officers. Abandoning her to her death throes, they plunged into the water and started swimming for shore. They were halfway when the flagship capsized to port, her burning hull setting fire to more of the oil on the water. Her bow went down first and for a brief span her stern rose and her three bronze propellers glistened in the morning sun. To the horror of the watching Norwegians, it was now realised that many men who could not swim still clung to the rudder and shafts and were going down with her. They listened as over the clear water the men sang 'Deutschland, Deutschland uber alles ...' until they vanished beneath the water. A few minutes later there was a terrific underwater explosion and a massive, burning bubble erupted on the surface, setting fire to the remaining unlit oil and killing many of the last to leave.

Norway had made its first and most significant kill. The *Blücher* proved that German might was not all it could be. But the victory would be wasted and Norwegians would later wonder what had been the point of the loss of so many lives in the cold waters of the Oslofjord.

THE SUFFERING OF OSLO

The Norwegian authorities were never comfortable with their role as warmongers and it was a depressing state of affairs that not long after the tremendous defeat of the *Blücher* around 300 Norwegians, including the crew at Oscarsborg, surrendered to fewer than fifty Germans. The town of Karljohansvern was first to go; a brazen ploy by German soldiers who had succeeded in surviving being shipped to Norway won them the day. They threatened Kontreadmiral Smith-Johannsen with a bombing attack on the civilian population if he did not capitulate.

As evacuations had barely begun, Smith-Johannsen decided the death toll would be too high and agreed. Despite the Germans maintaining a bluff that they were there to save the Norwegians from British invasion he was not convinced, but decided his hands were tied. Because of his actions he effectively handed the defensive fort system of Oslofjord to the Germans. It was all over – the Narrows were safe and Oslo was wide open to attack.

All that remained now were the airfields of Sola-Stavanger and Oslo-Fornebu. As they were not under the control of the RNN they remained operational, though it is debatable how much of an asset that was. Just like the rest of the Norwegian military, the airfields were undermanned and woefully outdated. Even so, Hitler decided to strike them with all the might the Luftwaffe could muster.

In the early hours of 9 April, reports came in of German planes over Oslofjord, and Fornebu scrambled its small force of Gloster Gladiator biplanes. Designed by Henry Philip Folland, the Gladiator was the last British biplane fighter, but also the first to have an enclosed cockpit. Introduced in 1934, it looked like a relic of the last conflict, but sold well to numerous countries in the pre-war years. Equipped with four machine guns and a Mercury engine, it could achieve speeds of 257mph and was used by Allied forces in the early stages of the war, though largely in peripheral campaigns where it stood a chance against equivalent planes; against the Luftwaffe it was simply outclassed.

Even as the Gladiator was being introduced it was already obsolete, with the new generation of monoplanes such as the RAF Hurricane and Spitfire already taking its place on British airfields. Despite this, the RAF bought 483 and converted nearly 100 of them to seaplanes. In 1939, fifty-four of these sea Gladiators were still in service with the Royal Navy's Fleet Air Arm. However, in other aspects of the wars of the skies it was apparent that the Gladiator would be hopeless, particularly against the German Messerschmitt, several of which (along with Junkers and Dorniers) would be sent to take Fornebu.

Fornebu's small Gladiator force took off just before 7 a.m. and went in search of the Germans. It took them 40 minutes to find them and, to their horror, leading the invasion were eight Messerschmitt Bf 110 heavy fighters followed by around fifty bombers. The shocked Gladiator pilots knew they had no chance of stopping the invasion (outnumbered as they were ten to one); all they could do was inflict as much damage as possible on the Germans and hope to survive the skirmish.

The one advantage the Gladiators had was their nimbleness; the crews of the Bf 110s later reported they were stunned at how easily the Gladiators outmanoeuvred them. The Germans were using tracer bullets and this made it easier for the Norwegian pilots to avoid the shots. Even so, it was like a handful of wasps stinging at a hungry pack of lions. Two Bf 110s were shot down by the fast-flying Gladiators and two more were badly damaged. Two He 111s were also lost, but they were minor losses to the overwhelming German forces. It was not long before the Gladiators were out of ammunition. One was hit by return fire and had to make an emergency landing, the remaining fighters landing wherever they could once they were of no further use. All were damaged and none would see battle again.

Despite anti-aircraft guns taking out a Junkers 52 and damaging most of the planes in the first wave, it was quickly apparent that Fornebu was about to be overrun. The Norwegians fought bravely to defend the airfield, many remaining at their posts until they were out of ammunition – even as the first German aircraft began landing.

The combined efforts of Gladiators and AA guns had killed or wounded fifty to sixty German soldiers or aircrew within the planes, but now the little fighters were grounded and out of ammunition the Bf 110s could turn their attention to the AA gunners. They started strafing the machine guns; the crews returned fire, only leaving their posts briefly to duck when the German tracer bullets came too close. No one was more than lightly injured. Their bravery meant little, unfortunately, as the AA ammunition did not seem effective against the well-armoured German planes. It appeared to be bouncing off the hulls of the aircraft as long as they stayed high. At the northern end of Fornebu the two light machine guns were the first to run out of ammunition and, as no one seemed to know where the key to the depot bunker was, the guns had to be abandoned. At the south-east, hunkered down in concrete pits, the machine gun crews had a stockpile of ammunition and were determined to hang on to the very last.

The plans of the Germans were not going well either. There were supposed to be twenty-nine Junkers carrying paratroopers who would be dropped over the airfield to mop up the resistance, making it safe for the heavier planes to land. The Junkers, however, were nowhere in sight and the Messerschmitt Bf 110s were running low on fuel, making landing imperative. Suddenly, at 8.20 a.m., three Junkers finally appeared, much to the relief of the Messerschmitts' crews. This quickly turned to astonishment when the lead Junkers began to descend to land instead of dropping its paratroopers – apparently it was under the impression that the airfield was in German hands. Norwegian Sersjant Tellefsen saw the Junkers lumbering in to land and fired into its hull with his Colt machine gun. The Junkers pilot instinctively slammed forward the throttle to take the plane back up, but several troopers were already dead. Tellefsen looked on in astonishment, hardly believing what he had done.

For the Bf 110s there was no choice remaining but to run the Norwegian gauntlet and land. Leutnant Helmut Lent was ordered to try first while the other Messerschmitts strafed the AA gun crews and kept them out of action. Lent was down to one engine, having shut down his starboard one to conserve fuel, so landing the cumbersome Messerschmitt was far from simple. He came in too fast, bouncing onto the runway in a hail of bullets. His undercarriage broke off and he sailed along the runway, down a grass verge and through the picket fence of a nearby house. Luckily neither Lent nor his navigator were injured.

The remaining Bf 110s were quick to follow him and, despite the Norwegian machine guns, were all landed safely and parked to the north of the runway, where some of the rear gunners dismounted their machine guns and took up defensive positions.

Several of the Junkers crews now believed the airfield was under full German control and started to land. They were easy targets for the Norwegians who severely damaged the arriving planes, killing and injuring those inside; but there was no longer any way to prevent the inevitable. Signals were being sent that Fornebu was in German hands, even if it was a little premature. More and more Junkers landed; some still took heavy damage from the machine guns, but these were fast running out of ammunition. Other Junkers were lost simply because Fornebu was small, awkward to approach and lacking air control. It is known that at least fifteen German transport aircraft crashed fatally at Fornebu that day trying to land, and others collided on the tarmac. It was a chaotic and costly arrival. But the Germans had done what they had set out to do; as the machine guns fell silent and the Norwegians were ordered to fall back, Fornebu came under German control.

Twenty-five German He 111s flew over Oslo as a demonstration at dawn on the same day that Fornebu was captured. They were soon joined by fourteen more, designed to intimidate the Norwegians into a bloodless surrender. It worked. Prime Minister Nygaardsvold, though safely evacuated himself, gave permission to surrender the city. At 2.30 p.m. German soldiers marched through Oslo, the stunned residents watching on. Despite numbering under 1,000 and lacking any heavy weapons, the Germans in Oslo were fully in command and any hopes that Britain and Norway had had of preventing an invasion were long gone.

There had barely been time to evacuate the Norwegian administration so that a government in exile might be maintained, or for the British at the embassy under Minister Dormer to destroy their records and run. Margaret Reid, assistant to head of MI6 Frank Foley, who had arrived in Oslo in 1939, recorded the events of the day in her diary:

> I slept soundly while the Germans were sailing up Oslofjord until the ... telephone brought me leaping from my bed ... 'Come to the office at once, will you – and be ready to go!' [MI6 officers Foley and Newill] were tearing files out of their drawers in the open safes ... [at the British Legation] we saw a great bonfire before we reached the grounds ... and were soon frantically rending code books and files to feed the flames.

DAMAGE LIMITATION

On 9 April, the British Government woke to the news that Norway was lost. Instantly the War Office came together and decided air reconnaissance was its first vital move, along with preparations to retake Oslo, Bergen and Trondheim and to regain control of Narvik. At 2 p.m. the Admiralty issued orders that any Norwegian or Danish ships in Allied harbours should be immediately taken under British protection and detained to prevent them returning home. Merchant ships spotted sailing for the Scandinavian coastline were to be redirected to Kirkwall, Scotland. The Admiralty was taking the first step towards salvaging Norwegian forces in British waters for future assaults against the Germans. It could not foresee at the time how vital this would prove to be.

Meanwhile Kaptein Thore Horve of the ancient Norwegian destroyer *Draug* was having similar thoughts. The destroyer had been operating as an escort up and down the coast since the Norwegians had begun their 'Neutrality Watch' – an effort to monitor and maintain their own neutrality from outside breaches. Like so many of his colleagues, Horve was out of the loop when it came to the main events happening around

Oslofjord and Narvik. He had received messages to suggest a German invasion attempt was imminent late on the afternoon of 8 April and had orders to the effect that he was on his own when it came to decision making and had to act according to how he judged the situation. It was troubling news for Horve, who took it to mean that the Germans were closing in and there could be hard times ahead.

Based alone in Haugesund to patrol the Leads, Horve's position was unenviable. Still, he was determined to do his best and ordered the *Draug* to be hastily reloaded with coal for the boilers and ammunition to be brought to the guns. Then all he could do was wait.

Just after midnight, signals came from Bergen that the forts of Oslofjord were in battle. They did not state who was attacking but, unlike many, Horve deemed it obvious that it must be the Germans. But still he waited. A German ship carrying the state flag appeared during the night and was allowed to proceed up the Leads unescorted and at its own risk, but when more appeared, Horve began to feel uncomfortable and was not prepared to allow them to pass so freely. He ordered the ships to wait and made unsuccessful attempts to contact Bergen. Communications were down – he could only guess why – and inevitably his mind turned to the worst scenarios. But Horve was a courageous man and until he heard otherwise he would not allow the German ships to pass.

An uneasy stand-off commenced. The Germans were impatient: their ships contained supplies for the invasion and, faced by the small and old-fashioned *Draug*, they felt frustrated as well as irritated by the Norwegians. At last someone's patience snapped and the merchantman *Main* made an attempt to hurry through the sounds.

For Horve it was an obvious breach of neutrality and he set off in full pursuit despite a 12-degree list to port because the *Draug* had not finished taking on coal. He caught up with the *Main* in the waters just north of Haugesund and two warning shots finally ceased her run. Horve sent over his First Officer to inspect the ship's papers and cargoes, but the Germans were cagey. They were supposedly carrying an unspecified mixed cargo of 7,000 tons destined for Bergen, but had covered their hatches with coal to prevent inspection. The First Officer was not impressed and the *Main* was seized, her captain was escorted back to the *Draug* for further questioning and her radio room was sealed off.

Meanwhile Horve had taken the *Draug* back to the depot to finish loading coal and had finally managed to place a phone call to Bergen. He spoke to Orlogskaptein (Commander) Sigurd Arstad and was astonished when Arstad explained that a German officer was standing next to him as he spoke and he was now a prisoner of war. The line abruptly went dead. Bewildered and distressed, Horve hurried back to the *Draug* where he discovered a Norwegian MF 11 seaplane had landed. Norwegian pilot Stansberg filled in the gaps in Horve's limited knowledge of the invasion, then refuelled his plane and took off for further reconnaissance to the north.

Horve was a pragmatic man who was aware of the limitations of both his ship and the Norwegian military in general. If the Kriegsmarine was sailing up the Oslofjord there was little the valiant *Draug* and her crew could do about it. She was an old girl, outdated, poorly armed, and simply not cut out for modern warfare. The more Horve thought about it, the more he realised that any defence he tried against the Germans would be nothing short of suicidal. Perhaps another captain would have chosen a heroic, if pointless, demise, but Horve saw the broader picture and he wasn't prepared to sacrifice his men for nothing more than posthumous glory. He made a brave decision. He would cross the North Sea, taking the *Main* with him as a prize, and hand his crew and the *Draug* to the British. He was certain that Norway, if it had the opportunity, would enter the war on the Allied side, and with the Germans nipping at his heels he was not prepared to wait for further orders – *if* any came at all.

Horve sent the captain of the *Main* back to his ship, telling him they were headed for Bergen to mask his real intentions. At 9 a.m. the *Draug* and *Main* left coastal waters and Horve turned his ship westwards. As he expected, the *Main* stubbornly remained on a northerly course, so Horve turned back and threatened her with guns and torpedoes until her captain reluctantly agreed to follow them. The *Main*'s captain was not a happy man – he was under strict orders not to allow his ship to be captured or to surrender to the enemy, and now he had done both. He was desperate for any opportunity to either escape with the *Main* or sink her so her supplies would not fall into enemy hands. Around 40 miles into their journey he had his chance when a squad of six planes appeared out of nowhere and one attempted to drop two bombs on the *Main*. Neither hit, but the captain ordered his men into the *Main*'s boats, ensuring that the ship's seacocks were wide open so she would take on water and sink.

Looking on in astonishment at the mass evacuation, Horve then turned the *Draug* to collect the sailors (including a Norwegian pilot who had been doing his job of guiding in the *Main* before her capture). It took time in the rough seas to collect the sixty-seven men and by then it was clear that the *Main* was doomed. Horve finished her off with six shots aimed at her waterline, then carried on to Britain. The *Main*'s German crew, unable to fit below decks on the *Draug*, stood on deck for the journey, thoroughly seasick and fed up.

Horve arrived at Scapa Flow on 11 April, having unloaded his German cargo at Shetland. By 12 April, he was in talks with Rear-Admiral Halifax and was asked to become a liaison officer aboard a British destroyer. Horve agreed and around fifteen of the *Draug*'s officers and NCOs were also recruited to join ships in the Fourth and Sixth Flotillas preparing to head for Norway.

WAR ON NARVIK

Remote and peaceful, the ore town of Narvik became a symbol of the horrors of the Norway operation. No one within the town had expected war to impact directly upon them, though in retrospect the high value and significance of the location should have provided a warning had the locals only been prepared to have less faith in neutrality.

Norvik had grown from a settlement of around 300 in 1898 to close to 10,000 by 1940, helped mostly by the building of a railway line between the town and the Kiruna-Gällivare iron-ore district. Narvik boasted an ice-free port. Even in the harsh winter of 1939–40 when roads were completely blocked by hard-packed snow and even the railway lines occasionally had to be closed and cleared, the fjord beside which the town is built remained ice-free. Narvik was a vital wintertime lifeline for iron exports.

Narvik was not entirely ignorant of its value nor the danger its biggest customers posed. Just before the First World War work had begun on a fort at the entrance of the Ofotfjorden, the narrow 48-mile long channel that leads directly to Narvik. The route to the town through first the funnel-shaped Vestfjorden, then the Baroy Narrows and lastly Ofotfjord was, in theory, highly defensible. In parts Ofotfjord is only 2–3 miles wide, making its negotiation by larger ships difficult. Good defences could easily hammer battleships trying to sail the Narrows and inflict heavy damage without their opponents being able to manoeuvre around them. Patrol vessels could also be situated at the head of Vestfjorden to monitor and prevent traffic from entering the Narrows and further defend the town.

However, as with much of Norway's defences, lack of funding and a reluctance to pursue military matters had left the town exposed. The fort had never been finished; when the First World War came to its conclusion work halted and the various guns intended for two batteries along the fjord were placed into storage.

When the invasion of Norway began, Narvik was still considered a neutral port, unlike most of the major ports in the country which had been placed under wartime conditions. This was designed to prevent problems dealing with international traffic, but left the town open to disaster. On 8 April, there were twenty-six civilian ships sheltering from the freezing weather at Narvik, ten being German. Fritz Wussow, Vice-Consul to Germany, stationed in Narvik, regularly reported news of the various ships entering and leaving the harbour to his masters and was a familiar sight in the evenings wandering the hillsides of the town with his binoculars. As the Germans ramped up their plans, he could report that Norwegian warships had arrived at Narvik.

Though the odds were against them, the Norwegian defenders put up a valiant response when the Germans finally arrived. Kommandørkaptein Willoch of the Norwegian panzership *Eidsvold* showed particular bravery, challenging the German fleet of destroyers heading his way even though he was hopelessly outmatched. An awkward stand-off commenced, the Germans being under strict orders not to fire unless the Norwegians did so first. As the tension mounted and Willoch endeavoured to negotiate for the invaders to leave peacefully, German patience failed. The German destroyer *Heidkamp* launched torpedoes which impacted on the thinly armoured hull of the *Eidsvold* with devastating results: Willoch along with 177 men perished as their ship went down, having failed to fire anything but a warning shot at the Germans.

Before the defence had really begun, the battle was over. The destroyers pulled into Narvik harbour and disembarked their cargo of German and Austrian soldiers. The Norwegian troops on land, left with no specific orders, failed to comprehend the danger now approaching. The Germans dispersed about the town and set up machine-gun positions, while in his headquarters local commander Konrad Sundlo heard explosions from the harbour.

While known to be German-friendly, it was probably a lack of clear orders from above and the impressive numbers of Nazis swarming into Narvik that convinced Sundlo that any defence would be costly to civilian life. The Germans wanted Sundlo to surrender the town and were threatening to use the armaments of the destroyers to reduce Narvik to rubble if there was any resistance. Sundlo had been told he would have to decide for himself what to do based on his previous orders, and in the face of the mass of Germans, unable to communicate with any of his superiors, he conceded defeat. He would later face a court martial for surrendering the town, viewed as a traitor to Norway by his superior General Carl Gustav Fleischer. In truth, Sundlo had very few options on that day in April and any form of resistance would have been disastrous for the thousands of ordinary people still in Narvik. Based on the circumstances and the lack of definite orders he probably made a wise decision. The Supreme Court believed this and cleared him of the accusations.

However, Sundlo was far too helpful to the Nazi occupiers during their time in Norway, and though he could be spared charges over Narvik, other decisions he made during the occupation were viewed less favourably. He was eventually sentenced to life imprisonment with hard labour and stripped of his later rank of colonel.

4

'IN THE NAME OF GOD, GO!'

The instant impact in Britain of the invasion of Norway was a disappointing attempt to restore the balance and save face. British troops were sent to try to retake the airbases and significant ports – a brief resurrection of Plan R4 – but it was a useless exercise. Unprepared for Arctic fighting, under-equipped and outnumbered despite assistance from French and Norwegian soldiers, the British waddled around in the thick furs and clothing the Army had provided them with like rather clumsy bears. From the start there was a lack of enthusiasm and full support for the mission. When it failed and the troops had to be hastily evacuated it was hardly a surprise.

Britain mused on the disaster. In a reversal of its own plans since the start of the war it now found itself short of iron ore. The Nazis controlled Narvik and, as a result, could control supplies being sent from Sweden. Since December 1939, Britain had had a representative in Sweden to oversee the export of important war goods. This was Arctic explorer and United Steel Companies man George Binney. Settled in Stockholm, Binney had set about ensuring via Swedish contacts that Britain had a steady supply of raw and semi-finished materials for its war effort – until 9 April 1940, that is.

Binney heard about the disaster at his offices in Stockholm. The Germans announced that they were blockading the Skagerrak, the main body of water that ran along the southern Norwegian coast and had to be negotiated to reach the North Sea. Sweden was therefore cut off. The Germans had a clear idea of how they would ruin the British war effort; they sent threats to Sweden to make it plain that they had mined the Skagerrak to protect the country from the British (of course) and that regular air patrols and armed trawlers would be watching the waters.

Unimpressed but far from disheartened, Binney would try everything possible to fulfil his responsibility to get iron to Britain. He explored the possibility of shipping less bulky goods through Norwegian ports and paid a visit to Namsos at the same time as the British expedition to recapture Norway was evacuating. Seeing the British troops hastily fleeing under the cover of the short Norwegian nights, Binney realised that the Norway route was out of the question. For the time being he was stumped.

CHAMBERLAIN'S LAST DAYS

Neville Chamberlain was a tired and weary man as he entered the Houses of Parliament on 7 May 1940. Already suffering from the cancer that would snatch his life away at the end of the year, the 71-year-old Prime Minister was now realising his attempts to limit the aggressive advance of Nazi Germany through diplomacy had failed.

Chamberlain had been in power only three years, yet in that time he had already made dangerous decisions that would later brand him as an ineffectual, weak and foolish politician. In 1938, he had signed the Munich Agreement returning the Sudetenland region of Czechoslovakia to Germany, leaving the fragile fledgling country vulnerable not only to internal politics but also to the greed of other nations. Hungary and Poland would both eventually annex portions of Czechoslovakia.

On his return to London, Chamberlain found the public response to his negotiations positive. The press was uncritical of his actions and while opponents such as Churchill felt he had failed his country and left them in even greater danger of war, Chamberlain addressed a cheering crowd from an upstairs window at Number 10: 'My good friends, this is the second time there has come back from Germany to Downing Street peace with honour. I believe it is peace for our time.'

Yet it was only a matter of months before public favour was turning against the champion of peace as the Nazis showed their true colours and began their policy of aggressive expansion. Portions of Czechoslovakia were swallowed first, followed by Poland. Up until the last moment Chamberlain hoped for appeasement, but the general public were against any form of negotiation with Hitler and were starting to feel unease about their own war leader. Members of Parliament had similar views; Churchill helped brand Chamberlain as a weak and ineffectual Prime Minister who had sent the country into an uncontrollable dive towards war.

On that spring morning when Chamberlain met his own ministers to defend his Norwegian decisions, he had to know it was already hopeless. The men who faced him were angry and hostile. Members of the Opposition wanted a debate on the matter, but their fury went deeper and voices were already whispering that Chamberlain should resign. As the Prime Minister tried to address the House and defend his decisions, he was interrupted by a mocking voice that reminded him of his speech of 4 April, when he had unadvisedly stated that 'Hitler had missed the bus'. The gloves were off. Speaker after speaker, from both sides of the House, hurled accusations at the Prime Minister and were rewarded by cheers of agreement from the other members. Sir Roger Keyes stood up and criticised the Naval Staff (Churchill among them) for failing to recapture Trondheim, Norway. It was a metaphorical public execution for the strained-looking Chamberlain, who took the abuse and insults with dignified calm.

The final blow came when Mr Amery stood and quoted words from a speech by Cromwell, when he was dissatisfied with the parliament of his time: 'You have sat too long here for any good you have been doing. Depart, I say, and let us have done with you. In the name of God, go!'

It was the end for Chamberlain. A second debate on 8 May confirmed that both parties had lost confidence in him and, at this time of national crisis, there was no room for a man who could not summon respect and loyalty among his political troops. Chamberlain took aside some of his ministers, including Churchill, and debated the matter privately. The country needed a national government that could work as one in this time of crisis. One party alone could not shoulder the burden. 'Someone must form a Government in which all parties would serve, or we could not get through.' Chamberlain was not the man to do it. When he sent word to the Labour Party, having its conference at Bournemouth, to ask whether it would serve in a national government under his leadership the answer was a clear no. Chamberlain looked around for a suitable replacement for himself and finally settled on Winston Churchill who, ironically, had played a part in the downfall of Norway and subsequently Chamberlain's disgrace. But that had been in part due to error and in part due to having his hands tied by a government set on a course of appeasement.

In any case, Churchill was the right man for the job. Chamberlain, on the other hand, retired to nurse his failing health and to find himself vilified. In July 1940, only two months after the resignation of Chamberlain and the handover to Churchill, and riding on the back of the Dunkirk evacuation which seemed once again to put Britain on the back foot, Victor Gollancz published *Guilty Men*, a book that attacked fifteen important British figures for their support of the appeasement policy towards Germany. Chamberlain was obviously a leading target for abuse in the work. While mainstream retailers refused to touch it, news-stands and street-sellers took up the volume and it sold in its thousands, going through twelve editions in the first month.

Chamberlain had still been working within the government despite his removal as Prime Minister and was still influential, but his health was failing rapidly. By the time *Guilty Men* hit the shelves he was in constant pain. He visited hospital for surgery, where it was discovered that he had terminal bowel cancer. His doctors made the decision not to tell him and the poor man returned to work in mid-August, unaware his death was imminent.

The pain returned shortly after, and the start of air raids on London, meaning Chamberlain had to spend his nights in an air-raid shelter, took away his last reserves of strength. Chamberlain finally offered his resignation to Churchill on 22 September. He retired from public life, spending his last few weeks angry at the public's reaction towards his retirement and weary of the criticism the press constantly flung at him. He died on 9 November. After the funeral Churchill remarked, 'Whatever shall I do without poor Neville? I was relying on him to look after the Home Front for me.'

CAPTURE AT NARVIK

The first that William James Escudier, Mate on the SS *Mersington Court*, knew of the invasion of Norway was after 5 p.m. on 9 April, when he heard gunfire and commotion while he was below decks. The Court Line-owned cargo ship had weighed anchor in Narvik early that morning, having sailed in to Norwegian waters at the end of March. She had just fulfilled her part in a small British convoy that had started out from Southend and her crew were resting before her next perilous voyage across the U-boat-patrolled Atlantic. Escudier hardly expected trouble in the neutral harbour as he relaxed below decks on the 5,141-ton steam ship. Word had yet to spread of the advance of the Germans.

As evening came on and strange noises could be heard outside, Escudier wandered onto the deck to take a look. As usual at that time of year, a heavy snowstorm was making it impossible to see anything beyond the stern of the ship, except for a few random bright flashes of light.

'What's happening?' Escudier hollered to another crewman who was also on deck. It happened to be the ship's gunner.

'I think a submarine stationed in the harbour is torpedoing the ships!' the gunner cried back.

Escudier peered into the thick white swirl. There was a temporary pause in the snowfall and he could just glimpse two German destroyers near the jetty at the entrance to Narvik. To his astonishment they were firing torpedoes at two Norwegian cruisers, which he believed were the *Norge* and the *Eidelfelt* – in fact the latter was the *Eidsvold* captained by the valiant Odd Willoch. Hardly believing the Germans had so suddenly decided to disregard the neutrality of Norway, he watched horrified as the *Norge* was struck and sank in under 2 minutes. Some of her crew, over 200 men, jumped for their lives into the icy waters, swimming to any ship that was near. The Nazis were utterly merciless in their victory and machine-gunned the survivors; 105 men were killed in the disaster; and a further 96 were rescued by the nearby merchant ships.

Stunned by the scene, Escudier wrongly calculated that 800 men had jumped into the icy waters, of whom only a handful were saved, some by two German vessels. While the final toll was nowhere near as high, it was still a deeply felt tragedy among the Norwegians. Out of the *Eidsvold*'s 185-man crew only eight survived, four being pulled from the water by the whaler *Martha Heinrich Fisser*. Willoch went down with his ship.

As the confusion died down, Escudier spotted what he thought were two British destroyers entering the harbour. His relief was instant; he cheered at their approaching saviours, gladdened that the Nazis would not have it all their own way that day. Then the snows cleared a little more and he saw the Nazi flag flying from the masts of the destroyers. Jubilation quickly changed to anxiety. The decks of the destroyers were so thick with soldiers that they appeared black in the evening light. As one aligned herself with the wharf, the troops began to disembark and swarm into Narvik. It wasn't just a breach of neutrality, Escudier realised, this was all-out invasion.

Nazi soldiers were hastily transferred to lorries that, worryingly, had been awaiting their arrival, and were taken inland, while others swarmed along the quay front and up onto the cliffs, cutting off any chance of escape for the merchant ships now trapped in their safe harbour.

The British vessels SS *Blythmoor* and SS *North Cornwall* determined to make the effort, however. They lowered boats and sent men off in them. Escudier lost sight of the escapees but, from the lack of response by the Germans, thought the little boats might have made it by going the long way out of the harbour. Several men remained aboard their vessels, including Second Mate C. Boylan of the *Blythmoor*, who could only stand by miserably as his ship was boarded. Escudier too could do nothing but stand back as grey-uniformed Germans boarded the *Mersington Court* and demanded to see her captain.

'You are all prisoners,' the Germans explained. 'And if anyone attempts to leave the ship they will be shot. Captain, where aboard your ship can we imprison your crew?'

Glumly, the captain indicated the fo'c'sle and the saloon as possible locations. The body of the crew were locked in the former, while the captain, officers and engineers were locked in the saloon with guards at the exits.

Escudier struggled to know what would happen next. He wondered if any men from the *Blythmoor* and the *North Cornwall* had actually escaped. They were perhaps their only hope of reporting quickly to Britain what had happened. Were those that remained about to be shot, despite being civilians?

When the Germans returned and marched the crew of the *Mersington Court* ashore, Escudier feared the worst. They were taken through Narvik, the town's residents looking on nervously, and shut in a room of the school house for a few hours. The waiting was depressing as well as worrying. Finally the captain and officers were removed by the Germans and those that remained, including Escudier, were reunited with the remainder of the crew from the *Blythmoor*, among them Second Mate Boylan. They spent a miserable night in the school house. With no blankets or a fire it was cold and dark. The Germans brought no food or drink, and the men had to shiver and make do as best they could. It was quite a difference from the restful night that Escudier had anticipated.

Morning came slowly, and the prisoners were cold, thirsty and hungry. A mild protest rose among them and they complained to their captors. Reluctantly the Germans agreed to allow two men to leave the school house and buy food for the prisoners, but they would have to do it with their own money. Hastily the prisoners pooled their funds and gave it to two men they could trust. They went out into occupied Narvik and sought out any shopkeeper who would open their doors to them on that miserable morning. When they returned they had managed to buy forty loaves of bread and a little sausage – far from adequate for the large group of hungry men.

It was only now that the British began to wonder about the crews of the other ships in the harbour. There had been five British ships at Narvik that day, SS *Mersington Court*, SS *Blythmoor*, SS *North Cornwall*, SS *Riverton* and SS *Romanby*, all of roughly equal tonnage and age. Moored alongside them, as the neutrality permitted, were ten German merchant ships mostly used for shipping the vast quantities of iron ore that the Germans required. Alongside *them* were five Norwegian vessels, six Swedish vessels (including two harbour tugs) and a Dutch ship. Had the German merchant vessels known what was coming? What about the other Norwegian and British crews?

In fact, the SS *Romanby* had left Narvik on 8 April, but had encountered German destroyers and had been sent back.

When British destroyers entered Narvik on the same morning, Escudier was sharing sausage and bread with his fellow prisoners, their random shelling would strike more than the Germans – the *Blythmoor* was a British casualty and six of her crew died. The German merchant vessels and crews took the heaviest toll, however. Out of the ten in the harbour, eight were hit by British shells or torpedoes, four were sunk, while five were scuttled (one actually on 9 April by her own crew who ran her aground and set fire to her). Four were later salvaged.

But the retribution the British meted out to the shipping in Narvik harbour failed to extend to the ground troops and there was no triumphant retaking of the town. Escudier remained at the school house for most of the day, the noise of shells a distant reminder that something was happening offshore. In the afternoon the British crewmen were once again forced to march, this time to the Café Iris, where they were locked in a room on the top floor with 100 other men.

Escudier's new surroundings were not a great improvement. The room was overcrowded, with no facilities for washing, and windows could not be opened to allow in fresh air. Yet again, blankets were not provided but he managed to sleep as best he could on the bare boards of the floor, with his legs crossing over his neighbour's due to the limited space.

The day after their arrival at the Café Iris, the German guards brought them a humble meal of thin bread and margarine. The guards tried their best to improve the lives of their prisoners. One was good enough to find them tobacco and cigarettes, but there was only so much he could do without getting himself into trouble. What surprised Escudier more was the despondency of the soldiers. They believed unerringly that Narvik would be in the hands of the British within days and were resigned to the fact. Some even asked the British sailors how they would be treated in England.

This general disbelief in the Nazi ability to hold Norway filtered through to the German merchant sailors, who chose to scuttle their ships rather than see them fall into British hands. How ironic that at the same time as the Germans were expecting imminent attack and capture, the British Government was close to cutting its losses with Norway and accepting that it was now in enemy hands.

THE BRITISH RETURN

Not long after the taking of Narvik the German tanker *Jan Wellem* crept into harbour. Her mission was not as dramatic as her counterpart ships, but she was no less vital. The *Jan Wellem* carried a cargo of oil ready to refuel the German destroyers now sitting in Narvik.

It had never been part of the German plan for the destroyers to remain stationed at Narvik for any more than one night. They were desperately needed elsewhere; Hitler's fleet was stretched thin and he could not risk having essential destroyers sitting idle in Norwegian waters. But to return to Germany the destroyers needed fuel, having expended most of theirs just by sailing to Narvik. Without oil they were trapped in the fjord.

The *Jan Wellem* was supposed to be accompanied by another tanker, the *Kattegat*, but she had been spooked by stories of British mines in the Vestfjorden and had decided to wait to the south until the captain could clarify the situation. She was stumbled upon by the Norwegian auxiliary *Nordkapp* and was scuttled by her own crew rather than be captured. Throughout the Norway campaign the Germans had proved very jumpy.

From the windows of the Café Iris, William Escudier could see the *Jan Wellem* entering the harbour. When Escudier asked the harbour master what this new ship was, he was told she was a whaler. Escudier was sceptical; he believed she was a supply ship, perhaps carrying more German troops. But, in fact, the harbour master was not lying as the *Jan Wellem* had formerly been a whaler before being upgraded to a tanker. Unfortunately for the Germans she was also rather slow: her pumps would take 8 hours to fill the fuel tanks of the German destroyers and she could work only on two ships at once. Worse, she did not have enough fuel to supply the U-boats that were loitering around Narvik in desperate need of oil as well. The decision was made to prioritise the destroyers. The subs could wait.

Escudier wasn't sure what to make of the new arrival, but the general decline in morale among the Germans suggested he could still hope for British intervention. He did not know that the Germans were suffering from the new disappointment that the batteries that Quisling had promised were on the cliff-tops were actually non-existent. The Germans had hoped to capture them and use them against the British; now they felt uncomfortably exposed.

Some of their fears were quite justified. As early as 10 April, there was intervention from the British when young Captain Warburton-Lee led the Second Destroyer Flotilla into the harbour and torpedoed enemy boats. The *Hardy*, *Hotspur*, *Hunter* and *Havock* had taken turns in the cramped harbour to assault the Germans. The *Heidkamp* had been their first victim, the German flagship being hit on her port stern, igniting her aft magazine and causing a huge explosion that killed eighty men instantly, including her commander and most of his staff.

The destroyers still hitched to the *Jan Wellem* for refuelling were easy targets. The *Hermann Künne* attempted to move away, ripping off the hoses and moorings from the *Jan Wellem* as she went. However, when the *Anton Schmitt*, a destroyer not hitched to the *Jan Wellem*, was torpedoed for a second time the shockwaves from the underwater explosions crippled the *Künne*'s engines and she drifted into the wreckage of the *Schmitt* where she remained a sitting target.

The initial ease of the first assault gave Warburton-Lee too much confidence and he failed to move out of the harbour while he retained the advantage. Instead he was almost trapped by a rescue party of German destroyers heading up the fjord, in much the same way as he had cornered his victims. The ships of the Second Flotilla were suddenly fighting for their lives and *Hunter* and *Hardy* were lost, the remaining ships escaping (just) to lick their wounds and rethink the whole matter.

Saturday 13 April started for Escudier in much the same way as the last few days had. The confined men were bored and dreadfully hungry, kept on starvation rations by their captors and slowly losing hope. They were cold, uncomfortable and deeply worried. As each day passed, their German masters seemed to grow more settled in their position in the town. Cut off and with no knowledge of what was happening elsewhere in Norway, the men could only glumly speculate about their future.

Around 11.20 a.m. Escudier heard the boom of guns outside. There was sudden elation among his party. Had the Royal Navy at last come for them? Over the course of the next 2 hours they listened eagerly as the noise increased, reaching a crescendo in early afternoon when the old and ramshackle Café Iris quaked on its foundations. A ripple of fear passed through the men that it might tumble down upon them. Then, as dramatically as the noise had begun, it went silent. Looking from the windows of the Café Iris, it was obvious that the Germans had suffered a heavy toll. The damage of the first British assault had been repeated and improved upon. There did not appear to be a single German destroyer left intact in the harbour.

This new assault was being led by Vice-Admiral Whitworth, who was not intending to make the same mistakes as Warburton-Lee and had amassed a sizeable force for the assault. His 'Force B' was comprised of the *Warspite, Bedouin, Punjabi, Eskimo, Cossack, Kimberley, Forester, Icarus, Hero* and *Foxhound*.

Around 2.30 p.m. the prisoners at the Café Iris could see three British destroyers moving into the harbour and heading for the wharf. The Germans fired at them from the shore with machine guns, but they could do little damage to the heavily armoured ships and the British gunners returned fire. Escudier spotted a small German ship bravely defying the odds and shooting continuously at the British until she was hit by two salvoes of shells and 'just crumpled up and sank'.

The damage to the Nazi ships was immense. Whitworth's orders had been to ensure no German destroyers were left intact and he had undertaken his mission faithfully, though not without heavy damage to the British force. The *Eskimo* in particular had been badly hit and had to limp out of the fjord with her bow blown away and the remains hanging vertically into the water. That she sailed at all was remarkable.

The men aboard the *Hero* and *Icarus* were having a better time. When they spotted the remains of the *Hans Lüdemann* still afloat they mounted a race between them to see who could board her first. The party from the *Hero* won and proudly marched the decks of their captured vessel, amazed at the standard of the German ship. She seemed more like a yacht than a destroyer. There were worries that the ship might explode, so the men did not stay long. They conducted a rapid search, collected some souvenirs of their victory with the Nazi ensign on them and found a German petty officer, badly wounded but alive, on deck. They took him with them back to the *Hero* and then watched as their captain ordered that the *Lüdemann* be destroyed once and for all. A torpedo sent her to the bottom of the fjord at around 4.55 p.m.

At the Café Iris, Escudier was watching excitedly as three destroyers came right into Narvik harbour and one made for the jetty. The German soldiers began firing again, but the action was hopeless and the British crews retaliated. He felt certain that 'there must have been a lot of slaughter amongst the German crew because we could see lots of ambulances collecting the injured'. The resistance finally faltered, and the destroyers moored in the harbour three abreast. Escudier elatedly turned to his comrades. Everyone was convinced that during the evening they would be rescued by the Royal Navy. They rejoiced and sneered at the pathetic attempt by the Nazis to conquer Narvik.

Aboard the flagship *Warspite* Whitworth's men were settling down to a post-action supper of tea, eggs and corned beef.

They were allowed up on deck to watch the sun setting over the snow-covered mountains and to admire the town they had saved from the Nazis. Vice-Admiral Whitworth was still on his bridge sending a report to Admiral Forbes that he had succeeded in destroying all the German ships in Narvik. Privately he was wondering about landing a party in the town itself and securing it in British hands. Commander Sherbrooke of the *Cossack* was keen for more action and was convinced the Navy could retake Narvik.

Whitworth was more reticent. Under the misapprehension that there were around 2,000 Nazis in Narvik, he decided that he did not have sufficient men to send ashore. It also concerned him that the *Warspite* would need to remain close to shore to provide covering fire for the landing party, and the last thing Whitworth wanted was to be pinned down in the closed harbour, a sitting duck for any German counter-attack. Had he known there were only a few hundred soldiers in Narvik itself, the rest being spread widely around the perimeter, and that many were poorly armed and so spooked by the shelling from the British fleet that they had fled into the mountains, his decision would no doubt have been different. Though whether the British ever could have held Narvik successfully without further back-up is debatable. In the end, Whitworth chose to consider his mission over and ordered his flotilla to sail away from Narvik.

William Escudier awoke the following morning and looked out of the café window only to see the harbour empty. His countrymen had not come for him. Beside him, Boylan stood miserable. His ship, the *Blythmoor*, had been sunk in the action and there was no sign of her. The *Romanby* had also been sunk, while the *Riverton* and *North Cornwall* were badly damaged and sat listing in the harbour waters – they would take three days to sink. The German *Bochenheim* was on fire and other ships were either missing or floating wrecks.

Throughout the day British planes flew over the town and dropped bombs on the harbour front. Escudier saw German tracer bullets from the machine-gun posts soaring into the air, trying to catch one of the aircraft, but their successes were minimal. One British plane flew in very slowly; Escudier assumed it was reconnoitring. It dropped five bombs and was slightly caught by German bullets, its fuselage being damaged as it flew seawards. Whether by luck or design, the Narvik powerhouse took a direct hit and went up in flames, engulfing several adjoining buildings.

The Nazis still had a foothold in Narvik, but they were miserable about it. The supply ships that had sailed separately from those carrying troops and were meant to ensure the Army was well equipped for taking and holding Norway had either failed to arrive or had not been as well stocked as promised. Food was short and the Germans had well over 100 prisoners to share their meagre rations with. Escudier and his fellow captives found their meals reduced to one half-inch slice of mouldy bread. They cut off the green mould and ate the stale bread, which 'was like eating compressed sawdust'. Even the regular flights of German planes dropping medical and food supplies over Narvik failed to improve matters.

Sat among the confused and worried merchant sailors was a dashing young man, with dark hair and a stern stare. This was Giles Romilly, a journalist for the *Daily Express* and nephew to the man about to become Prime Minister, Winston Churchill. The 24-year-old Romilly had been serving as a war correspondent for the *Daily Express* when Narvik was taken. The Germans had quickly picked him out for special attention and after several sessions of close questioning had learned of his significant connections.

Romilly was earmarked for Germany, destined to stay in Colditz castle as the first of Hitler's *Prominente* – important political prisoners afforded special, luxury treatment. A few days after the British attack on Narvik, Romilly was removed from the Café Iris at around 8 a.m. to be flown to Germany. Escudier did not expect to see him again, but when he was returned a few hours later it was a pleasant surprise. The seaplane had suffered engine trouble and Romilly had been escorted back to the Café Iris. Unfortunately for Romilly his transport was fixed and he was shortly removed once again and sent to Germany. He was unlucky, as a few days later his fellow prisoners were released.

The situation for Germans and British alike at Narvik had become impossible. Food was scarce, the Café Iris was cold and uncomfortable and not even clean. Escudier had been confined there for fifteen days already and was going stir-crazy. The sailors regularly complained to the officer in charge of them.

'You will either have to feed us or liberate us!' they demanded.

Eventually, on 23 April, the German officer had had enough. He came to the sailors and told them he had barely enough food to feed his own men, let alone prisoners, and his troops would have to come first. As a result, he had come to the conclusion that the best thing to do would be to release the sailors and send them to Sweden. The sailors were elated. The German officer picked out sixty-nine, including Escudier, who were to march from Narvik at 1 p.m. The remaining sailors would wait an hour and then follow. An awful air raid was raging as Escudier left the Café Iris with the others under a German escort. Despite the noise and explosions, everyone was in good spirits to be heading away from their prison and onwards to Sweden.

They marched along the cliffs of the fjord, deep in snow at times. After an hour and a half had passed, they spotted a French and then a British destroyer out in the water. Exposed on the cliff-tops, the sailors thought that they had been recognised when the British ship gave a blast on her siren. Not long afterwards the destroyers opened fire on them, mistaking them for Germans. Thankfully, by falling into the snow, the sailors escaped any casualties.

Ten long hours of marching brought them to a train station. The party was wet, cold and fatigued, but freedom was in sight. As they bundled into the train, sitting five abreast in the overcrowded carriage, they were served a measly portion of soup, but at least they were headed for neutral territory.

Escudier was exhausted, and even the sight of a submarine officer with a machine gun trained over the prisoners could not prevent the fatigue of the last few days catching up with him. As he rested, his wet clothes sticking unpleasantly to his skin, he clung to the knowledge it would soon all be over.

5

A SHADOW OVER SWEDEN

George Binney found life behind his desk in Sweden as a representative for the British iron and steel industries a trifle dull, though the events in Norway had certainly added a new touch of drama to his existence. Sweden was nervous; its people were anxious that not only Norway's but also Belgium's neutrality had been completely ignored by the Nazis, not to mention the invasion of Finland by the Russians in which the Germans were complicit. The Swedes could not help but wonder if they were destined to be next.

Sweden's place in Scandinavia had for many centuries been one of rivalry with its nearest neighbours. At various times there had been wars with Russia or Norway. On occasion Sweden had been ruled by a Norwegian king and, in contrast, had at some points in history had its own king as joint ruler of Norway. At times Sweden had sided with Norway against the Russians; on other occasions it had defended Russia's interests; but over the last century or so Sweden had been developing a survival strategy in the form of neutrality.

The First World War had been Sweden's biggest test, when it had stood its ground and remained neutral while the nations about it seemed determined to descend into chaos. It had been a difficult and dangerous strategy and had earned Sweden a good number of insults from both sides, who felt that it had sat on the fence during the conflict, but Sweden had avoided the brunt of the war. It had survived and, in comparison with other nations such as France, had very little war damage to mend. However, the damage to its reputation among the fighting nations was another matter.

No one was particularly surprised that Sweden chose neutrality once again as the twilight war finally ignited into true conflict. Binney had been sent to Sweden in 1939 with this in mind. There was no doubt that Sweden would stick to its (peaceful) guns and refuse to take sides, but that didn't mean it couldn't be swayed to act in Nazi interests. Germany was a lot closer to Sweden than Britain and could exert a great deal of pressure on the country. Binney was there to make sure the Swedish authorities did not renege on any contracts they had with the British because of Nazi threats.

It was a tense time, yet few predicted in those first quiet days of war that Hitler would prove so aggressive and that neutrality would suddenly become so fragile.

Now Norway was lost and it didn't appear, certainly not to Binney, that the British were going to do anything about it. In Sweden he was near enough to hear the latest rumours and news about the events in Norway and to wonder if he was soon to become a Nazi captive. Binney was not greatly troubled by the risk of imprisonment. He was described by those who knew him as 'a true Elizabethan: a merchant adventurer'. Just missing out on the First War, Binney had had to find his own adventure to compensate. While a student at Merton College, Oxford, he helped to organise three Arctic expeditions between 1921 and 1924.

This was the great age of exploration and Binney took full advantage of the patronage of his college and the support of the Royal Geographical Society to fulfil his own dreams of adventure. Even today Arctic exploration has its risks, but Binney travelled in an age when cold protection came from furs, when power was provided by dogs and where rescue if things grew bad was virtually impossible. Only nine years before the first of Binney's Arctic explorations, Robert Falcon Scott and his party of explorers (including the famous Captain Oates) had perished on the return journey from the South Pole.

The 1921 expedition took Binney to the island of Spitsbergen, off the Svalbard archipelago in Norway. Spitsbergen had served as a whaling post in the eighteenth and nineteenth centuries before being abandoned. It was redeveloped for coal mining in the early twentieth century, but was largely under-explored, and Binney's expedition had the goal of conducting various surveys and experiments in the Arctic environment to increase popular understanding. In fact what Binney succeeded in doing was learning about better survival in Arctic conditions and how to train men to cope with the extreme cold. This information would later be used by the British Army when it fought through heavy winters in Europe against Germany.

Binney was involved in a second Spitsbergen expedition for Merton College in 1923. Among his party was keen sportsman and excellent rower Andrew 'Sandy' Comyn Irvine, who was making his first foray into Arctic exploration. He proved impressive with his natural adaptability to the harsh environment, and the expedition leader, Professor Noel Odell, asked him to take part in a forthcoming attempt he was organising to climb Everest. Irvine would last be seen by Odell as he headed for the summit of Everest with George Mallory in 1924.

That same year, Binney was undertaking his final Arctic expedition, heading for Nordaustlandet (often referred to as North East Land) – an uninhabited, 90 miles square, ice-covered island north-east of Spitsbergen. The island was remote and dangerous; a German expedition sent to explore it in 1912 had perished in the attempt. However, Binney was finding his feet in Arctic exploration and the challenge appealed to him. He also made a point of having an aerial survey team, something he had used sporadically in his last missions to great success. Binney was a pioneer of using seaplanes to chart unexplored areas, and for his 1924 mission he had secured an Avro seaplane with a new Siddeley Lynx 185hp air-cooled engine. It had been adapted to have an enclosed cabin with a sliding roof and to carry not only a sledge and five weeks' provisions for three men but also a collapsible boat. This had all added to its weight and Binney had had to compromise by not equipping it with skis to its undercarriage for landing on snow. Instead its normal floats for sea landings had been altered to enable the plane to make emergency landings on ice.

The plans for the expedition were as audacious as the equipment. Binney wanted to co-ordinate three sledging parties, along with the Avro, to map a large chunk of North East Land. He also wanted to beat the current record for sailing farthest north in navigable waters and to explore the Josef Archipelago, 'where practically no work has ever been attempted and where there is reason to suppose unknown land exists'. Binney was one of those great minds of an age of adventure and exploration when nothing was deemed impossible.

The expedition left Newcastle in June 1924 aboard a 300-ton Norwegian whaler, the *Polar Bear*, accompanied by a small Norwegian sealing sloop. Binney was at home on the ocean and his enthusiasm for the mission was at full throttle. Walking into the mess room of the *Polar Bear* he could stop and admire a silver shield presented to him by the Prince of Wales for his expedition to Spitsbergen, which wished him and the twenty-two men in his party success.

As Binney prepared to face the unknown, he spoke to the press for what could easily have been the last time:

> [The *Polar Bear*] will go where no other ship has sailed, and it may well happen that new land may be discovered. The arrangements for wireless should ensure better contact between the various sections of the expedition than has been obtained previously. We hope to receive the

British Broadcast programmes during the whole period of our absence from civilisation. We expect to return in September. The seaplane we are taking if successful may attempt to fly back to England by easy stages. Meantime we are stocking the ship with a year's provisions in case the ice closes down before we are able to leave the island.

The journey into Arctic waters would rapidly leave Binney and his men out of immediate communication with any form of help, though they could use the wireless on the *Polar Bear* to send back reports. In this way Binney intended to communicate a series of articles to *The Times* on his adventure.

Very quickly misfortune found them, but Binney considered it quite usual during an Arctic expedition for problems to rapidly mount up. When it was discovered that their seaplane pilot could not cope with Arctic flying conditions he had to be shipped back to England and another man sent for. That was a minor inconvenience as the seaplane had to be assembled on site first before it could be flown, and Binney anticipated the replacement pilot arriving before he was needed. More disheartening was news of the loss of young Irvine on Mount Everest. Binney took it as a personal blow, remembering the 'light-heartedness, resource, and endurance' Irvine had brought to his 1923 expedition. It also came as a stark reminder of the dangers that his own team faced. Every man knew death could await him in the Arctic, either through accident, injury, illness or sheer bad luck. The cold was a killer and they were dependent on the quality of the provisions they had been issued with for survival.

Time was always against them. Binney realistically stated, 'In all probability we are over-reaching ourselves, and attempting too much work in too little time.' But that wasn't going to stop him from trying.

The new seaplane pilot arrived and Binney was eager to try out the specially built Avro. On 14 July, he joined the pilot as the Avro flew from Green Harbour, where the seaplane had been constructed, to Liefde Bay, where it was intended aerial operations would be based. The Avro never arrived at its new berth. In early afternoon it became obvious to the crew of the *Polar Bear* that something was wrong. They began a search but it would take them until midnight to find the little plane, which had been drifting for 14 hours in freezing water with her two passengers. Thankfully both Binney and the pilot survived this first ordeal unscathed.

Disaster after disaster now began to plague Binney. Not long after his dramatic rescue, both the *Polar Bear* and the smaller sealing sloop hit a sunken reef and were almost impossible to refloat. Then an anticipated first landing at Brandy Bay became impractical and they had to divert to Wahlenberg, now Wahlenbergfjord Bay to drop off two sledging teams. Sickness started to affect the men; Captain Helmar Hansen, part of the third sledging party, contracted blood poisoning in the face, though fortunately the ship's doctor was able to ensure his full recovery so his party could be landed before the encroaching ice made it impossible. Less happy was the sudden illness of Mr Law, the wireless operator, which temporarily made communications a problem. Law was suffering from pleurisy and eventually had to be sent back to England. The only ray of light in all this darkness was that the Avro seaplane had been completely repaired and had made her first successful flight since her forced landing three weeks before.

Slowly things improved. Binney happily sent home photographs of the expedition, including a picture of himself, in what counted as Arctic clothing for the time, gathering seagull eggs. His picture appeared in *The Times* beside images of a sheep dog trial, a Zeppelin flight and the Devil Worshippers of Mosul. But then the weather turned against the explorers. Binney reported by wireless that they were experiencing the worst weather that had hit the region in fifteen years. The seaplane was covered in snow and one survey party had briefly been lost in a blizzard while out on a motorboat. Pack ice was threatening the *Polar Bear* and Binney had put in place emergency evacuation measures for their base camp. For readers of *The Times* back home the fortitude of the men in such horrendous conditions seemed unimaginable, but Binney knew how to lighten his reports. He finished one gloomy report with the remark that they had managed to hear every recent concert broadcast by station 5XX 'quite distinctly'. Britain liked to know how wonderful and far-reaching its influence was.

Despite the conditions, Binney set out with a sledging party and through fog, blizzards and high winds they managed to drag themselves across an unexplored section of the island. They named a glacier after Eton College and traversed a range of crevasses, the dog teams proving more of a hindrance than a help, until they reached the western coast of the island. It had taken them eleven days and, as far as they were aware, they were the first to do it. They were expecting the Avro to greet them, as the day was bright and the skies clear, perfect for aerial photography. The sealing sloop eventually found them and brought them the news that the seaplane had crashed yet again.

It took eight days to restore her, but Binney was determined to prove the worth of aircraft on Arctic exploration. It flew on several more reconnaissance missions, eventually flying the furthest north any aircraft had ever gone. Then it was autumn and the weather was too poor for flying. The Avro was dismantled on the shores of the Reindeer Peninsula and abandoned. The plane had justified its expense and the difficulty of transporting it; over the course of the expedition it had photographed 70 miles of North East Land despite the appalling weather.

When Binney returned from his mission his gains proved slight; he had mapped the interior of Wahlenberg's Bay and discovered a new tract of land which he named rather proudly the Oxford Peninsula, and he had collected eggs of the ivory gull and Sabine's gull, rare finds. But even Binney had to admit it was a minor haul for such effort and expense. 'Perhaps, we hoped for too much,' he said.

Binney's love for the Arctic was far from over; in 1926, he joined the Hudson's Bay Company and wrote *The Eskimo Book of Knowledge*, a rather cynical compendium designed to accustom the natives of the colder stretches of Canada to English life. Supplied with illustrations, it showed things like horses, which were described as four-legged animals that ate grass like a deer, and King George, called Atanek George in the Inuit tongue. This invaluable resource of Englishness was to be sold to the unsuspecting natives for the price of a few ermine skins. Even reviewers of the age found it hard to take the book seriously. 'It is extraordinary how impressive our own trite wisdom looks in Eskimo,' *The Times* reported. 'The White Men are tremendous fellows, no doubt, but they seem to have a trivial, snippety, jerky sort of language [compared with Inuit].'

Binney stayed with the Hudson's Bay Company until 1930 when he joined the United Steel Companies Ltd as export manager and continued his life of adventure travelling the world and securing contracts for them. He spent time in India, China and South America, and in the latter started to get a feel for the rising Nazi movement among the German immigrants. Unlike some, Binney was not inclined to spend a great deal of time philosophising about politics, and pursued his work with vigour while mounting tensions in Europe began to trouble the British Government. As late as 1938, he was securing complex contracts for 100,000 tons of exported railway materials and spending time developing business connections in Iran. When the twilight war threatened to cause problems for Britain's Scandinavian imports he was a natural choice to head to Sweden and begin the delicate negotiations to ensure Britain was not cut off and its war effort stifled. Once more, George Binney was heading for an Arctic adventure.

FROM PETSAMO TO NEW YORK

May 1940 found Binney in a depressed and miserable Finland, hoping to negotiate with the Finnish Government the establishment of British bases to export Swedish goods along the Arctic highway. It was hardly two months since the Finns had signed an armistice with Russia, ceding the entire Karelian Isthmus, their second largest city Viipuri (now Vyborg), and a large chunk of their industrial territory to the Soviets. Eleven per cent of their territory was lost, and 30 per cent of their economic assets, with 422,000 Karelians having to evacuate their homes and become refugees. Finland also lost a portion of Salla, the Kalastajansaarento Peninsula, and four islands in the Gulf of Finland.

From Binney's point of view, the only consolation was that the Soviets had returned Petsamo to the Finns after its occupation by the Red Army. He was full of optimism that Petsamo could be the base for exports from Sweden, or, at a push, the nearby Kirkenes might be used. The Soviets were still allied to the Nazis and Binney would have to avoid arousing their suspicions and alerting the Germans to his tactics. As it was, he was disproportionately optimistic about his chances for success, considering the Finnish people were still licking their wounds and reflecting bitterly on the complete lack of aid that had been sent their way either from Norway, France or Britain. The Allies had abandoned Finland to its fate, and now they wanted its help.

Still, Binney's early negotiations seemed promising and he returned to Stockholm convinced that he would soon have the export issue resolved. It was then he learned that the British had evacuated Narvik and the whole of North Norway was under Nazi control. His hopes were shattered. The Germans had almost total control of the Baltic shipping routes, so developing a commercial route from Petsamo to Britain was now impossible. With the Germans building up a blockade and the British conceding Narvik to them (despite their resounding victories on shipping in the harbour) there was no possibility for him to dodge the Nazis.

Rarely despondent for long, Binney attempted to send small shipments clandestinely under German noses using Finnish ships. They sailed from Petsamo to New York successfully enough, but their minor cargoes were a mere drop in the ocean for British needs. As the Nazi net spread further around the shores of Norway and began ensnaring Sweden's waterways as well, Binney knew he had to find another way to ship goods. Sitting in his cubby-hole of an office in Stockholm, he received a cable from the Ministry of Supply reminding him 'of the paramount importance for the Swedish war materials (particularly those connected with British Aircraft Production) to reach England …', as if Binney needed reminding. Yet everywhere he turned the Nazis had set up a barrier to prevent the British receiving their vital war supplies.

Binney's office was tucked away in the British Legation which Peter Tennant, fellow office worker and friend to Binney, described as resembling the set of a 'medieval mystery play with hell in the basement, home of printing and photography'. Situated on Laboratoriegatan, the building had originally been designed as the Office of Works. It was built between 1913 and 1915 under the supervision of a Swedish Count, and bore a closer resemblance to a residence in London than a Swedish home. When the British moved in they rapidly outgrew the space given to them and further offices were arranged at Strandvägen 82, an Italianate-style building overlooking the waters of Brunnsviken. Binney resided in a cramped room on the first floor of the Legation in the British minister Victor Mallet's residence alongside the Commercial and Service Departments. Below him on the ground floor were the reception, Chancery and Press Departments, while above was the attic where the radio operators and other secret personnel hid.

The Legation was a hotchpotch of people on legitimate and clandestine business: Tennant partially ran a propaganda operation from the building, and SOE eventually had rooms in the Legation. Unsurprisingly this attracted the attention of the Swedish security police who were working a little too closely with the Gestapo for British tastes. The Svestapo, as they were nicknamed, took over a barn opposite the Legation and from there photographed and detailed the Legation's comings and goings. In return, members of the Legation enjoyed taking their own photographs of the supposedly neutral police, which were published later in the war much to the Swedish Government's chagrin.

To get to his office, Binney had to go through an arch into a courtyard and confront at the main door Strandberg the Swedish Chancery messenger, who, along with his son, guarded the entrance. Just inside and on the right were the Chancery offices commanded by the archivist Mr G.A. Urquhart, who protected his domain fearlessly despite his close friendship with a long-serving member of the German Legation. Helping him was a fingerprint expert from Scotland Yard, Mr Battley, who insisted that Legation residents changed their safe combinations regularly, causing great consternation for those who had to remember the new numbers.

Along the left of the hall were the offices of Sir William Montagu-Pollock, Counsellor, and Archibald Ross, Second Secretary. Bill and Archie were career diplomats serving alongside the Minister, the Commercial Counsellor and the Consul-General, Ken White. They were later joined by George Labouchere as First Secretary. Bill Pollock was quite the character in the Legation and could often be found wandering around in sandals and one of his specially made green linen shirts or disappearing off on an expedition to collect edible fungi and snails.

On the first floor, Binney was kept company by Jack Mitcheson who was in charge of the Commercial Department responsible for implementing the War Trade Agreement, rationing Swedish imports and ensuring the safe conduct of ships. His burdens had become considerably heavier after the invasion of Norway and Denmark, and he spent a great deal of his time trying to prevent the Swedes from exporting iron ore to the Germans. Though quiet and modest, Mitcheson was a tireless supporter of Binney in his blockade-running exploits. Aside from the main names, the Legation was overflowing with various attachés, who regularly came and went, like the unfortunate air attaché who became paranoid about being bugged by the Abwehr and suffered a nervous breakdown.

Gradually over the course of 1940, the fledgling SOE acquired rooms in the Legation, starting in the kitchen, and took over the co-ordinating of certain operations, including Binney's brainchild of blockade-running. Binney's cubby-hole put him in direct contact with his superior, Victor Mallet. Mallet had replaced Sir Edmund Monson (not a terribly respected character) and had been viewed with slight suspicion by the mishmash of workers under his command when he was first appointed. Son of a former lady-in-waiting to Queen Victoria and one of Her Majesty's many godchildren, he had married Peggy Andreae, daughter of a banker. Peggy was a keen hostess who took great care of all her charges in the Legation, at one time arranging for the wife of a Polish refugee to have her baby in the building so there could be no debating its British nationality.

Mallet got on well with the Swedes, some thought a little too well, but he was British to his core and would give no quarter to his neutral friends. The day before his forty-seventh birthday he had celebrated the apparent British naval victory of the sinking of the *Rio de Janeiro* by the Polish submarine *Orzel*. When he woke up the next morning it was to discover that the Nazis had invaded Norway and there was little the Royal Navy could do about it.

Binney did not always see eye to eye with Mallet and they had regular heated arguments, especially concerning Binney's more ambitious schemes to sneak iron ore away from the Germans. It wasn't helped by Binney considering it prudent to keep his superior mostly in the dark about his plans, leaving Mallet often red-faced before the Swedish. Ultimately, however, they remained firm friends and Mallet admired Binney's courage.

This was the strange mismatched world Binney worked in, surrounded by an assortment of eccentrics and free-thinkers who very often worked in isolation or in contradiction to each other. There was rivalry between the various departments, but also co-operation, and if sometimes things were overlooked or duplicated, it did not affect matters greatly in the larger scheme of things. But however Binney looked at it, when it came to getting Britain its iron, he was mostly on his own.

MARCH TO SWEDEN

While George Binney wrestled with his iron ore issues William Escudier had other concerns on his mind, not least of which was getting back to England. After boarding a train from Norway the Nazis had transported Escudier and his fellow sailors to the Swedish border. Their reprieve from marching had been brief. In the early hours of the morning they were ordered off the cramped train, pleas for a drink of water being treated with scorn by the submarine officer touting a machine gun. 'Get out you English swine!' he snapped. Submarine crews were known for being the most ardent Nazis and the hardest of men.

Escudier had vainly hoped that they would arrive somewhere close to civilisation, but the Germans dropped them apparently in the middle of nowhere. The snow was knee deep in the shallowest places and the route the Nazis indicated the men must follow was entirely uphill. Tired and stiff from sleeping in damp clothes, the men resigned themselves to the journey and began the arduous trek towards what they hoped was warmth, humanity and food. None of them realised that to reach their destination they would have to walk 31 miles, half-starved, inadequately clothed and numb from the cold. The Germans had abandoned them at the limits of their newly won territory. Trespassing into Sweden was a step the troubled invaders were not about to take. As the men marched off they could look back and see their captors leaving.

The journey was tough, the sailors helping each other when necessary, but the snow sapped their meagre energy reserves and the only thing that kept Escudier on his feet was the thought of freedom ahead. After a gruelling uphill struggle they came to a frontier post guarded by soldiers. For Escudier this seemed like the worst part of the whole ordeal; so close to freedom, they were now delayed for five long hours while the Swedes decided if they should be allowed to pass. The frontier post did not boast luxury facilities and the men had to shiver and ache in the cold, not even able to warm themselves by the constant movement of walking.

When the Swedes finally made their decision and lifted the barrier, the sailors were escorted to what had been a tourist hotel but now appeared to be occupied by the military. A Swedish officer stood on the front step and was stunned at the sight of the half-frozen sailors marching towards him. He yelled out to his men to give assistance and suddenly the sailors were surrounded by a swarm of helping hands. For some it was too much and they collapsed, having to be carried into the hotel by the helpful Swedes. Escudier managed the last short distance on foot and with great relief found himself in the warm confines of the hotel. It seemed a long time since he had last enjoyed civilised living and now the Swedish soldiers hovered about the sailors providing food and drink. Twelve of the Englishmen were immediately assessed to require hospital treatment and were whisked away, the rest settling into the hotel for the night.

'The Swedes definitely deserve full marks for their reception of us,' Escudier later remarked, but despite the consideration they were shown, every man was anxious to get back to England now that it seemed true war had arrived. Escudier tried to wire the Ministry of Shipping to get advice; when that failed he tried a number of other names he knew, but there was no response and yet again he felt he was on his own.

The next morning found Escudier and his shipmates back on a train, this time headed for Gällivare. There they spent two days while the Swedish authorities scratched their heads and tried to figure out what they were going to do with this raggle-taggle bunch of ex-captives. Finally they were sent to Jörn where everyone was bundled into an old dilapidated house for accommodation. Escudier was unimpressed. 'The treatment we received there was not so good and we started to complain to the consulate who then made arrangements to billet us.'

The billets were a great improvement and, for the time being, the men were content. But the consulate was troubled by their continued presence and, on 25 July, had them sent to a specially prepared camp at Helsingfors. Were they prisoners or refugees? Perhaps neither. In any case, Escudier didn't mind the camp where he met up with survivors from the *Hunter*, one of the ships that had caused such havoc to the Germans at Narvik but had been sunk in trying to exit the harbour. There were about 170 men in the new camp and the Swedes offered them paid work to keep them occupied in the form of road-making. Escudier found himself surprisingly happy with the new arrangement. It seemed that there was no immediate way of returning to England and at least the work prevented the men from sitting around idle. He did wonder what the future held and whether this was the way he would spend his war, but for the time being there was little he could do, and it was certainly no use complaining.

THE HEADACHES OF WAR

How was Binney going to get the desperately needed iron ore to Sweden? Britain was in urgent need of ball bearings and other supplies for the manufacture of tanks, aircraft and weapons and the Germans were, so far, doing a good job of preventing them from being delivered. Could the Nazis 'starve' Britain into surrender before the war had hardly begun?

Binney cast around for any options he could find. He looked briefly to Russia, which, despite being an ally of Germany, was in the process of arranging a trade agreement with Sweden, but

so far nothing had been concluded and there seemed no prospect of using either the Trans-Siberian railway or a route across
the Persian Gulf to get goods to England. He also did not have a
lot of faith in Russian reliability.

Meanwhile the Swedish iron and steel works, knowing that
they could not fulfil their British contracts as the Nazis made
delivery impossible, had ceased production of British-ordered
goods. This was exactly what the Germans had hoped for.
As a side benefit of the invasion of Norway they had predicted
Sweden would be forced to allow the Anglo-Swedish War
Trade Agreement to lapse, crippling Sweden economically and
throwing it back onto the mercy of German trade. Fortunately
the Ministry of Economic Warfare could see the danger and
agreed that, as far as possible, Sweden would honour its contracts. Binney was instructed to negotiate a settlement for the
remaining outstanding British contracts with the Jernkontoret
(the central body of the Swedish iron and steel industries) and to
press forward production of materials essential to the British war
effort. Then all he had to do was find a way of getting the goods
to Britain.

Binney was beginning to feel rather stumped when some
Swedish friends told him the story of the *Nora*, a small Swedish
vessel which had been sitting in Gothenburg loaded with a cargo
of timber prior to 9 April. The cargo was destined for England,
but when Norway fell it seemed that any attempt to transport
the timber would be pointless. For almost two months the *Nora*
sat in Gothenburg while her master contemplated his prospects.
Finally, at the end of May, he decided to take a chance and run
the German blockade of the Skagerrak. Remarkably the little
Nora, assisted by the cover of night, eluded Nazi attention and
made it safely to England to deposit her load of timber.

Binney was impressed. If the *Nora* could escape the blockade,
why not other ships? Blockade-running was an old tactic, though
in modern warfare, with the risks from planes and U-boats, it
was a very dangerous business. Binney reported to Steel Control

in London, having to communicate by telegram or wireless as the Germans had cut the telephone connection from Sweden to Britain. He explained the prospects of sending shipments of iron from Gothenburg under the cover of the long winter nights; it would be the best chance of securing bulk loads of materials for Britain. There was no opportunity at the moment because the summer nights were so short, though he was considering chartering a small vessel to load with cargo and run the blockade as an experiment. If luck was on their side, she might reach England with vital supplies. Unsurprisingly the desperate Steel Control agreed.

There was only one slight hitch. Binney was still effectively working as a civilian outsider. It was time to legitimise his role within the British Legation and to secure its help. Since the only way to communicate with Britain now the Nazis had kindly disconnected the phones was via the Legation, which had a team of wireless operators stationed in the attic to send encrypted messages, it seemed only logical that Binney should become an 'official' part of the team. Mitcheson took up his cause and persuaded Mallet that, with the agreement of the Foreign Office, Binney should be appointed assistant commercial attaché. Binney took residence in the cubby-hole that would be his workspace throughout his time in Sweden, refusing adamantly to leave it even when offered better accommodation.

Sweden had become a strange place to live since the invasion of Norway. Before the war, Sweden had been upheld as an enviable ideal of a socialist paradise. The country had managed to live in peace and avoid taking part in warfare since the time of Napoleon. Neutrality had become a habit to the Swedish; they did not see any other course of action when the first sabres were rattled between Germany and the rest of the world. But neutrality was tenuous. While Hitler was aware that it was better to keep the country unoccupied and neutral, Sweden lived under the constant fear that one day the Nazis might come marching across its borders and take over.

There was also a strong German influence in Sweden. Throughout its history, the country had encouraged ties with its Teutonic neighbours and Germans had regularly emigrated to Sweden and played a significant role in its political history. Through much of its history, Sweden had in fact had a better relationship with Germany than Norway, which it was regularly in conflict with. Therefore there was a strong element of pro-German and pro-Nazi feeling among certain sections of the population, particularly the old noble families and the upper classes. While politicians realistically perceived it would be safer, and politically more advisable, to side with the Allies if they had to, there were many who were working against them.

Public opinion shifted continually during the war, and the disastrous losses of Poland, Finland, Denmark, the Netherlands, Belgium and ultimately France, disillusioned the Swedes and had them favouring Germany. The successes of Germany in north Africa and (initially) Russia turned the tide in their favour even more. These changing attitudes, along with concerns about German aggression, saw Sweden making favourable concessions to the Nazis, including permitting troops to cross its country to reach Norway. Germany was allowed to base warships and troopships in Swedish neutral waters, and air space was allowed for euphemistically described 'courier flights'. Not to mention the channel Sweden cut for the Germans through Falsterbo, giving vessels a shortcut to England and enabling them to avoid a large number of British minefields. And there always remained the ball bearing issue. Despite Allied pressure, Sweden continued shipping iron ore and ball bearings to Germany. In contrast, Swedish authorities put up endless obstacles to prevent Britain claiming its own, paid for, ball bearings and iron.

Being a Briton in Sweden started to become awkward after the invasion of Norway. Aside from general shortages natural to a country that had almost been hamstrung by a threatening neighbour (including fuel; wood for heating and power was stockpiled and cars converted to gas), Swedish authorities set up 'defence zones' which were forbidden to foreigners. The Swedish security police were heavily influenced by the Germans and eventually became infiltrated and dominated by them. They posed the biggest problem to Binney and his fellows. They were often followed and the Legation monitored. Binney found a hidden microphone in his office in Stockholm (not the one in the Legation; Strandberg would have been mortified if he had allowed such a breach of his security). Another was discovered hidden in a chimney when it began to smoke right in the middle of Binney discussing his operations. Traitors were another issue, and good Swedes were sometimes offered as helpers to the Legation only to report back to the Germans.

Sweden made muted attempts to limit free speech under pressure from Hitler. There were both anti- and pro-Nazi newspapers published during the war years. Swedish authorities tried to pass legislation to limit their influence and the owners of the papers were frequently arrested for their work, but few received more than a slap on the wrist. Peter Tennant was arrested and released for reporting war news in the paper which he published.

More of a hazard for Binney was the red tape Sweden could throw up concerning British-bound ships. Throughout the war there was an ongoing legal battle concerning the right of passage, ownership and armament of vessels carrying cargo for Britain. Sometimes the only way to get around it was to hide the truth. In short, Sweden was comparable in many ways to an occupied country. Some of the conditions Binney had to work under were similar to those experienced in occupied France by Resistance workers, even down to the fear of falling into Gestapo hands.

6

A FRIEND IN THE HOUR OF NEED

B ehind the darkness of betrayal and obstruction there was a genuine desire among many in the Swedish Government to see Britain succeed, even if it meant bending the rules of neutrality. July to October 1940 was a bad time for the Swedes. There was great anxiety that any British activity that ran contrary to German perceptions of Swedish neutrality would lead to reprisals, perhaps even invasion. Victor Mallet had his hands full trying to calm these fears. When Binney first approached him with the idea of running the blockade he knew there was no way he could do it without securing the support of the Swedish Government. Through confidential negotiations and conferences he ensured the goodwill and co-operation of the government. It even warned Mallet when the German Government became aware of Binney's plans.

The Gothenburg branch of Lloyd's shipping company was less helpful. It declared that the operation 'was folly and the fiasco which it foreshadowed would seriously affect British prestige in Sweden …'. Binney astutely ignored it.

Binney could not, however, operate in isolation from Britain. He reported to the British Steel Control on 9 April:

We are left with two logical alternatives – either on the grounds of force majeure to leave everything in the hands of the Swedish makers for them to dispose of as best they can, i.e. to Germany, or alternatively to settle with the Swedes on a reasonable commercial basis and to stock that portion of the material at the bottom of the North Sea which we are unable to ship successfully to England.

In Britain the responsibility to get government approval for the scheme and to co-ordinate the facilities and services necessary for its success fell to three men. First there was Deputy and Assistant Steel Controller, Mr C.R. Wheeler, effectively Binney's boss, who gained the co-operation and support of two other, Charles Hambro and H.N. Sporborg. Both would eventually have ties with the fledgling SOE.

THE LAST ACT OF A DYING MAN

New Prime Minister Winston Churchill had plans to do away with the 'gentlemanly' attitudes towards warfare many of his ministers had, which were tying their hands in this very modern conflict. Just before his predecessor died, he persuaded Chamberlain to sign a document that would found an entirely new organisation designed for subversion, sabotage and secrecy. It was so controversial a concept that Churchill kept many of his fellow ministers in the dark until it was too late to do anything about it. Officially formed by Minister of Economic Warfare (MEW) Hugh Dalton on 22 July 1940, it was exactly the sort of organisation that Binney needed to help him with his plans.

SOE had a remit of espionage and sabotage. There were various departments dealing with the different countries involved in the war. While the Scandinavian branches could only claim minor successes, SOE proved its worth in occupied

France where it fuelled the Resistance, provided trained wireless operators and agents and eventually landed Jedburgh teams (special forces units) on D-Day to support the guerrilla activities of the Maquis. Sabotage was another of its specialities, with timed explosives on railways particularly popular for spreading disruption.

Hambro joined MEW and thus SOE at the outbreak of war and was placed in charge of operations concerning Scandinavia, putting Binney's plans instantly within his remit. Meanwhile Harry Sporborg, a city solicitor, was put in charge of supervising SOE business in northern and north-western Europe.

Binney needed the support of SOE if he was going to pull off his plan. SOE would act as co-ordinator for his scheme, securing funding from the Treasury to pay for the iron and the support of the RAF and the Royal Navy. It also ensured the co-operation of the Ministry of Shipping and the Norwegian Shipping Mission. Binney suddenly found himself with the funds and the means to pull off one of the most daring civilian-manned missions of the war.

Hambro went to Stockholm in the autumn as the nights were drawing out and making the plan possible. He could see for himself the trials that the staff of the Legation were under and the risks posed by the pro-Nazi elements of Sweden. Hambro was no stranger to warfare in Europe. Born in 1897, he left Eton in 1915 and went immediately into the Royal Military Academy at Sandhurst, becoming an ensign in the Coldstream Guards. Sent to the Western Front in 1916, he finished the war with a Military Cross for conspicuous bravery in action. Between the wars he served in banking and fought a triumphant personal battle against oral cancer. When he found his way into SOE he was faced with a very different war from the one he had fought as a young man of nineteen. The static warfare of trenches and prescribed battlegrounds was long gone; now combatants had to deal with a secretive, wide-ranging conflict, where civilians could as easily become aggressors as soldiers.

The changes in Sweden did not entirely surprise him. He remembered how the country had played for neutrality in the Great War and survived as a result. But Sweden wasn't passive in its side-stepping of conflict. It was re-arming and reinforcing its military forces as fast as it could and was prepared to defend its right to neutrality with aggression. Even so, Hambro was not afraid to risk the country's wrath and back Binney's audacious scheme. He gave his advice on the various hazards Binney faced and returned to London knowing that should the worst happen and the mission fail, full responsibility would fall on his shoulders.

German influences in Sweden represented a real problem. There were Abwehr agents and informers everywhere and they were monitoring the British for the slightest sign of any attempt to run the blockade. Binney concluded he would have to give his mission a Swedish façade if he wanted to achieve anything with even a modicum of secrecy. His pre-war trade contacts enabled him to get in touch with Messrs Carl Setterwall & Company and ask them to play the role of the British Iron and Steel Corporation's general agents. He was also able to get Messrs Wilson & Company of Gothenburg to act as shipping agents for the project. Both companies had close ties and commercial interests in Britain, so it was to their benefit to assist and Binney made this plain, but they were also loyal supporters from the first to the last, and did all they could to ensure that the mission was successful. As a result, they were blacklisted by the Germans.

THE VALIANT *LAHTI*

Binney had promised an experimental mission in the summer months and in July 1940 that was exactly what he was attempting. The delicate M/S *Lahti*, a Finnish vessel, was found sheltering in Gothenburg harbour and it did not take much on Binney's part to persuade her master to attempt to run the blockade for Britain. The *Lahti* was loaded with 300 tons of war materials, mainly tubes for the aircraft industry, but also machine tools and desperately needed ball bearings.

The *Lahti* set sail with the short nights and clear weather of summer stripping her of all cover. Surprisingly she reached the outer limits of the Skagerrak without any problem, but she was then spotted by a German air patrol. The *Lahti* was too small and lacking arms to risk challenging the Nazis, so she quietly turned tail and obediently allowed herself to be shepherded back into Kristiansand.

Binney had expected as much, but the attempt clarified in his mind several important points for his ultimate operation. For a start, it was pointless making attempts in summer when the short nights and good weather helped the Germans to locate errant ships. Secondly, the Germans had made a big noise about having laid minefields in the Skagerrak, but as both the *Nora* and *Lahti* had navigated the expanse of water without incident, and had also passed fishing vessels happily trawling the waters, it seemed to Binney that the 'German minefields, if they existed, enjoyed a greater reputation than their efficiency deserved'.

There was another issue on Binney's mind: logically he should use fast ships to clear the span of the Skagerrak as quickly as they could and take full advantage of the long winter nights. Yet fast ships also naturally meant large ships. Binney had ideally wanted to make the crossing with several small ships to spread his losses should any be sunk. But he had to judge the odds and everything fell in favour of fast vessels.

Swedish regulations also concerned Binney. Under Swedish maritime law it was impossible to load the cargoes in secret (unless Binney was prepared to step on neutral Swedish toes far more than he already had), so the vessels would be loaded in full sight of the watching Germans. While precautions to keep publicity to a minimum would be made, there was no hope of preventing the Germans from knowing something was afoot.

What of the ships' crews? Binney was disappointed at the meekness the *Lahti*'s master had shown when she was spotted, but he could hardly deem it surprising. 'Neutral crews, even supposing they were not previously suborned by German agents, could hardly be expected to undertake the voyage with requisite determination.' He had serious doubts whether, if challenged, the crews would try to fight through or scuttle their ships to prevent the Germans obtaining the precious cargo. He had a nasty hunch they would be more likely to surrender peacefully like the Finnish *Lahti*. That could not possibly be allowed.

While mulling over his crew problems, Binney learned in early August that twenty-six Norwegian merchant ships were lying up in Gothenburg and other Swedish ports. These were refugees from the invasion which had been away from home when the Germans attacked and had subsequently seen little point in making their way back to an occupied country. They were lying idle, their crews enjoying some R & R on full pay.

Binney made some enquiries and learned that the vessels were under the authority of Nortraship, the Norwegian Government Shipping Mission in London. Even better, a number of the ships were modern cargo liners with diesel engines, perfect for blockade-running as they were fast and did not throw out telltale smoke from the raising of steam prior to setting sail. Of course there was always a hitch; this time it was due to the vessels being under the supervision of the Norwegian Legation via the Gothenburg Consulate. 'The Norwegian Consul in Gothenburg is a reputed Nazi,' Binney groaned as he reported the problem. The Consulate held considerable influence over the Norwegian sailors and would make life extremely hard for Binney if its political leanings were as he feared.

On 11 August, Binney wrote to Mr Wheeler:

The best chance of success in running this blockade lies in regarding it as a venture rather than as an ordinary commercial voyage, and it will be necessary to infect the Norwegians with this spirit. They tend to be rather feckless as allies and are very critical of our performance in Norway last April and May, and I think that by sharing the risk with them rather than by merely paying them to undertake an unpleasant voyage the chances of success will be increased.

Fortunately Charles Hambro had good relations with Nortraship in London and was easily able to secure an agreement to use any Norwegian vessels Binney chose. Nortraship also appointed a Norwegian Vice-Consul, Mr V. Fuglesang, whose loyalty to the Allies was unquestionable, and entrusted to him all the work previously under the auspices of the Consulate. The Norwegian Consulate was now completely out of the picture.

Money remained the main concern. Binney had no intention of stealing his iron. All his supplies would be paid for up front and further orders placed with the relevant firms. Not only would this encourage the co-operation of manufacturers, it would also remove any added criticism the Germans might try to level at him later. Binney needed an accountant and one appeared from inside the Legation in the form of Mr H.W.A. (Bill) Waring. Bill was a refugee from Norway, having fled to Sweden with his wife Anne and son Patrick after the German invasion. From 1939 he had been attached to the British Consulate in Oslo and was strongly pro-Allies. Like so many of those who served the under-cover needs of the Allies, Bill was a mixed bag of professionalism and imagination. He spoke with a stutter, which did not hamper him being fluent in both his native Norwegian and German. He liked to write fairy stories, which he one day intended to publish alongside illustrations by his old friend and Legation colleague Peter Tennant.

Born in 1906, Bill spent his early years in Asia where his father served in the Indian police, and trained as a chartered account-ant, eventually working for Whinney, Murray & Co. in Berlin and Hamburg. In the early 1930s Bill had met Peter Tennant, a Cambridge graduate with a passion for Scandinavian culture and language, who was press attaché to the British Legation, a keen supporter and friend of George Binney and an ardent anti-Nazi. They met in Oslo while Peter was doing post-grad-uate research and Bill was busy with the liquidation of Ivar Kreuger's match empire, after Kreuger's suicide. They remained firm friends thereafter and it was Peter who introduced Bill to Binney when the latter was desperate for a reliable accountant.

If Bill needed any more credentials of his loyalty to the British cause, it could come from the adventure he had endured just getting to Sweden. On 9 April, he was in Norway as word spread among a disbelieving public that the Nazis were invading. He sent Anne away immediately with Patrick while he was sum-moned to Oslo to burn important British papers in the middle of the night. By morning Bill was not prepared to wait any longer for the Nazis to appear and set out for Trondheim, first on foot then on a bicycle he bought from a bicycle factory he passed. He reached Hamar that first evening and made it to Elverum the next day only to see it destroyed by the Luftwaffe. Finally he made it to the Swedish frontier and found his way to Stockholm. No sooner had he arrived and reported to the British Legation than he was off again, this time to assess a possible trade route through Finland via the Arctic highway to Petsamo, the only remaining passage between Scandinavia and the US, and sub-sequently Britain. His investigations ran parallel to Binney's. Both crossed into Norway and both realised the hopelessness of the situation when Britain evacuated its troops from Narvik. However, while Binney returned to Stockholm, Bill double-backed into Finland where he was promptly arrested.

For a fortnight Bill was the guest of a Finnish General in a hotel on Lake Inari. His imprisonment was light-hearted and more of a holiday than true captivity. His guard was a Finnish officer who had a passion for drinking brandy and Swedish punch all night long. When he finished his last bottle he often took it into his head to shoot the rapids down into the lake in a rickety boat. Bill's 'holiday' came to an end and he travelled back to Sweden. He was rather depressed at the events around him, especially as his plans to travel to England had been ruined.

Fortunately the Legation took him and Anne into the Cipher Department and he worked there until Peter mentioned to Binney about his old friend Bill.

The chance conversation led to a remarkable friendship and working relationship. Peter described Binney and Bill as 'perfectly matched'. They complemented each other. Binney was stocky and sturdy, his complexion ruddy from years of Arctic exploration and outdoor activities. His blue eyes sparkled from beneath his grey hair. In comparison, Bill was dark-haired and dark-eyed, with a thick moustache and heavy horn-rimmed glasses. He was also rather thick-set, having once been a keen rugby player, and was another lover of the great outdoors. Fortuitously the two men shared a similar sense of humour and were passionate about writing. George was a stickler for precision and grammar, often taking hours to compose his reports, which shine with his passion for a good adventure story. Bill was a keen reader and wrote when he could. The two men only truly differed on their religious beliefs – Binney, son of a vicar, held onto a simple faith throughout his life, while Bill remained a sceptic.

They came together in August 1940 and would quickly prove themselves the ideal blockade-busters. Bill handled the finances surrounding the operation, ensuring payments were made on time and keeping a check on any expenditure relating to the shipping side of the mission. He was indispensable in his humble way; he freed Binney from being bogged down in details and kept a handle on the administrative side of the scheme. Binney remarked that 'much credit is due to him for the ultimate success attained'.

LESS THAN PERFECT FRIENDS

With the go-ahead coming from Britain for the operation, Binney had to start putting out feelers to Norwegians and Swedes to look for their help. This was the dangerous part of the procedure, because any man he contacted could prove a traitor.

He needed the Norwegian captains of the ships he hoped to use on his side and ideally someone in authority. But Sweden's upper echelons were crawling with Nazi sympathisers, so any approach had to be carefully considered.

Vice-Consul at the British Consulate, Mr P. Coleridge, was set the task of finding suitable allies for the recently named Operation Rubble after the Consul became ill and could not attend to his work. He had the hard job of securing an engineering crew that could be trusted to work on the various ships. But his biggest triumph came when he contacted Captain Ivar Blücker, Chief of the Gothenburg Harbour Police, and secured his help. Blücker quickly proved himself not only pro-British but the best asset Binney could have.

In his role as Chief of Police he had the freedom to patrol the docks, inspect anything he deemed suspicious and keep a close eye on anybody he thought was working for the Germans. When Binney first heard about him from the Vice-Consul he was suspicious that the man was merely a tool of the Swedish Government which was quietly turning a blind eye to British operations, while also discreetly helping them. Binney underestimated the man; Blücker had received instructions from his superiors to ensure that neutrality was strictly enforced in Swedish waters, but he chose to stretch the meaning of his orders to the limit (and beyond) to give all his assistance to the British. He patrolled the harbour to ensure sabotage was not attempted by the Germans and was always alert to potential Nazi agents being planted among the engineering teams. He posted men to guard the ships night and day, and rounded up known Nazi agents and jailed them.

Not long before Operation Rubble was due to proceed, he caught two Swedish naval officers passing information to the Germans about the whereabouts of one of the Rubble ships. He arrested them and both men received seven-year jail sentences.

Blücker's enthusiasm appealed to Binney and it wasn't long before he took him into his confidence and explained the whole plan. Blücker, an ex-sea captain, was keen on the idea and believed firmly that it was entirely practical. He was also determined to do anything he could to ensure the success of the mission. Binney could not get access to Swedish meteorological reports, but Blücker could. He took it upon himself to secure the reports and co-ordinate them with British reports to produce a detailed picture of the forthcoming weather. He picked out a fjord he felt would work as the best hiding place for the ships before they made their dash across the Skagerrak and he made trips along the coast – forbidden to foreigners – to confirm the weather was favourable for their operation. He even secretly sent a message to Britain, via Gothenburg, that the attempt was about to take place and the Royal Navy should be ready at the outer end of the Skagerrak. To conclude his efforts he cut the phone lines for long-distance calls from Lysekil, so that no news of the ships' departures from Gothenburg could be transmitted easily to the Germans.

In comparison with Blücker's enthusiasm and loyalty, the Norwegian captains were a huge disappointment. Binney had been informed by Mr Sunde of Nortraship that the captains of the detained Norwegian vessels 'were all loyal men and ... the majority of them were anxious for the opportunity to take their ships to England'. Binney quickly learned that Nortraship was over-optimistic in its assessment.

Taking a flat in Gothenburg, Binney began the task of inter-viewing the captains of the ships he was interested in. These included the *Elisabeth Bakke*, *John Bakke*, *Tai Shan*, *Taurus*, *Dicto*, *Lionel*, and *Flint II*. Several meetings took place in the flat to convince the captains to join in with the scheme. Only the acting captain of the *Tai Shan* showed any enthusiasm; the others were more inclined to remain in Gothenburg enjoying full pay for the duration of the war. Binney could not induce in them a feeling of patriotism for Britain, or their own country. They had become completely disillusioned and preferred a quiet life to one of adventure. Binney could hardly be surprised. The disastrous British response to the invasion of Norway had left a great deal of ill-feeling. The Norwegians felt that they had been cast aside and forgotten, left to suffer their fate while Britain sat back and mouthed sympathies without moving into action. Why should they now help those who had so blatantly abandoned them?

With their ships safe in harbour and their owners content to leave them there until the end of the war, the captains had no incentive to move. Despite being paid by Nortraship in London, they were loyal to their bosses in Norway. They had no interest in their own exiled government and while they recognised a certain feeling of duty to their king, it was not enough to persuade them to get off their backsides and risk the Skagerrak blockade.

Disheartened, Binney swore the men to secrecy over the operation and started to cast around for new options. Almost immediately he realised his mistake in speaking so openly with the captains before their help was assured. Captain Knutson of the *Dicto* thought he should warn his employer of the intentions of the British and sent a telegram to Oslo very clearly stating the plan. Someone in the telegram office was more loyal to the Nazis than the Norwegian shipping forces and delivered the message directly into the hands of the German political police. The *Dicto*'s owner was informed by the Germans that he must go to Stockholm and do everything in his power to prevent his ship from sailing. This fell in with his own wishes and he hurried off, making a brief stop at the Norwegian Legation to warn it that if any ship was to try to run the Skagerrak it would be captured and either confiscated or destroyed.

Binney was angered at the breach of trust, but pragmatic. Keeping Operation Rubble a complete secret had always been an impossibility and since he had no intention of listening to anything the Norwegian authorities said, he brushed off the *Dicto* situation. Leaks now began to spring everywhere. At the Gothenburg shipyards the Norwegian inspectors supervising the building of new ships were in regular contact with captains and chief engineers of the Rubble vessels and despite secrecy they gossiped about the bizarre British plan. The inspectors in turn reported everything they learned to Norway.

Rubble looked liable to be over before it began. With the exception of Isachsen, acting captain of the *Tai Shan*, all the Norwegian masters refused to sail unless the British guaranteed to send the Royal Navy through the Skagerrak to Gothenburg to escort them. Of course this was utterly absurd and impossible. Binney now had no captains to sail his fleet.

SPEAKING OF THE BRITISH

William Escudier was content at his road-building, even if he still hungered to escape Sweden and get back to Britain. Germany and Sweden had come to an agreement that any German POWs finding themselves in Sweden would be allowed to make their way home, and this was taken by Sweden to also include British POWs they had received from the Germans. Escudier and his fellows were free to find their way back to England, but that was easier said than done. The Germans, at worst, could walk home; the British had an ocean to cross.

Escudier settled to his work and waited for an opportunity to present itself. At the end of October he learned that a man named George Binney had arrived at the camp and had dinner with the various British captains interned there. It had been agreed that the next day he would present himself to the refugee crews and ask for volunteers for a daring mission he was organising. Binney initially had asked the four captains who remained among the prisoners to join Rubble and they had agreed, but the next morning they regretted the decision and declined, believing the risk too great.

Binney presented himself to Escudier and the other sailors, explained the mission and asked for volunteers. Escudier had been waiting for just such an opportunity to arise and didn't hesitate to volunteer. Several crewmen and engineers followed suit. To the disappointment of many, it was then explained that the ships ran on new diesel engines rather than steam, and none of the engineers had any experience of the former so would have to sail at the reduced rank of greasers. This was a blow as Binney would have to fall back again on Norwegian or Swedish engineers, but at least he had part of his crews. Remembering the leakages at Stockholm he had the men sign an agreement:

> We being the officers of the SS *Blythmoor*, SS *Romanby*, SS *Mersington Court* and SS *Riverton* now stationed at Halsingmo, have been asked whether ... we will volunteer to man Norwegian vessels now lying at Gothenburg ... and to run these vessels through the German blockade of the Skagerrak to England with cargoes of steel, pigiron and other materials urgently required by the British Government for war purposes.
>
> Mr Binney has explained to us in detail the risks entailed in the voyage, namely enemy submarines, destroyers, armed trawlers, aircraft and mines. He has also emphasized to us that we can expect no protection from the British Navy at any rate until we are in the North Sea ...
>
> We are unanimously agreed that it is our special duty to uphold the traditions of the British Merchant Service ... and if we are given the opportunity to do so we shall put to sea in good heart ...

Binney returned to Stockholm feeling buoyed by the patriotism of his fellow countrymen. They might have no engineers, but all four of the wireless operators present among the stranded sailors had volunteered – a huge boon since they would play a key role in the subsequent operation and needed to be entirely trustworthy.

A NORWEGIAN AFFAIR

The Scandinavian winter was pulling in as, reluctantly, the masters of the trapped Norwegian cargo ships were summoned for a final meeting with Binney. They had hoped the affair might have ended with their refusal to help, but it seemed that the determined Englishman had other plans for them. Standing in an office at Gothenburg, Binney presented himself too cheerfully for a man who had just had his ambitious schemes quashed and the masters began to feel worried.

'It's all right chaps; as you are unwilling to take your ships out, I propose we man the *Elisabeth Bakke* and the *John Bakke* with British crews.'

The Norwegian masters were naturally appalled.

'That is illegal, Mr Binney!' they protested.

'On the contrary; Mr Hysing Olsen, the Director of Nortraship, has agreed to this unprecedented step and has induced your government to telegraph instructions to the Norwegian Legation in Stockholm stating the same.'

The Norwegians were stunned, but they also had their hands tied. A quick visit to the Legation proved Binney was correct: the telegraph sat before them, giving explicit instructions from the exiled Norwegian Government that the masters were to hand over their ships to the British.

Binney wasted no time in replacing Norwegians with British men. Andrew Henry, Chief Officer of the *Romanby* was appointed master of the *Elisabeth Bakke*, while William Escudier was made master of the *John Bakke*. So far there were only two full British crews Binney could call upon, but Einar Isachsen, First Mate on the *Tai Shan*, was all too eager to participate and, as his ship was already partially loaded with 4,500 tons of general cargo originally destined for South Africa, he was accepted. The Norwegian ship *Taurus* was another matter. She had been sitting in Malmö and her captain had been persuaded to sail her to Gothenburg with a Swedish escort to take part in the Rubble scheme. He was not a happy man. The instant he landed at Gothenburg he resigned and made active and vocal attempts to oppose the British operation, managing to persuade a number of Norwegian officers to leave their ships and refuse to help.

The *Taurus* was left without a qualified master. Binney scoured his contacts in the harbour to no avail. German influence was now falling heavily on the Norwegians and no master was prepared to stand up against them. Eventually attention fell onto Carl Jensen, First Officer of the *Taurus*, who was showing a keen interest and enthusiasm to help the British. He was not a certified captain, but he begged to be put in charge of the vessel, certain he could pilot her safely to England. Binney's options had run out; he accepted the offer a touch dubiously, but was comforted by the obvious excitement and loyalty Jensen showed for Rubble. 'He seems to have entered into the spirit of the venture,' Binney remarked.

Meanwhile, Andrew Henry (now called Captain Henry) had set foot onto the *Elisabeth Bakke* only to find her old master still aboard and very disgruntled. Making protests, he left his vessel to her new captain, but an atmosphere of antagonism between the Norwegians and British seemed to have fallen. No one was more concerned about this than Binney, who realised that German agents were now trying to wheedle their way into the remaining Norwegian crews and spread dissent. Both the *Taurus* and *Tai Shan* retained their Norwegian sailors, but if they were persuaded to walk off at the last moment it would ruin Operation Rubble, and there was no doubt that was exactly what the Germans were aiming for. What Binney needed was a British captain to take part in the plan, bringing his already loyal crew with him.

In early November, Binney fetched Captain J. Nicholson from Hälsingmo and took him on a tour of the Rubble vessels. Captain Henry and Captain Escudier were very helpful in generating enthusiasm for the plan in the good Captain Nicholson, who finally agreed that there could be hope for the endeavour. Promising his assistance, he returned to the camp to organise a third British crew which could take over a vessel at the last minute should the worst happen and the Norwegian sailors flee.

Binney was no fool to assume even the British might falter at the last moment if there was no other incentive than pure patriotism.

They were, after all, civilians; loyal yes, but not Navy men who had accepted the dangers of their occupation. Fear of the worst happening could take over. Binney met with the men and gave them his final (and financial) assurances:

> All crews will be given an additional 20% to their normal wages in view of the special discipline required of them on this mission. Each ship will receive a bonus of £1,500 on safe arrival in England and the captain will receive £500, while the Chief Engineer and Chief Officer will receive £75, other officers £50 and the crew will receive £30 each. In the event of death, disablement or capture, compensation or maintenance will be given to the sailor's family, in accordance with the British or Norwegian tariff, whichever is higher.

Binney was arranging other small matters to ensure co-operation, when a Norwegian second engineer protested against participating as his pregnant Belgian wife could not bear to be parted from him. Binney took the unusual step of appointing the woman Chief Engineer so she could sail with her husband. Both parties were delighted at the arrangement, not least because as Chief Engineer the wife would receive a £75 bonus when they reached Britain successfully!

Running out of Norwegian engineers to recruit, Binney looked for Swedish men, deciding to pay them an advance of £100 when they signed a contract to sail with the ships. Anticipating that they would spend the money almost instantly and would then have no means of paying it back, he felt that they would be tied to the British until the operation was over. Three Swedes were brought into the mission this way, but Binney never had to resort to reminding them of the £100 inducement they had taken to join the British.

Binney now had enough loyal men to crew the *Tai Shan*, *Elisabeth Bakke*, *John Bakke* and *Taurus*. The four cargo vessels began loading their precious stores of iron and ball bearings. This in itself was an open invitation to the Germans, who could observe the proceedings and wander past, making dark comments to the crews about their ships being bombed out of the water if they tried to leave the Skagerrak. Tension was high. Binney knew there was no way he could prevent the Germans from learning of the scheme, and the only secret he could keep was the exact date of their departure. Everyone had their eyes open for potential sabotage attempts, and the British and Norwegian masters had a tough time keeping their crews' morale high.

Just before Christmas the four Norwegian vessels sailed to Bro Fjord, where they would hide until the order came to make a dash for Britain. The Norwegian nerve had held and Binney was able to place his spare third crew on the motor tanker *Ranja*. While she carried only ballast, she was a valuable ship if she could be brought to Britain. Operation Rubble was close to execution. As Binney settled down to a quiet Christmas at Bro Fjord he could not help but feel satisfied at the arrangements he had prepared and brought together. Even if every ship sank to the bottom of the North Sea during the attempt, at least he had proved that he could bring such a grand and complicated plot together. Besides, Binney had a healthy optimism for their success and did not even contemplate losing a ship as he sat in his cabin aboard the *Tai Shan* and watched the snow falling outside.

7

OPERATION RUBBLE

C aptain Henry sat aboard the *Elisabeth Bakke* bored with waiting. The heavy skies of a Scandinavian winter threatened further snow and the water around his boat had turned to thick ice that scraped and creaked against the *Bakke*'s hull. Things did not look promising. Crews from the various ships had taken to visiting each other by trotting across the ice, and to all intents and purposes it looked like the defiant little convoy was about to spend the winter stuck in the Swedish ice.

Behind the scenes frantic telegrams were passing between Binney and Britain, particularly with the Ministry of Economic Warfare (MEW) which naturally had a vested interest in the operation. Binney promised the ice was not as bad as reports made out; it mainly existed at the head of the fjord and a brief spell of good weather would quickly disperse it. He still believed that the right moment would come for their attempt.

Henry's men were beginning to look rather glum. They had not left the cosy camp at Hälsingmo merely to stand on the deck of a freezing cargo ship trapped in ice. Sailors they might be, but they had been promised action and now it was like being stuck in Narvik all over again. Morale among the Norwegians was even worse. If they did not sail soon, Henry feared they would either abandon ship or turn tail at the first sign of trouble. Impatiently he turned his attention back to the weather and prayed for a perfect night to storm the Skagerrak.

The *Elisabeth Bakke*, along with her four comrades in the escapade, had been hastily altered to stand a better chance of survival on her daring mission. Arming merchant ships was against Swedish neutrality and could cause a great deal of political problems. It would also give the Germans the excuse to do all they could to sink the ships and claim it was because they were armed vessels. However, if the vessels were not armed, or at least defended, then they had no means of saving themselves if they were attacked before reaching the Royal Navy.

Binney had chosen to be cautious on this occasion and the ships remained unarmed, but they were fortified with 6in blocks of concrete surrounding the bridges. Crews were confidently assured that this would provide protection from air attacks. In case of disaster the crews had been told to sink their ships rather than allow the Nazis to get hold of the precious cargo. It had been impossible to obtain explosives for scuttling ships so a resourceful Binney, in consultation with a Lloyd's surveyor in Gothenburg, arranged for eight valves to be fitted in the holds of the ships. Operated from the 'tweendecks, the valves would ensure that the ship would sink within an hour of them being released, and the handles were detachable so they could be removed and thrown overboard once the process began. Nothing would stop the ships being scuttled if necessary.

For secrecy purposes the ships had been individually sailed to Bro Fjord and painted grey. Windows were blacked out and other precautions taken so that no light would accidentally show and give them away. The Svenska Lloyd Shipping Company had loaned every British sailor a Swedish life-jacket which consisted of a loose-fitting rubber overall, securely fastened at the neck by a zip. The garment included weighted boots and gauntlets. Designed specifically for sailors operating in Arctic waters, not only was it deemed unsinkable but it would keep a man inside it warm for a considerable time, preventing death from exposure in the frozen waters. Costing £10 each, they were a pricey life-saver, but the sailors saw an instant problem with them. They were cumbersome and made any operation fiddly. The heavy boots prevented easy movement and the heavy gauntlets caused men to fumble their tasks. While it was feasible for men on deck to wear the suits, for men working in the engine room it was not only near impossible but dangerous. Despite this, every sailor was issued with one; the British had them on loan from Lloyd's, while Nortraship had purchased one for every Norwegian sailor.

By 23 January 1941, Captain Henry's nerves were frayed and his men on edge. He doubted that they could wait any longer without it seriously compromising their morale. The skies were still bleak, but a ray of hope arrived with Ivar Blücker and a Swedish weather report which promised that the coming night should be perfect for a clear run. The ice in the water was reasonably broken up and the ships could traverse it. Snow and fog would mask the attempt, and the night promised to be moonless, providing extra cover. Suddenly every man was at action stations.

At 2 p.m. pilots were supposed to arrive to escort the ships out of the narrow fjord, but no man arrived for Henry's ship. He took the decision to risk the waters alone and follow the other ships ahead of him. The slow *Ranja* had gone first, forcing her way out through 8 inches of ice. Henry brought up the rear, uncomfortably alert to the dangers he was about to face. It took him until 5.30 p.m. to sail clear of the ice. 'Then it was every man for himself and we scattered.'

The weather at first appeared favourable to the British. Blücker had promised a gale, ideal for keeping the Luftwaffe at bay, but as the journey progressed the skies grew clearer and clearer. Henry called for the *Elisabeth Bakke* to be brought up to her full speed – 17 knots – and at 5.32 p.m. he was chugging swiftly away from the other vessels. Rumours of a minefield in the Skagerrak kept him in deep water, never less than 100 fathoms, and his eyes were constantly looking upward for the first sign of an enemy aircraft.

He spent the long night sailing alone, unaware that behind him William Escudier on the *John Bakke* was being tailed by a German plane. For Captain Henry the voyage was unremarkable. At 8.45 a.m. he spotted two destroyers nearby. With nothing to signal with except a small Morse lamp, he decided to run up a white flag with the letters 'OB' on it in black. The destroyers spotted them at once and approached. Henry held his breath, hoping that he had signalled the correct ships and was not about to come under fire from patrolling Germans. As the vessels drew closer they signalled their own message:

'Where are the others?'

Captain Henry was filled with relief; these had to be the British destroyers the Navy had promised to send. He answered back that four more vessels were following him. The destroyers asked for his speed and course, and once he had satisfied them that he was heading at full speed to Britain they turned away to look for the remaining ships. Captain Henry pulled away and set course for Kirkwall. It would take him a full day to reach Scotland, but when he anchored outside the harbour entrance at 9.30 p.m. that night he realised with jubilation that not only was he home but he had brought with him his most important cargo ever.

For Escudier the voyage was about to become more eventful. The German plane followed the *John Bakke* for 4 hours, clearly under the mistaken impression that she was taking her cargo to Germany. Escudier was flying the Norwegian flag and had no intention of disabusing the plane, which at once was a blessing and a curse. On the one hand, he had his own private escort, which would hopefully convince other passing patrol planes or boats that he was working for the Germans; on the other, at any moment the pilot might realise his mistake and open fire. As he reached the end of the Skagerrak he knew that he would soon have to show his real intentions when he turned in the direction of Britain rather than Germany. To make the situation even more uncomfortable, his crew had spotted British planes flying nearby – his genuine escort! – which in the darkness of the night had failed to realise that the plane on his tail was actually German.

Escudier could hardly believe his bad luck as he turned for his course to Britain, surprising the Luftwaffe pilot behind him and finally alerting the German to his error. Suddenly the plane opened fire with its machine guns. Everyone took cover, the bullets chipping and grazing the protective concrete around the bridge as the plane flew over them from starboard to port. For a moment the plane moved away, then it swooped in again and dropped two bombs. Fortunately bombing accuracy at sea was abysmal and the bombs fell wide, exploding harmlessly in the water. By now the British planes were too far away to realise what was happening and Escudier was on his own as he pushed the *John Bakke* to her full 13½ knots and headed for the rendezvous with the destroyers as fast as he could.

Abruptly his German escort fell back, and a few minutes later the destroyers were in sight. At last the Luftwaffe pilot was fully convinced that he had been assisting British ships, but with the armed destroyers ahead he wasn't about to risk another attack on the *John Bakke*. Instead he flew 8 miles astern and started machine-gunning the slow *Ranja*. It turned out that 6in concrete was no match for Luftwaffe aircraft cannons and it was now that the unfortunate Nils Rydberg received his fatal injury. (Reports differ as to whether he was struck by bomb shrapnel or machine-gun bullets.)

Even so, the approaching destroyers prevented any concerted attack and the plane had to turn for home shamefaced at being so easily fooled. Slowly the little convoy regrouped and, with the big destroyers shepherding them, they sailed for Kirkwall and safety.

TAKING STOCK

Standing on the harbour side at Kirkwall, George Binney puffed himself up with pride over the success of his first mission.

Inventories were being taken of the stock he had secured: over 24,000 tons of invaluable supplies, among them more than 2,000 tons of ball bearings destined to go into the construction of weapons, tanks and planes for the continuing British war effort. He had every reason to feel pleased with himself. More importantly he was already contemplating a repeat mission. If it had worked so wonderfully once, why not again?

Binney told SOE and MEW:

I see no reason to regard the first attempt as an isolated fluke. While the Germans will be more on their guard to frustrate a second attempt, the means at their disposal, aircraft patrols, armed trawlers, submarines and E-boats, are not necessarily a match for the elements of fog and snow upon which we rely.

There were plenty of ships trapped in Swedish waters that would be ideal for a second Rubble. Aside from more Norwegian vessels there were even a few Polish, Dutch and Belgian merchantmen available to him. And while minefields were a worry, he was fairly confident that the Germans were exaggerating the extent of those they had laid. After all, they had to use the same waters to sail supplies to Germany. They would not mine their own routes, so logically the minefields were not as widespread as claimed.

'While the nights are shortening, the weather for blockade running is improving,' he continued enthusiastically. 'Long nights are in themselves an unnecessary luxury if the days are thick and the wind sets in a favourable quarter.'

Binney had ideas on how their operation could be improved as well. Coastal Command would need to play a stronger part in scouting out Swedish waters in daylight to spot any threats and, ideally, the Royal Navy would rendezvous with the convoy 50 miles closer to the mouth of the Skagerrak. He also wanted machine guns to be provided for the ships, despite the consternation this would cause politically, and smoke candles which could

be lit when a ship was under attack to fool the enemy into thinking she was already hit.

Finding a good crew would be problematic. The methods he
had used for Rubble would be unlikely to work again, but if an
air route was established between Britain and Sweden, Binney
was confident that many of the Rubble men would volunteer to
be flown back for the next operation.

As Operation Rubble had just secured Britain £1 million
worth of war materials the temptation to repeat it was all too
high. The goods they had might support manufacturing for a
year, but then what? Even if 50 per cent of a subsequent cargo
was lost during the mad dash to Britain, the goods that survived
would make the operation a success.

Already plotting for a March operation, Binney was looking
at bringing over a 1,000-ton cargo of ferro-chrome and he had
earmarked ships, including the tankers *B.P. Newton*, *Buccaneer*,
Realf and *Rigmor*, along with the motorboat *Dicto* which he had
lost from Operation Rubble due to legal difficulties. There was
also the possibility of 'rescuing' the newly built fruit ship *Pacific
Express*, currently laid up in Malmö and attracting the attention
of the Germans for her potential to be used as an armed raider.

Binney was ecstatic about the possibilities, but there were
problems not far ahead.

RIBBENTROP BECOMES IRATE

'A British convoy comprising five Norwegian merchantmen has
recently run a consignment of essential war materials to this
country from Sweden,' began the rather vague and emotionless
press release compiled by the Ministry of Supply after the success of Rubble. It was destined never to be released to the papers
as the full backlash of the mission hit.

The unfortunate Head of the Commercial Department
from the Swedish Ministry of Foreign Affairs was in Berlin in

February 1941 when the first news of Rubble came out. He was confronted by the Germans, and Victor Mallet reported in a telegram, 'He was vigorously attacked for alleged help given by Sweden to us but was able to argue that Swedish conduct had been entirely neutral. German Admiralty particularly furious.' The Swedish Government sent a plea to Britain that publicity of Rubble should be suspended, as this would 'much embarrass' the government and 'might prejudice Swedish plans in connections with ships [Britain is] allowing to bring cargoes to Gothenburg'.

It now became apparent that another operation would not occur that winter. While Binney was accepting a knighthood for his efforts, Ivar Blücker, the helpful Chief of the Gothenburg Harbour Police, was on the verge of being sacked. Sweden had gone heavily into damage control, fearing that at any second Hitler might order an invasion of the country. The government was hardly to know that the Führer had already realised Sweden was more valuable to him unoccupied.

Joachim von Ribbentrop, Foreign Minister for Germany, was particularly harsh in his criticism of Sweden and volatile in the threats he made to Swedish ministers. He stormed from meeting to meeting lashing out at the men he deemed culpable and making increasingly difficult demands on Germany's behalf, backed by talk of reprisals and invasion. The Swedish Government started to worry.

In August 1941, the Swedish Secretary-General summoned British diplomat William Montagu-Pollock to his office urgently. Montagu-Pollock had been in Stockholm since 1939 and was rather popular among the Swedes, not least for his enthusiasm for local cuisine and his eccentric personal appearance. He had sailed through a number of diplomatic storms in his time in the country, not least the crisis Rab Butler caused in 1940 by implying to a Swedish envoy that Britain was ready to make peace with Germany.

Montagu-Pollock was unfazed by the panic now brewing within the Swedish Government in the face of German aggression. The Swedish Secretary-General explained:

> The German Government is about to make some further demands of the Swedish Government the nature of which I cannot divulge, but that the reply which the Swedish Government has decided to make to these demands is one which cannot do otherwise than cause the German Government great displeasure.

The Secretary-General was clearly forlorn about the prospect of further browbeating and animosity from Ribbentrop:

> I sent for you urgently as I have heard that you are intending secretly to run some more Norwegian ships to the United Kingdom from Gothenburg and that some of them were due to leave immediately?

No response was made to the allegation. The Secretary-General continued:

> This would annoy the Germans so much that I am convinced my government would not survive the incident unless the ships were postponed for the moment. I realise that you are perfectly free agents in the matter and my government would not put obstacles in the way of you carrying on lawful activities of this kind; nevertheless I beg you to arrange for action to be postponed until the incident has blown over.

Montagu-Pollock had no hesitation in assuring the Secretary-General that, under the circumstances, the ships would not leave in the immediate future. It was hardly skin off his nose, since no move would be made by the British until the Scandinavian winter crept on with its longer nights and foul weather anyway.

A short time after he had given assurances to the Secretary-General, Montagu-Pollock was to discover that he was not alone in playing coy games. He learned that the Germans had demanded that Nazi troops be allowed to travel through Sweden from Norway to Finland. In itself, that did not surprise him. The Swedes had already started playing a dangerous game of allowing German troops to cut across their country when either marching to Norway or heading home. While this delighted the Germans, it inflamed Allied opinion against Sweden, particularly in the US, even if there were still several months before the attacks on Pearl Harbor would finally give Roosevelt the excuse he needed to launch his country headfirst into the war.

No, troop transits did not surprise Montagu-Pollock. What did was that Germany had demanded additional Swedish shipping to be put at its disposal. Ships sitting idle in the Baltic would be temporarily given to the Germans for business use. Even though the matter was yet to be decided it was worrying, as it had been kept secret from certain Swedish ministers favourable to the Allies. Montagu-Pollock sent details home via his diplomatic bag, outlining not only the demands but the threats that the Germans were making. The Nazis had insisted that they would cancel their outstanding contracts with Gothenburg if the Swedes allowed Britain to make another 'Rubble' attempt, and no doubt their plan to take over idle ships was another way in which they hoped to eliminate, or at least hamper, British attempts.

Sweden was in an awful dilemma: it needed the income from German trade to survive the war, but it also wanted to keep Britain on side. For Montagu-Pollock this again meant interviews where, on the one hand, he was assured all help would be given to aid the British if they made a second Rubble attempt, while on the other, the Swedes continually stated that it would be much better if the operation was postponed indefinitely.

In September 1941, the British Legation sent its own damning report on the matter. Germany was making continual mention of the Rubble operation to Sweden's ministers, harping on about its outrage and fury. By now the Germans were well aware that Britain was planning a second blockade run; they had to be, after the success of the first. Binney was back in

Stockholm, having turned down a job with the British Supply Ministry in Washington, which would have kept him quite safe for the remainder of the war. His presence in Sweden amplified German fears and they turned to the government, complaining about the liberties the British were being allowed. Sweden shrugged its shoulders and declared that it was up to the Germans to stop British ships sailing on the high seas.

A nonchalant response it may have been, but behind the scenes Sweden was deeply concerned. Sir Orme Sargent of the Foreign Office wrote that he feared reprisals being taken against the country's shipping in Gothenburg. He believed that Germany would mount another blockade and prevent Swedish trade with South America, which would be utterly disastrous. More apprehensively he wondered whether Germany would consider a military or naval coup should Britain be allowed to continue. Deeply troubled he might have been, but the Swedish Government was not yet ready to tell Britain to abort its plans, though secretly it wished that it would. Yet again it begged for a delay.

At the beginning of September, the Swedish Secretary-General had an unexpected visitor. Dr Karl Schnurre, German diplomat and a member of the German Foreign Office in Berlin, had just arrived in Sweden with a special message for its government. Addressing the Secretary-General, he made it plain that should Britain be allowed to continue its arrangements and operations, Sweden would face the direst consequences. Though his threats were veiled, he left the Swedish minister in no doubt that Germany intended violence if Sweden failed it again.

Miserably, the Secretary-General went to a pre-arranged dinner with Victor Mallet and, as their meal concluded, confessed to the unexpected visit by Dr Schnurre.

'His message was couched in more unpleasant language than any delivered to the Swedish Government since the outbreak of war,' the Secretary-General described grimly, 'and he indicated that if the convoy sailed there could be no further hope of friendly benevolence.' Despite this, the Swedish Government was remaining firm in its support of the British. To the Germans they said simply they had no legal right to interfere with British shipping unless the Norwegian ship owners took the matter to court and obtained an injunction against their own government. So far only one Norwegian had been sufficiently pro-Nazi to attempt this, but the Secretary-General was still depressed at the thought of his country falling into German hands.

'Perhaps the German Government are bluffing,' Mallet suggested. The Swede shook his head.

'That seems unlikely; bluff is not their usual form. I can hardly imagine them attempting a campaign now, but they might contemplate one during the winter when the Russian campaign was quiescent.'

Mallet could not assuage him and the next day he met the Swedish Minister for Foreign Affairs who was equally downcast. With a wan smile, he remarked to Mallet that he wished all Norwegian ships had left last winter.

Things were just starting to hot up. At the end of September, Mallet learned that Ribbentrop had personally sent for the Swedish Chargé d'Affaires and told him that if any ships left Swedish harbours for Britain it would be viewed as a definite hostile act. Still, the Swedes stayed strong; partly it was their hopes for a British success, but it was also because they feared that if they caved in now they would be stepping onto the threshold of absolute surrender.

8

PLANNING A PERFORMANCE

Binney was unperturbed by the political fallout from his operation. Safely ensconced in the minister's residence, from which he and Bill Waring refused to be moved despite offers of better accommodation in the main Legation, he was plotting away as merrily as ever. His return to Sweden had not been welcome to the Swedish authorities, who looked upon him as the British red rag being waved vigorously before the maddened Nazi bull. There was little choice in the matter. Binney had turned down Washington and nothing, not even a bad bout of jaundice contracted shortly after his arrival in Kirkwall, was going to stop him returning to the country where he felt he could do the most amount of good – at least for the British.

The last few weeks had been filled with excitement. Binney had met with King George VI, who had been so fascinated by his adventure that he had asked to read the full report. He had also been touched by the story of the valiant Blücker, whose efforts had to go unrecognised because of his position in Gothenburg.

The king had paused for a moment to consider.

'Would Mr Blücker accept a pair of cufflinks with the royal cypher in recognition of his actions?' he asked.

Binney was certain that he would. Quietly the king removed the cufflinks he was wearing.

'I hope he will not mind a second hand pair.'

When Binney arrived in Sweden he had with him the same pair, securely parcelled up by Henry Hopkinson of the Foreign Office, and accompanied by a message from the king to express his 'appreciation of all that [Blücker] did to help in the achievement of that very successful operation'.

Binney's ties with SOE were also becoming stronger. Under the cover of its front department MEW it was gently stretching its wings in Sweden and had been involved behind the scenes of Rubble, largely dealing with correspondence and shipping arrangements. Now Binney found himself firmly an honorary member of the organisation and SOE intended to take charge of any future blockade-running operations. He was happy enough. As long as Charles Hambro, who still dealt with the Scandinavian divisions of the secret body, did not overtly interfere with his work he was quite content to let SOE deal with all the nitty-gritty of running a clandestine operation. It did however occasionally take liberties with his tolerance.

During 1941 Binney became accustomed to receiving unexpected SOE visitors and accepting parcels on behalf of the organisation. One evening several Norwegians appeared with a long, large parcel and asked him if he would look after it in his office overnight. Of course his office was a cubby-hole in Victor Mallet's residence, so effectively the minister was accommodating the parcel. But no matter, Binney waved them in and allowed them to deposit their oversized load. Not long after the Norwegians left, Binney grew curious as to what could be inside such an awkwardly shaped parcel. SOE had been sending small shipments of steel by air and such parcels had appeared in Binney's office before, but this one was too light to be a package of steel. Too curious to leave well alone, he carefully opened the packaging. He found himself confronted by a corpse. The dead Norwegian (or maybe he was Swedish) was on some secret mission even after death. Binney replaced the packaging and left the contents well alone from then on. The stranger's body was retrieved in the early hours of the next morning and Binney never did tell Mallet that he had housed a corpse overnight.

SUPPLY AND DEMAND

Shortly before his return to Stockholm, Binney had attended a meeting with Hambro and Sporborg of SOE and several ministers and officials involved with supplying Britain's war effort. Mr Wheeler of the Ministry of Supply made the situation very plain to the men. Binney's miraculous mission had provided a bounty of material, but even so, it would be used up by the autumn of 1941. Plans were in place to reorganise the British manufacturing calendar to enable factories to rely on American supplies and dispense with Swedish sources, but this would not be achieved until late 1942 at the earliest. The ministers were looking at a period of twelve months or more when Britain could not make a single plane, tank or gun because of a shortage of basic materials. The situation was plain: however much it had sympathy with the Swedish dilemma, Britain was fighting for its survival and only a blockade-run, no matter the consequences to the neutral Swedes, would save it. A minimum of 7–8,000 tons of Swedish special steels, ball bearings, and other components was required by the autumn for making aircraft engines alone, which were now creating a bottleneck in plane production. Without another Rubble-sized shipment, Britain would not be able to replace its aerial losses and Hitler would have the upper hand.

The Norwegian Government was equally keen to see Binney succeed in running the blockade again. The exiled ministers and Norwegian king were fighting a war an ocean away from their occupied country and there was little love lost for Sweden. They might have briefly formed a united Scandinavian front in the early twentieth century, but there were always tensions between the two nations, and watching troops march into your home territory having amicably crossed your neighbour's ground

1 One of the goals of the invasion of Norway was to occupy the country's airfields in order to give the Luftwaffe easier access to attack British shipping near Sweden. Here several German seaplanes can be seen at Stavanger. *By kind permission of Wikimedia: The Imperial War Museum*

2 Though resistance was slight, it was also deadly. Here German soldiers take cover in Norway while under attack. Notice the abandoned bicycles that the soldiers were using as transport. *By kind permission of Wikimedia: Fenrik Kvaals*

3 A soldier stands by a signpost in Norway giving the relative distances to various locations. Note Narvik at the top; this was the Germans' prime target as most iron ore traffic in winter went through that town. *By kind permission of Wikimedia: German Federal Archive*

4 Completed in 1929, the *John Bakke* was one of the newer ships in Binney's fleet. She had a top speed of just over 13½ knots which made her slow for blockade-running, but she could carry a large load. *Roger W. Jordan collection, by kind permission of warsailors.com*

5 The *John Bakke* sailed the Skagerrak unscathed and unmolested largely because of bad weather that kept the Luftwaffe grounded. She survived the war, but was scrapped in 1964 after running aground. *Alan McKnespiey, by kind permission of warsailors.com*

6 The *Tai Shan* was Binney's flagship during Operation Rubble. She had a top speed of 14½ knots and could carry eight passengers. There were 147 people aboard during Operation Rubble. *Markus Berger, by kind permission of warsailors.com*

7 The *Taurus* successfully ran the Skagerrak and continued to serve in convoys. However, in 1941 she was attacked in Scottish waters by a German plane and the resulting damage sunk her. Fortunately none of her crew was harmed. *Bjørn Pedersen, by kind permission of warsailors.com*

8 The *Elisabeth Bakke* had barely served four years as a cargo ship before she became involved in Rubble. With a top speed of 16 knots, she was one of the fastest in Binney's fleet and led a charmed life as a convoy ship throughout the war. She was eventually broken up in 1974. *Roger W. Jordan collection, by kind permission of warsailors.com*

9 The *Ranja* was a slow, heavy tanker and carried no cargo during Operation Rubble, just salt water ballast. She had the unenviable role of being a decoy ship to lure the Luftwaffe's attention away from the other ships in the convoy. *Sverre Johansen, by kind permission of warsailors.com*

10 There was only one casualty during Operation Rubble and that was the unfortunate Nils Rydberg aboard *Ranja* (above), who was injured in the abdomen during an air attack. Sources vary as to whether he was caught by a bullet or a fragment of shrapnel. He later died in Britain. *Bjørn Milde, by kind permission of warsailors.com*

11 This portrait of George Binney from an unknown periodical shows him in his prime just before the war. He was always a robust person, who was keen on adventure. There is a later portrait of him in the National Portrait Gallery. *Author's Collection*

12 Initially, aircraft tried to drop bombs on shipping, but this was very inaccurate and a direct hit was due more to luck than judgement. Later, planes were fitted with torpedoes – a real hazard to Operation Performance. However, it still took skill and a deal of courage on the pilot's behalf to dive and launch torpedoes. *By kind permission of Wikimedia: German Federal Archive*

13 The Performance vessels were attacked by various aircraft including the larger Junkers Ju 88. The Luftwaffe proved an extremely deadly opponent during Binney's second blockade-running attempt. *By kind permission of Wikimedia: German Federal Archive*

14 Swedish newspapers were prone to publishing scandalising news about Binney's operations and favouring the Germans over the British. This was despite there being no restriction on the freedom of the press in Sweden during the war. *By kind permission of Wikimedia: Trondheim Byarkiv*

15 Though Sweden had military equipment and well-trained soldiers, the country had no intention of taking part in the war. Rather, its soldiers were to protect the country's neutrality. Norway had tried the same and failed. *By kind permission of Wikimedia: Hd-Se*

16 After the *Dicto*, the *B.P. Newton* was carrying the most important load of Operation Performance, so it was a relief that she managed to be one of the two vessels that survived the crossing of the Skagerrak. Sadly she was not to be so lucky in 1943, on a convoy back from America, when she was torpedoed and a number of crew were killed or badly burned in the subsequent fire. *Markus Berger, by kind permission of warsailors.com*

17 The *Charente* was scuttled during the Performance mission and her crew captured by Germans. Her British temporary captain, James Donald, made an attempt to go down with his ship, but was dragged off at the last moment by a Norwegian crewman. *Oswald Bergstad, by kind permission of warsailors.com*

18 The legal wrangles surrounding the arrest and then release of the *Rigmor* had gone on for months before Operation Performance, so her crew were delighted to finally take her out to sea. Unfortunately she was attacked and sunk, though her crew were lucky enough to be rescued by British destroyers. *Øistein Eriksen, by kind permission of warsailors.com*

19 The *Storsten* was sunk during Performance and her crew divided themselves between two lifeboats, one motor-powered. A mystery arose when the men in the latter craft vanished into thin air. They were probably lost in a storm trying to reach Britain, but the belongings of one man later turned up in another lifeboat off the coast of Norway. How they got there no one knows. *By kind permission of warsailors.com*

20 The *Dicto* was Binney's flagship for Performance and carried the biggest load of the whole fleet. Binney eventually decided not to risk her across the Skagerrak and sent a wireless message to his other ships to do the same. He returned to Gothenburg unaware that his radio had been sabotaged and his important message had never been sent. *Roger W. Jordan collection, by kind permission of warsailors.com*

21 The only oth.er Performance vessel to return to Gothenburg rather than risk the Skagerrak in clear weather was the *Lionel*. She was subsequently trapped there and prevented from leaving. Britain could not sail her out of Swedish waters until May 1945. *Oswald Bergstad, by kind permission of warsailors.com*

22 The *Lionel* came to Britain in 1945 to unload her cargo of steel, then she returned to Norway. She was not seen again until 1964 when she came to Grays shipyard to be broken up. *Ørjan H. Johansen, by kind permission of warsailors.com*

23 Binney's later operations usually involved specially refitted MGBs. They were small but fast, and though they could only carry small loads, they could sneak back and forth across the Skagerrak. They really only proved themselves through the winter of 1943–44, as the weather was too bad during the next winter to enable them to sail. *By kind permission of Wikimedia: The Imperial War Museum*

24 The *Gay Viking* was the first MGB to reach Sweden during Operation Bridford. Unfortunately during Operation Moonshine fellow MGB *Hopewell* collided with her and she was abandoned. She appears to have been salvaged and subsequently used as a pleasure cruiser. *By kind permission of Wikimedia: The Imperial War Museum*

25 Hugh Dalton served as head of SOE for a time, and together with Charles Hambro he kept Binney's operations running despite many difficulties, including the unreliability of the MGBs. *By kind permission of Wikimedia: The Imperial War Museum*

26 The MGBs were horrible craft to sail in. They blundered through the waves and made the whole crew seasick, those in the engine room being particularly badly affected as they also had to contend with the diesel fumes of the engine. *By kind permission of Wikimedia: The Imperial War Museum*

27 When the Germans signed their official surrender it was an immense moment for all those countries involved in the war. VE Day was celebrated at once. Shortly after, Brian Reynolds made one last trip in an MGB and vanished, presumably having hit a mine. *By kind permission of Wikimedia: Ras 67*

28 Some of the Performance men found themselves captive at Bergen-Belsen, one of the most horrendous of the Nazi concentration camps. Typhus was rife and some would not survive to see the end of the war. *By kind permission of Wikimedia: Common Good*

29 Even after the liberation of the camp, healthy prisoners helped to carry the dead. The scenes were horrific. The Performance men were removed by Red Cross lorries shortly before the camp was officially liberated. *By kind permission of Wikimedia: Smial*

30 Other Performance men found themselves at Sonnenburg, but were transferred before the Russians arrived to liberate the camp. They were lucky. Most of the remaining prisoners were executed, and only three were found alive when the Soviet Army stormed in. *By kind permission of Wikimedia: German Federal Archive*

was hardly conducive to sympathetic feelings. The Norwegians were anxious that any of their remaining ships stuck in Swedish waters should be rescued and brought to Britain where they could at last be of use in the war effort. Norwegian consent was given to the plan, provided it had a reasonable chance of success and adequate sea and air support were given.

Binney was already a step ahead. He was looking at securing the 5,000-ton *Dicto* which had been unable to join the Rubble mission, and the 5,000-ton *Lionel*. Though not the speediest of vessels (the *Dicto* could achieve 13½ knots, *Lionel* 11 knots) they were within reach and could carry a good load, unlike the *Pacific Express* which he badly wanted to capture but looked liable to fall into German clutches. She had the promising speed of 20 knots, but carried 1,000 tons less than the *Lionel* and *Dicto*. All being well and with the inclusion of three 500-ton tankers, the Ministry of Supply could look forward to 12–15,000 tons of materials in autumn 1941.

Back in Sweden, Binney set to work making preparations. The flat he had used for interviewing the masters for Operation Rubble was retained, and it seemed that this time there would be little difficulty in piecing together crews. Not only were the men from the Rubble mission eager to participate again but a number of Norwegians twiddling their thumbs in Gothenburg were now showing interest. The only issue was that many of these men were desperate to get out of Sweden and some had ominously applied for Russian visas.

The Swedish Government needed to be informed of the new plan and thus there was little hope that the Germans would not catch wind of it, especially with their agents crawling all over the harbours. Binney flew home to England in June to finalise orders; then he was back in Stockholm chartering ships. He now had the *B.P. Newton* (a 10,324-ton tanker), the *Rigmor*, *Buccaneer*, and *Storsten* (all tankers of around 5,000 tons), the *Lind* (462 tons), the *Dicto* and *Lionel*, two coal burners of less than 1,000 tons each, and the whaler *Skytteren* (12,000 tons).

Everything was looking promising. Not only were Norwegian and British merchant seamen volunteering for the mission, but 500 British volunteers who had gone to Finland before the armistice with Russia and had become trapped there had just been evacuated to Sweden and were eager for action. In the background the Nazis had turned their attention to their one-time ally Russia, and were in the process of launching nearly 4 million troops at the Soviets in Operation Barbarossa. The Finns were acting as co-belligerents in revenge for the Winter War, and the world seemed to have turned upside down again. At least for Binney this might mean Germany was distracted and less attention would be paid to his own operation. Militarily this might be the case, but the Germans had other tricks up their sleeves and had no intention of letting Britain have its own way.

THE WALLENBERG VISIT

Marcus Wallenberg, a Swedish banker and influential businessman, had arrived in London with one mission in mind – to forestall the actions of the British which he believed could be disastrous to his country. Marcus, along with his brother Jacob, were part of the prestigious banking family who owned Enskilda Bank, not only the first private bank in Stockholm (and claimed by its founder to be the first to employ women) but one of the most influential during the dire financial years of the 1920s and '30s. Jacob Wallenberg oversaw trade agreements and the business portfolio of the bank in Germany, while Marcus took care of its interests in Britain. In one fell swoop the two brothers were at the heart of money matters concerning the two enemy countries.

Despite US allegations in 1945, neither Jacob nor Marcus was pro-Nazi. Jacob became a long-standing friend of the German resistance group headed by anti-Nazi Carl Friedrich Goerdeler. Goerdeler was hanged for his part in the Stauffenberg plot against Hitler in 1945. Marcus had his own secretive connections.

In 1912, Enskilda Bank was one of the founding owners of the British Bank of Northern Commerce which merged with another British bank, C.J. Hambro & Son, in 1920 to form Hambros Bank, with Enskilda holding shares in the new company. Among the men responsible for the merger was a certain Charles Hambro, later to be Sir Charles Hambro, head of SOE. And the connections between the Wallenbergs and the secret side of the British war effort continued. In 1936 Charles got married for the second time, to Dorothy Helen Mackay, once wife to Marcus Wallenberg. Marcus was also a close friend of Victor Mallet.

Marcus had the unpleasant task, because of his connections, of acting as a go-between for the Swedish Government when it came to negotiations on sensitive topics, such as the new operation Binney was plotting. Marcus was pro-English (his first wife Dorothy had been English) but his loyalties were to his country, and though members of the British Legation jokingly referred to him as 'Charles Hambro's brother-in-law by divorce', there was an unspoken tension caused by his presence. The Foreign Office resented his friendship with Mallet and took it as evidence that the minister was far too much in the pockets of the Swedes and not playing fair to Britain.

Binney had had an unpleasant encounter with Marcus just before the commencement of Operation Rubble. In a fiery row started because Marcus insisted that the British should pay for their orders when they were completed and *before* they were loaded onto ships (a riskless venture for Sweden which would have put Britain at a serious disadvantage), Wallenberg told Binney that 'Britain was finished and her credit was rotten'. In a fury, Binney retorted by telling Marcus exactly what he thought of him and declaring that 'as a free man and not a diplomat, he would personally sign an agreement … between them and the British Steel Industry, to the effect that goods would be paid for when delivered over the side in Gothenburg'. Marcus had impugned Binney and his country's honour, a slur he would never entirely forget.

Marcus's arrival in London would have hardly endeared him to Binney either, as he was seeking an indefinite postponement of the new operation (now codenamed Performance), along with British promises to assist Sweden with aircraft should the Germans attack. Mallet had kindly paved the way for a visit with the Secretary of State, another black mark against the minister in the eyes of the Foreign Office.

Meanwhile, Hambro was busy making the case for the defence of Performance, including apprising the British Government of the dangers involved in giving in to Swedish demands. If allowed to continue they would eventually completely hamstring the operation with all their little requests. The warning had its effect. Mallet was claiming that renewed diplomatic approaches could resolve the issue with the Swedes. Hambro and his colleagues made it plain that this was not the case and also stated, 'It would clearly be a mistake to respond to Swedish overtures, or to let the Swedish Government think that we are pleased with them.' In short, the Swedes had pushed too far.

Binney would no doubt have been satisfied to know that Marcus had received a cold reception in London. The Secretary of State suddenly refused his visit, objecting that he was too busy with other matters, and several ministers whom it was suspected he would try to seek out were warned not to talk politics with him. Instead, it would be preferable to remark on how displeased the British were with Swedish behaviour. Britain was bored with the same old appeasement arguments from Sweden and its patience had worn out. Letters did the rounds of ministers friendly with Marcus to remind them to keep their mouths shut.

Marcus's visit was in fact pretty disastrous. Not only would no one speak to him, but when he stayed for the weekend at Anthony Eden's country house he suffered a bad stomach upset (Eden blamed it on the Spartan diet the Swedes had been existing on, which had not prepared him for the rich dinners of England) and spent the whole weekend in bed. He made a half-hearted attempt to bring up the subject of Anglo-Swedish relations and why Sweden was so unpopular in Britain – a fact he seemed unable to comprehend. Eden thought 'he was a very chastened person compared to the last time I saw him about 18 months ago'.

LIFE OF BRIAN

It had been a muted war so far for Brian Reynolds. On a chilly spring morning in England in 1940 he had listened to the rousing words of his new commanding officer, American Kermit Roosevelt, son of former president Theodore Roosevelt, as he stood with hundreds of British volunteers headed for Finland. Roosevelt viewed his campaign to save Finland from occupation as a crusade. 'I felt that in fighting for the Finns I should be ranging myself against the O.G.P.U. [Soviet Intelligence and secret police] and the Gestapo and all the forces which are troubling the world today,' he declared to his waiting audience, every word scribbled down furiously by eager newspaper reporters.

Roosevelt stood before his troops, an imposing man with a high forehead and a thick moustache. He had just resigned his commission as a major in the British Army to lead the expedition, composed entirely of volunteers and with an average age of 31. It was not the first time Roosevelt had volunteered for a war that his home country was virtually ignoring. In 1939, when war was declared on Germany, he left America to sign up with the British Army, having previously served with the British in the First World War. Now, as Britain seemed prepared to leave Finland to its fate, he was once again ploughing into the unknown.

Brian Reynolds had his own sympathies for the troubled Finns and was too eager for adventure and action to stand back when volunteers were called for. Not overly tall but with striking curly red hair, which he tamed into a moustache and beard, he came from a background of horse racing at J.V. Rank's stables (brother to the film magnate and also breeder of champion Irish wolfhounds) and was known for being daring and a risk-taker. With Britain in the depths of the twilight war, it seemed there was nothing for a keen soul to do but sign up for the Finnish campaign.

For Reynolds things were all about to go horribly wrong. Roosevelt was truly on a crusade – a losing one. His volunteers arrived in Finland just days before the armistice was signed with Russia. The volunteers were trapped, unable to go home, as the Nazis rolled into Norway and arrested nineteen of the volunteers who had failed to leave Oslo in time. Reynolds could only sit back and watch as the war he had expected to fight came to an end and, in its place, Britain's true war began. He had wanted action; instead he had blundered straight into enforced peace.

Through the next year he made various attempts to escape Finland via Petsamo, failing on all occasions and ending up in a Finnish jail. Bitterly he reflected that his commanding officer had missed out on this disaster. Roosevelt had not yet reached Finland at the time of the armistice. He had been free to return to England and rejoin the British Army while hundreds of his volunteers were cut off. He later earned distinction during a raid into Norway and had then been sent to north Africa where there was little action. Roosevelt had proved the leader of a crusade that was over before it began. It would have been cold comfort to Reynolds to know that his valiant, earnest leader was battling alcoholism and depression; he had been dismissed from the British Army in May 1941, despite appeals to his old friend Winston Churchill.

Reynolds felt little joy when he learned in his cold cell that Germany had turned on its friends the Soviets and that Finland was now united with the Nazis. The people whom he had volunteered to save were now his own country's enemy. There was one ray of hope: along with many of the trapped volunteers, he was at last extradited to Sweden. He was still a far cry from England and getting back into the action of war, but he was at least one step closer. Reynolds introduced himself to the British Legation as soon as he could and became an odd-job person for it. He was instantly popular; with his striking hair and bold demeanour he attracted the girls of the Legation, who fluttered around him and took turns to curl his moustache with old-fashioned moustache curlers. They nicknamed him 'the Lion' and he quickly fell in with the activities of SOE on an informal basis.

Binney saw a lot of himself in 'Brian the Lion'; bold, courageous, adventurous and up for any challenge, he recognised a fellow explorer and comrade. As the preparations of June swung into action, he approached Reynolds with an offer. Would he care to take part in Operation Performance?

Reynolds could not have been keener. At last here was real action and right under the noses of the Germans! He agreed without hesitation and quickly discovered that he was to be more than just a bit player. Bill Waring could not be spared from his duties ashore to participate physically in the operation, so Reynolds was made Binney's second-in-command while afloat. Put in charge of acquiring and placing scuttling charges in the various ships to be used and sneaking aboard Lewis guns for defence, he quickly settled into clandestine life and selected and trained men to handle these devices. Binney had now crossed a line. Sweden would not allow the British to arm any ships they were using, as it was against the terms of neutrality and would have the Nazis jumping up and down in fury. But that meant that in the open waters of the Skagerrak the British were sitting ducks for the Luftwaffe, German E-boats or U-boats, with no means of defending themselves. Binney refused to send his men into a potential trap unarmed.

His determination meant that he now had to work clandestinely not only against the Swedish and Germans but also against his own minister Victor Mallet. Mallet would not have sanctioned the guns, so Binney simply did not tell him. While Mallet was happily assuring Swedish ministers that the ships were maintaining strict neutrality by being unarmed, Binney was smuggling gun after gun aboard. Some came in the most amusing fashion. English conductor Malcolm Sargent, about to go on a visit to Sweden to conduct orchestras in Stockholm and Gothenburg, was politely asked if he would mind bringing over an extra couple of suitcases when he came. He willingly agreed and transported two unusually heavy cases on an overnight train between Stockholm and Gothenburg. He never asked what was inside them, even as he delivered them to the Consul-General, which was just as well considering that they contained more of Binney's armaments.

AN ARRESTING PERFORMANCE

The Norwegian ships had spent most of 1941 lying idle in Swedish ports. Rumour was rife that they would not be still for much longer. It was September and the long Scandinavian winter was approaching. German eyes had spotted cargo being quietly loaded and strange packages being delivered to the ships by a red-haired man, and there were far too many British seamen loitering about. They decided to make their move.

Victor Mallet received a worrying communiqué early in October. The Swedes were denying visas to British captains despite being happy to grant them to Norwegian masters. Without a visa the British masters could not go aboard and sail the Norwegian vessels they had been assigned. Under a demise charter established in July 1941 between the Norwegian Government and Britain, British masters were allowed to commandeer any idle Norwegian vessel whose own master was not prepared to sail her. It was a legal ratification of the actions Binney had taken during Operation Rubble when he had evicted troublesome Norwegians in favour of Captains Henry and Escudier. But now it appeared that the Swedes were pointedly ignoring the charter, even going so far as to consider it unjust and illegal. There was no doubt that German pressure was behind the move.

Mallet was given the unpleasant task of changing Swedish minds while also keeping Operation Performance hush-hush. Talking to Binney he learned that Sporborg at SOE had been sent a message from the Swedish Commercial Counsellor yet again asking for a delay on the operation. Mallet was torn; as a career diplomat he did not like such awkward wrangles where both sides were so set on their course of action. News that the Germans had imprisoned several Norwegian ship owners and demanded powers of attorney over their vessels hardly encouraged him. All of a sudden, and somewhat remarkably, a secret wartime operation was about to be legally challenged in court.

On 26 October, an application was made by the Norwegian owners for all vessels in Gothenburg harbour to be arrested. The owners were also suing for damages against certain captains. It was an astonishing turn of events that could have happened only in Sweden. Britain sent over lawyers and legal advisors to plea immunity based on the demise charter, and Sir William Brown of the Ministry of Supply found himself giving evidence. He was particularly required to discuss the arrangements involving *B.P. Newton*:

In the early months of 1941 Sir George Binney was authorised by the then Minister of Supply to purchase in Sweden ... certain raw materials ...

Subsequently arrangements were made for the importation of the materials ... by means of certain Norwegian vessels lying in Swedish waters which were chartered by the British Ministry of War Transport from the Royal Norwegian Government acting through the Norwegian Shipping and Trade Mission.

Amongst the vessels so chartered is ... *B.P. Newton*. The cargo loaded or to be loaded on the said vessel consists and will consist solely of materials, etc., purchased by Sir George Binney in accordance with the arrangements set out above.

But the Swedes were not listening. They had seized the *Rigmor* in late September and this was turning into a legal catastrophe alongside the broader matters of the arrest of all Norwegian ships. Mallet put on his best diplomatic hat and tried his hand at swaying the Swedish authorities, filling his communications with every formality and respectful term he could think of and grovelling in a manner Binney would have found appalling. He tried to convince Christian Gunther of the Ministre des Affaires Etrangères that Britain had every right to operate the Norwegian ships and that the *Rigmor* should be handed back to them. 'Your Excellency,' he began, 'I have the honour to request your Excellency to take such steps as will ensure the immediate release of [*Rigmor*] to His Majesty's Government in the United Kingdom.'

The grovelling worked and the *Rigmor* was released. Sir Montagu-Pollock followed up Mallet's letter with his own sweet-tongued response.

'I take this opportunity of expressing to your Excellency my satisfaction at the action which has been taken in regard to this matter. I have the Honour to be, with the highest consideration, Your Excellency's most obedient, humble servant.'

Unfortunately the Germans were also able to write flattering letters and as a result the Swedish Appeal Court overruled his Excellency's decision and declared that despite the immunity Britain was claiming, the Norwegian owners were perfectly entitled to have their own ships arrested. This was a highly dangerous situation; the decision could undermine all Britain's plans and completely scupper its war efforts. Understandably everybody was anxious.

Worse news almost immediately followed the negative verdict. Montagu-Pollock was sent for by Swedish minister Erik Boheman and was told that the Swedish authorities had decided that 'for fear of a German coup our ships could not be permitted to lie up on the Swedish coast awaiting a favourable opportunity to slip out. They must start from Gothenburg.'

This was disastrous. Leaving from Gothenburg would mean losing every element of surprise and any advantage the British had hoped to gain. Boheman added to the disappointment with his next statement:

A naval escort would be provided in territorial waters, the ships would be at liberty to leave the coast at any point but they must not loiter anywhere within territorial waters for fear of inciting German patrol boats to enter Swedish waters, and they could return to Gothenburg if departure conditions proved unfavourable.

It sounded reasonable enough, but the unspoken intention was to force the British to make a dash across the Skagerrak, any hesitation being viewed as an excuse to arrest them, and the offer to return to Gothenburg was tinged with the real worry that once back there the ships would never be allowed to leave again. Bitterly, Binney remarked, 'These restrictions do not of course apply to German mercy ships, which enjoy normal facilities in Swedish waters.' Here was the crux of the matter. While every obstacle was put in the way of the British, the Germans were merrily and freely shipping steel and other goods from Sweden to their own factories. It seemed a very one-sided form of neutrality the Swedes were endorsing.

Depressed, Binney told his superiors, 'You must fight these restrictions tooth and nail … if the Swedes refuse we shall do our best, but the dice are loaded against us.'

Demands for arrests were now being made against every ship Binney had previously chartered, and the matter became headline news. The *Göteborgs-Posten* led the publicity with 'Giant Arrest of Norwegian Tonnage Valued at Hundred Million Kronor! Ten boats in Gothenburg harbour. Norwegian shipping firms allege they fear flight of vessels at British Government's orders.'

It was all going horribly wrong. On the one hand, various international lawyers were working on Britain's behalf to prove the validity of the demise charter, while on the other, more arrests and damning claims were being made.

At 4.30 p.m. on 5 November, the Gothenburg harbour master and the town bailiff marched onto the *Dicto* and demanded that two engineers they had brought along be allowed to immobilise the engine by removing a vital part. On hearing of the demands, the Vice-Consul was appalled and rushed over to protest, declaring that it was an insult against His Majesty's Government, but to no avail. His lawyer convinced him that protests would do no good and that the *Dicto* had to be immobilised. Her crew looked on helplessly as the engine was pulled apart and essential components removed. The mutilation done, the bailiff and harbour master left. The Vice-Consul was promised by his lawyer that all attempts would be made to overrule the actions of the Swedes, but there was an ominous, unspoken concern hanging in the wind – if they could do this successfully to the *Dicto*, they could do it to every other ship Binney had chosen.

Yet in the midst of the horror the Swedes suddenly redeemed themselves. The following morning, 6 November, an abashed-looking town bailiff was back. With him was the *Dicto*'s engine part and, without discussion, he restored her engine and left the harbour as quickly as he had come. It seemed that the Swedish Government was finally stepping in to restore the situation. Even more surprising, the arrest orders were overturned and all vessels were freed. Immediately Binney put plans in place to clear and sail the *Dicto*, knowing full well that the Germans would hasten to appeal the decision.

Binney had no intention of sending the *Dicto* to England – that was too risky. On the contrary, he merely wanted to get her out of Gothenburg and 'test the waters' with the Swedish authorities. Would they try to stop the *Dicto* leaving? And what about the Germans? How would they respond? He was also hoping that Coastal Command would release aircraft to patrol the waters between Gothenburg and the Norwegian frontier to assess the German position.

The fate of the *Rigmor* was less positive. Caught again in the Swedish legal system, her captain had been removed and the Courts of Appeal were upholding the judgment that the British had no right to move her. Binney spoke with British lawyers, who were of the opinion that the judgment was based on the *Rigmor* being an oil tanker and, therefore, deemed only able to carry oil. Under Operation Performance she would be expected to carry steel, which the Swedish did not consider a valid use for her and thus had decided that Binney was not entitled to use her. The judgment was not only frustrating but controversial, as the courts had ignored all the Norwegian tankers either already loaded or being loaded with steel cargo, including by the Germans, who had even mentioned this in their plea for the arrest of the *Rigmor*! The only reason that the poor *Rigmor* was lying empty was because she had been seized before any cargo could be loaded. One of the lawyers reported that he felt 'the judgment [sic] of [the] appeal court is so patently fallacious that we should not abandon an immunity plea for the *Rigmor* …'.

THE SAGA OF THE *RIGMOR*

The unfortunate oil tanker *Rigmor* had found herself in the position of a pawn between the Swedish, British and Germans. The outcome of her case was liable to be significant to the other ships in harbour; her arrest, if it could not be overturned, could be used as a precedent for arresting every Norwegian ship the British laid their hopes upon. So, as the Scandinavian winter crept in, the *Rigmor* case began to absorb the attentions not only of the legal teams sent by Britain but also of Binney and his fellows at the British Legation and the Norwegian sailors trapped in Gothenburg, along with Swedish civilians, politicians and agitating German agents.

Binney pottered in his office, his eternal optimism refusing to allow him to see the situation as entirely negative. He would not believe that it was the Swedes' intention to prohibit the operation, but only to delay it until Marcus Wallenberg had had a chance to speak to the ministers in London. (As Binney considered this, Marcus was barely a week away from his British visit and unexpected bout of food poisoning.) Binney was certain that even if the *Rigmor*'s arrest was upheld, this would not automatically validate the arrests of every other ship, at least not until the case had been dealt with by the Swedish Supreme Court and the verdict was final. His opinions were all based on circumstantial evidence – the refusal to grant visas to the British, a temporary refusal to allow Norwegian crews out of their refugee camp, deliberately slow delivery of goods ordered, and pressure put on shipping agents to delay loading the goods. He told London, 'The Swedish authorities appear so obsessed by the fear of German reprisals that they ignore the possibility of British repercussions … an exceptionally firm and uncompromising action is required from London if "Performance" is to proceed.'

The British Government was less inclined to play down the Swedish fears of the Germans. After all, the Germans were the ones poised to invade if the mood took them, and everyone knew that Britain was not really going to attack Sweden. The War Office had its hands full enough already.

However, the British were not about to be played for fools. They were convinced, as were their lawyers, that the vagueness of the judgment against the *Rigmor* and the unexpectedness of it suggested a heavy influence from the Swedish Government on the Court of Appeal – all to delay Performance. They started to drop heavy hints to the Swedish Secretary-General that they considered this a distinct possibility. Their lawyers meanwhile were using reams of paper to report how unfair and illegal the Swedish ruling had been, quoting laws, charters and conventions of the previous decade to prove that Sweden was not behaving in either a neutral or unbiased manner.

Two could play at that game. Binney got to wondering that if no further arrests would take place until the *Rigmor* case was settled, why not use it to British advantage? If the Swedes dragged out the case, kicked their heels and loaded the courts with paperwork on the subject, then the remaining Norwegian vessels would sit idle but free in Gothenburg, and while they were doing that, they could be used for the operation.

Mallet, on the other hand, was meeting with the President of the Court of Appeal and came away a deeply worried man. His initial thought, that the court was judging the *Rigmor* on the basis of her 'nature' as an oil tanker rather than a cargo ship, was wrong. He now knew that the court really meant that because she was a merchant ship and not a man-of-war or fleet auxiliary she could not be used for an operation involving blockade-running. Mallet wasn't sure how this stood on a legal basis, but he realised the implications. The verdict was more serious than he first suspected. Even if Binney loaded all his ships with cargo (as he planned to, to skirt around the judgment) it would not prevent them being captured. Mallet, Binney and their lawyers had failed to realise the true danger of the verdict. It was more important than ever that Operation Performance began.

9

OPERATION PERFORMANCE

A board ten Norwegian merchant ships anxious British sailors waited for news. They had 'commandeered' the ships under the demise charter back in September, but now it was November and the owners of the ships were trying to have them evicted. It was yet another legal twist in the strange delay that had sailors sitting aboard loaded ships, uncertain whether they would ever sail them. The threat of arrest still hung over the vessels in Binney's little scheme. The *Rigmor*'s case was pending and another vessel, the *Rapid II*, was stuck in limbo, uncertain if she was under arrest or not. It looked increasingly likely that Binney's operation would never start.

Behind the scenes, things were not so bleak. Britain had scored a triumph when it was ruled in the Swedish courts that the immunity it had claimed over the ships was legal. Unfortunately the Swedish Navy, notorious for its pro-German feelings, had immediately stepped in to put every obstacle possible in the way of launching the ships. Binney had hopes he might be able to clear the *Dicto*, *Buccaneer*, *Storsten* and *B.P. Newton* before more trouble arose. The only problem was that under Swedish naval regulations he had to give the Navy seven days' notice of his intention to leave. The Navy was not about to be co-operative; under pressure, the Swedish Government rushed through legislation stating that any ship whose ownership was in question could not be moved. Binney's vessels were re-arrested and Gothenburg harbour was blocked by naval vessels to prevent their escape.

Lesser men might have given up at this point, but Binney was not to be defeated, nor was Mallet. The two men might sometimes have had their differences, even to the point of violent arguments and Binney operating behind the minister's back, but in this case Mallet was proving as dogmatic as his 'house-guest'.

In Britain, attitudes towards the Swedes were hardening. It was quite clear now that they were not equal in their neutrality and were kowtowing to the Germans. Hugh Dalton, then minister in charge of SOE, wrote to Anthony Eden to apprise him of the seriousness of the situation and how hazardous to the war effort Sweden's obstinacy could prove:

> The most important items [to be brought over by Operation Performance] are ball bearings and the machinery for their production since, both in this country and the United States, there is a serious deficiency in equipment for the production of ball bearings specifically for the war effort. Tanks and aircraft require in large quantities sizes of ball bearings not normally used in commercial industry.

It was hoped that a secret factory in Scotland might soon be able to start producing the ball bearings Britain badly needed, but they were far from ready for operation, and 'machinery which can only be obtained from Sweden and has never yet been successfully manufactured in this country or the United States' was necessary for the factory to function.

Britain set about appealing the decision. The ships remained idle, but now fully manned with around 430 Norwegian and British sailors and a handful of Dutch and Polish volunteers. It looked set to be another cold winter, the crews were bored and frustrated, and security was proving difficult as the men and harbour authorities were infiltrated by a number of traitors. Binney kept full details of the operation to himself, a genuine necessity that left the men wondering what was happening and caused their morale to decline.

December brought new issues; the Court of Appeal turned down the British application, leaving no option but to go to the Supreme Court – yet another delay. Adding to the confusion, the Russians suddenly appeared on the scene. Since the German invasion of their country they had been building ties with Britain. They were far from trusted, but their manpower and, frankly, the distraction value of having another aggressor combating Hitler, was much needed.

The Russians had been offered the option of loading cargo they required from Sweden onto the Gothenburg vessels supposedly in British hands. At first they had been uninterested; now, in December, they changed their minds and sent dozens of trucks from all over Sweden containing Russia-bound goods to Gothenburg. They wanted to load a cargo of 5,500 tons onto vessels already loaded with British orders. Somehow space was made and the new cargo added to the old, probably to sit forever in the icy waters of the harbour.

Russian Commercial Counsellor Nikitin also arrived in Gothenburg. An engineer and son of the famous Alexandra Kollontai, a Communist revolutionary and the first female government minister in Europe, his first thought on seeing the Russian cargo being loaded was purely financial.

'What about insurance?' he asked.

He was promptly told that the nature of the operation made the cargo uninsurable.

'I have no authority to load anything without insurance; it must all be off-loaded.'

Grumbling workers off-loaded the 5,500 tons of goods, while Nikitin prowled the docks observing the congestion the undelivered Russian orders were causing. A few days later he was back by the Norwegian ships.

'We've changed our minds,' he stated. 'Re-load the cargo without insurance.'

Nikitin need hardly have worried since the loads were going nowhere fast.

The winter of 1941 proved to be the coldest on record. The legal problems dragged on, coupled with increasing security issues. One evening, when Binney was sitting with Bill Waring and Peter Coleridge in the Gothenburg flat, the fire they had stoked to warm themselves began smoking badly. An examination of the chimney revealed a hidden microphone. Before destroying it the men entered into a fictitious conversation concerning their distress at receiving orders from England to abort the entire operation. There was no knowing if they were believed.

Sabotage was also a real danger. Sand was discovered in the main bearings of the *Skytteren*'s engines, one auxiliary engine was tampered with and a small fire started. She was not alone in being targeted. The *Lionel*'s auxiliary engine had its lubricating system tampered with, while the *Buccaneer* also suffered troubles with her engines.

The winter dragged on and temperatures plummeted to $-40°F$ with heavy frosts and clear nights. Bad weather for blockade-runners. The lawyers worked on and finally received a favourable verdict from the Supreme Court on 17 March 1942. It was a hollow victory. They had been delayed throughout the winter and now the days would lengthen again and any attempt to run the Skagerrak would be fraught with added dangers without the cover of dark nights. The Swedes had achieved their purpose; now they left it in the hands of the Germans if the British were foolish enough to try to break out.

THE SHOW MUST GO ON

The ice was thick in Gothenburg. Binney sailed quietly out on a harbour ice-breaker, heading to Vinga lighthouse to assess conditions. The ice was at least 2 feet thick in the fjord. Beyond, ice flows made sailing hazardous. The only consolation was that this would also slow the German patrols now said to be stationed at Kristiansand and Hantsholm. Binney gazed across the water with his Arctic explorer's sense of adventure and risk. They could do it; there was a channel left open in the ice, narrow but navigable. He sailed back to Gothenburg to rouse the captains.

On 28 March 1942, he wrote to SOE, 'All our ships are now lying at the mouth of the harbour in as advantageous a position as Gothenburg can offer, but of course they are easily seen by any watchers on shore.' Binney knew that there was no chance of a secret exit as had happened with Rubble. The Swedish authorities would not allow the ships to berth any further out than the outer limits of the harbour, where they were opposite the wharves of the belligerent Swedish Navy. Besides, Binney had been told that he must inform the Swedish Navy of the precise time of his departure and it would then put to sea ahead of him and alert the Germans. It seemed more and more likely the Swedes were determined to push the cargo vessels straight onto the guns of the Nazis.

The following day saw the Swedes trying to put naval ratings on the ships for the first half-hour of the voyage. Mallet protested, but the Swedes were adamant, stating that they also intended to put them aboard a number of armed German merchant ships that had recently sailed into the harbour. It was believed that these ships (notably allowed to remain armed in Swedish waters despite the contrary being applied to the British) would pursue the Performance vessels out of Gothenburg and give their position away to the German patrols. It was one small glimpse of fairness from the Swedes that they intended to ensure that did not happen and that wireless silence was maintained.

This one concession did little to off-set their next demand. The vessels would not be allowed to claim safety in Swedish waters except where the neutral shipping routes ran, and if any were to stop or anchor, other than to off-load a pilot or a naval rating, they would be forcibly returned to Gothenburg. By all accounts the situation looked grim, but Binney was stubborn and he had dug his heels in. Nothing was going to stop this attempt, not now.

Standing aboard his flagship *Dicto*, the vessel he had never quite managed to get out of harbour yet, on 30 March, he addressed the captains of the various convoy ships. It was late afternoon and this would be their final meeting. Weather reports had promised warmer, foggy conditions later that night, so it was intended that they leave that evening and sail along the Swedish coast until the fog descended. Binney could not mask the dangers they faced. The Royal Navy had been unable to promise the close support it had given during Rubble because of new minefields that had been laid and a tougher air and sea blockade by the Germans. Once in open waters each captain was on his own. He had to sail as he saw fit and if the worst happened he was to scuttle his ship rather than let its cargo fall into Nazi hands. There was apprehension among the men; they knew that a German attack would lead to capture or death, and there was an unspoken belief that should they be taken alive they would be delivered into the hands of the Gestapo. That was a fate none of them wanted to consider. Despite their fear, they were determined to stand beside the British and do what they could. That Binney would be sailing with them at least filled them with confidence and a sense of loyalty.

Binney issued copies of the order of the day to the ten ships about to set sail, among them the *Rigmor* which had finally been released from her captivity. The *Dicto*, *Buccaneer*, *Charente*, *Gudvang*, *Lind*, *Lionel*, *B.P. Newton*, *Rigmor*, *Skytteren* and *Storsten* stood ready as their crews read Binney's words:

To-day at long last we are going to England determined come what may to render a staunch account of our voyage as befits Norwegian and British seamen. Indeed we run a risk, but what of it. If we succeed, these splendid ships will serve the Allied cause and with their cargoes we shall aid the task of war supplies. To sink our ships and cargoes rather than see them captured by the enemy is, of course, our duty and on your behalf I have taken such measures as you would wish. Should we encounter misfortune at sea remember that in our homes and among our countrymen it will be said with simple truth that we have done our best for the honour and freedom of Norway and Britain. But I for one have never held with this blockade and look once more to our success, believing that before two days have passed your laughter will resound within a British port. So let us merchant seamen, 400 strong, shape a westerly course in good heart counting it an excellent privilege that we have been chosen by providence to man these ships in the immortal cause of freedom. God speed our ships upon this venture. Long live King George, long live King Haakon. MS *Dicto*, Gothenburg, George Binney.

It was typical Binney, but on this occasion even his eternal opti-mism could not ensure the success of the voyage. Back on the *Dicto*, he received the latest meteorological reports and read them with a disheartening sense of foreboding. The predicted fog now looked less likely; clear weather was rapidly moving over the British Isles, pushing the promised heavy weather ahead of it and meaning the fog would arrive sooner than anticipated – it would probably also evaporate sooner than hoped for too. Binney sat for a while with the meteorologist who had brought him the news and debated the implications. He could start the operation early, and at first this seemed the best option, but then the meteorologist hesitated; he could not stake men's lives on such an unpredictable thing as the foggy weather and advised against it. Binney decided to stick with his original plan. The ships would leave Gothenburg and hug the coast until 11 p.m. when Binney would receive a further weather report and make his final decision as to whether the operation would commence.

At 8 p.m. the first ship slipped down the narrow channel past the Vinga lighthouse and into open waters, the rest following in slow procession. Thick ice scraped and bumped on the hulls of the ships. There was no chance of their exit being unobserved; Swedish escort ships were following them with their lights full on. Ahead lay hope: the fog Binney had promised was visible as a thick bank some distance away but approaching. Even so, the attentions of the Swedish made their departure deeply uncomfortable.

Aboard the *Dicto* Binney was barely able to contain his temper as he watched the lights of the Swedes falling on his convoy. Had he not helped these people? Had they not promised that their true loyalties lay with the British? Right now it seemed that they were firmly favouring the Germans. Fear of retribution aside, it seemed there was far too strong a pro-German element among the Swedish authorities for Binney's or Britain's comfort. Still, the fog looked promising.

The *Dicto* was fifth out of the harbour and as she passed Vinga, Binney spotted the *Charente*, *Buccaneer* and *Lionel* steaming parallel to one another, a Swedish warship providing escort. The weather was disintegrating. The feared cold front was pushing over the Swedish coast and dispersing the cloud and fog. Visibility, Binney judged, was about 12 miles. It was around 11.40 p.m. and all the ships were out of the harbour. Binney could have called them off, made the decision that he had said he would hours earlier, but he wasn't ready to give up just yet. There were several hours of darkness yet; there had to be a chance still.

Though the weather was clearing, the ice certainly wasn't. The *Dicto* ran into a thick drift of ice and had to alter course until they found thinner ice they could sail through. Worryingly this pushed them outside territorial waters and they made an easy target sailing alongside the ice. Binney comforted himself that any attack could come only from the port side. The other ships were out of sight; communication was possible only via the wireless.

Shortly after 2 a.m. the *Dicto* rounded the Hallo Islands and was attacked by a large armed trawler. The *Dicto* veered into the coastal ice to avoid the shots and grazed her hull on the ice. The trawler moved off as quickly as it had appeared, but the *Dicto* was leaking and the prospects for making a breakout looked bleak. The latest weather forecast was disappointing; it looked likely that the fog would clear before the ships could reach the Royal Navy or air cover from Coastal Command. Binney decided it was time to warn the others. He sent out a wireless message at 6 a.m. on 1 April:

'Weather now unfavourable and likely to remain so for some days.'

He waited 15 minutes and repeated the message. He was crestfallen at the failure, but the captains would have to make up their own minds about risking the North Sea and, with the odds now so slim, it seemed pointless to make the run. Another 15 minutes passed and he sent the message again. Intriguingly, the Norwegian book *Nortraships Flate*, published in Oslo in 1976, contradicts this scenario and implies that Binney gave the go-ahead to the convoy. This, however, is not confirmed by the official record.

The coastal authorities on the Hallo Islands had spotted the *Dicto* and sent out a pilot. He was as obstinate as every other Swede they had encountered. When around midday they sailed into a patch of fog, he insisted that the *Dicto* drop anchor. Bitterly, Binney contemplated that they were being prevented from using the very weather they needed for escape. At 5 p.m. a Swedish destroyer approached them and a message was shouted across.

'Follow after me to Gothenburg, and if you do not follow I am going to use my guns.'

The *Dicto* was left with no option. Miserably, Binney watched the captain of his flagship turn her back to Gothenburg. He was angry and filled with resentment towards the Swedes. As he sailed back he could only wonder what had become of the rest of his convoy.

FATE TAKES A HAND

Captain Frederick Kershaw knew his temporary ship *Lionel* was never going to be the best bet for the ocean crossing. She was a slow ship, achieving a maximum of 10 knots. Even more dishearteningly, the bulk of his cargo was not even for the British, but was 3,690 tons of machinery and steel for the Russians. Alongside Kershaw was the Nortraship representative Hans Schnitler. Together they commanded a crew of forty on the long, lumbering vessel.

At 6 a.m. on 1 April all was quiet. Binney's message had failed to arrive and, as far as Kershaw knew, the attempt was still on. From where he stood on the bridge he could see thick snow flurries falling and decided it was a favourable time to attempt the Skagerrak. Just visible was the *Buccaneer*, also apparently making a move to head out to sea. By 6.40 a.m. the *Lionel* was 6 miles from the coast and making the best speed she could when the weather abruptly changed. Kershaw looked on in horror as the snow lessened and the skies suddenly seemed bright and clear.

Almost immediately the *Lionel* was spotted by a German armed trawler, one of the many Binney knew were patrolling in search of the escapees. She flew a signal to demand that the *Lionel* stop, but instead Kershaw ordered his ship around and headed as fast as he could back towards the coast. Aggrieved, the German trawler opened fire, but thankfully missed. Kershaw had no intention of placing his crew or the *Lionel* in the hands of the Germans and kept up the retreat until the German trawler decided that they had won and turned its attentions instead on the unfortunate *Buccaneer*.

Aboard the *Lionel*, Kershaw heard the distinctive sound of heavy gunfire and two loud explosions. He hardly dared wonder who had fallen foul of the Germans. The *Lionel* slipped back into Swedish territorial waters and stumbled upon the Swedish destroyers *Puke* and *Psilander* which had been quietly patrolling and watching the situation develop.

'Put to sea,' they signalled to Kershaw. That was the last thing he intended to do. Kershaw raised his own signal, declaring that he did not understand their message. The *Charente*, *Lind*, *Rigmor* and *Gudvang* were close to making their own dash and were in range to spot the *Lionel*. So were the Swedish patrol vessels, and they now began swarming around her. A patrol vessel broke away and her captain excitedly shouted a message across to the *Lionel*.

'Proceed West; you may not remain in Swedish waters.'

Unsurprisingly, Kershaw was beginning to develop the opinion that the Swedes were determined to throw him onto the guns of the Nazis. His experience as a seaman along the Scandinavian coast made him think there was no chance of a breakout that day and any attempt to cross the Skagerrak was sure to end in the sinking of the *Lionel*. He was now surrounded by patrol vessels ordering him to leave Swedish waters, with *Puke* and *Psilander* hovering ominously in the background. Kershaw ordered a signal to be sent asking if they could return to Gothenburg. Several responding signals quickly came. One told him unequivocally, 'Yes, but you will never get out from there again.' Another implied that he would be able to leave when he wanted. Kershaw had made up his mind. There was no point attempting the Skagerrak and, surrounded by the mobbing Swedes, he chose to make his slow way back to Gothenburg. Even that proved far from simple; as the *Lionel* passed Bottö a warning shot was fired towards her. Kershaw cursed and flew a signal asking if he could continue to Gothenburg. Atop the Bottö cliffs he could see the naval station that had fired upon him, and 16 tense minutes passed as he awaited their reply.

The Swedish seemed baffled as to how to deal with the Performance vessels and were confused about their orders. Eventually they made a decision and flew the simple response 'Yes'. Kershaw got his ship under way again and made the humiliating journey back to Gothenburg, arriving that evening. He had no idea how narrow an escape he had had.

NAZI WRATH

Captain James Reeve had stepped aboard the *Storsten* just before Christmas 1941. 'From the first moment [he] had the respect and esteem from the crew as only a man of his casting and mental structure deserved … His spirit was a constant encouragement to us and a great help for all of us …' some of his crew later wrote in a letter to his wife. Reeve's crew were far from conventional: his First Mate Finn Bie had brought his wife Mary aboard, who was heavily pregnant, and one of the sailors had also brought aboard his wife Bertha Olsen. They were, of course, all hoping to get to England safely. The remainder of the crew were mainly Norwegian, and Nortraship had sent a representative to join the voyage in the person of Ragnar Bull-Nilsen.

The *Storsten*'s escape began badly. On her way to Vinga a fault was found with the steering gear and Reeve had no option but to anchor his ship for several hours while it was repaired. His radio operator, Tor Jorfald, reported that the wireless had remained silent and, with no sign of the other ships which had steamed ahead, Reeve had to make his own decision about what to do. The weather seemed favourable enough, so he ordered them to sail further along the coast and then make a break for open waters.

The *Storsten* had a top speed of 10–11 knots, making her a slow-moving target for the armed German vessels patrolling the waters. Reeve had his eyes peeled for danger. At 10 a.m. on 1 April he made a dangerous mistake when he spotted three vessels approaching from the starboard side and mistakenly identified them as the *Skytteren*, *Rigmor* and *Lind*. He allowed them to approach far too close, when the smallest vessel began attacking. Reeve hastily ordered the *Storsten* to turn on a south-westerly course and managed to hide her in a fog bank. The German vessels lost sight of their prey and faded away. Reeve could thank his lucky stars that there was not a scratch on the *Storsten*.

For the next few hours Reeve stuck with the fog bank, relieved that the poor weather would prevent aircraft from taking off.

By 1 p.m. the *Storsten* was roughly 32 miles south-east of Kristiansand and had managed to avoid further attacks. The crew had settled slightly after their early nerves and the unexpected attack by the German vessels. Jorfald was still at his radio, but he reported that he had heard nothing – Binney's message had failed to reach him too. Reeve was at the edge of the Skagerrak. A few more miles and he could expect air and sea cover from the British, and he felt hopeful that his blockade-run was about to prove successful. That was when the fog began to lift.

The Luftwaffe had been frustratingly stuck at their bases by bad weather as news reached them that the British were making their attempt. They could do nothing but watch the weather reports as they sat grounded. Then at lunchtime the skies began to clear. A signal was sent that an aircraft could be launched and a jubilant pilot rushed to his Junkers 88 only too eager to set out on the hunt. Just after 2 p.m. he spotted a lone ship at the very edge of the blockaded waters. Aboard the *Storsten*, Reeve spotted the plane flying low. Within moments there was a tremendous explosion. Reeve thought they had struck a mine, either dropped by the plane or accidentally run into while distracted. It was equally likely that the Junkers 88 had dropped a torpedo.

Whatever the cause, the damage was horrendous – the foreship was ripped open on the starboard side, exploding a water tank and pushing water up and over the bridge. The drenched Kershaw looked on in horror at the ruins of his ship. The starboard life-boat was destroyed and the steering mechanism, an issue from the first day, was now completely wrecked. The reinforced concrete surrounding the bridge, which was supposed to protect against machine-gun fire, had exploded with the force of the strike. The helmsman had been thrown from the bridge onto the boat deck and Able Seaman Anton Andersen was injured by flying con-crete. First Mate Bie was dazed by the explosion, but came to his senses in time to see Reeve angrily, and pointlessly, firing at the enemy aircraft with his Colt pistol. It was just before 3 p.m. In the wireless room, Jorfald was trying to send an SOS message.

He managed to get out the name of his ship and 'torpedoed' before his machine stopped transmitting. It only took him a moment to realise that the enemy plane had disabled his radio set by destroying the antenna.

Across the ocean in Britain a radio station briefly picked up an SOS signal, while aboard the *Lind* a similar message was heard. Neither could respond or indeed aid the ship in distress. Jorfald was meanwhile trying to jerry-rig an emergency antenna. The deck of the *Storsten* was in chaos. The illegal Lewis guns were determinedly firing at the aircraft and in return the Junkers 88 was machine-gunning anyone in sight and dropping its bombs. One bomb crashed onto the deck but miraculously failed to explode, rolling overboard between the boatswain's legs. The emergency antenna was a pointless exercise and Jorfald retreated just as another bomb landed in the water a mere 70 feet from the ship.

Despite their dogged attempts to defend themselves, Reeve knew the situation was rapidly becoming hopeless. An armed German trawler had now appeared and was firing at the stranded ship. It was time to abandon and scuttle her.

Reeve went to find Jorfald. He discussed the plan for setting off the scuttling charges and informed Jorfald that he would be the one to push the button. Then Reeve went to see the port lifeboat, the motorboat and the gig being launched. Bull-Nilsen saw to it that the gig and lifeboat were fastened to the back of the motorboat and could be towed. The fifty-one members of the crew, including the two women, bundled into the craft, the last being Jorfald. He had to swim to the boats after setting off the scuttling charges. Under cover of the confusion caused by the attack, Bull-Nilsen towed away the two smaller craft. The last they saw of the *Storsten* she was surrounded by a swarm of Nazi aircraft.

Reeve's bedraggled crew baled water from their boats and clung grimly to the sides, cold, wet and suffering from shock. The decision was made to try to reach the rendezvous point with the British, as the motorboat could provide the necessary power and there was still hope that they all might reach England.

Around 6 p.m. they spotted a British aircraft; Coastal Command had been sending up planes to scout for the Performance vessels all afternoon without success. At 6.27 p.m. two Beaufighter crews reported seeing the *Storsten* lying idle in the water. She was listing badly to one side, a lifeboat lay ruined nearby, and there was no sign of life. Almost at the same time another Beaufighter spotted the crew of the *Storsten*. To the delight of Reeve and his men, the plane swooped low and they were able to wave at the pilot and brandish Norwegian flags. The Beaufighter moved away, reporting to base that it had spotted three boats in the water, the biggest towing the other two. He noted erroneously that there were 100 men in the boats.

The elation of spotting the Beaufighter did not last long when it became apparent that no rescue was imminent. Bull-Nilsen had the motorboat flat out, towing his passengers to the approximate location they hoped to find the British. As the evening drew in and high winds made the voyage even more unbearable, the motorboat's engines failed.

Bull-Nilsen dropped the weather anchor and held a conference with Reeve over what to do next. There was no point sitting out in the middle of the ocean, so the gig was abandoned after the three people aboard her were transferred to the lifeboat. Then Reeve had the lifeboat's sails raised and took the motorboat in tow, heading once more for the rendezvous spot. It took until the early hours of 2 April to get under way again and the strain of the adventure was taking its toll on the passengers. Bertha Olsen's mental state suddenly deteriorated, not helped by her husband's attempts to jump overboard. She became hysterical, insisting that the other men aboard the boat were trying to kill her. The nightmare worsened as strong winds made it impossible to maintain the sails and the two boats had to heave to once more until the weather improved.

Good Friday dawned with promising weather. The lifeboat's sails were once again raised and the two vessels drifted out further into the ocean. There was not a soul to be seen and any chance of a rendezvous with British ships seemed lost. No more planes flew overhead to bring consolation and, as the winds once more became impossible for the sails, the two sets of survivors had to make a decision.

Opinion was divided; a number of the crew in the motorboat, perhaps swayed by the sturdiness of the vessel even without its engines, wanted to continue to Scotland. Reeve could see land, and a rudimentary calculation of their position suggested that they were about 30 miles from Jøssingfjord on the Norwegian coast. The captain favoured landing there in small groups and trying to head back for Sweden. Eventually the decision was made that seventeen men in the motorboat would aim for Scotland, while the rest of the crew headed for the Norwegian coast. Trimmer Arne Borge asked to leave the lifeboat and go with those aboard the motorboat – he swapped places with Gustaf Nordstrom. The two vessels went their separate ways, both hopeful but afraid.

At 8.10 a.m. on 4 April, Captain Stork of the Royal Danish Air Service was flying his Lockheed Hudson off the coast of Scotland when he spotted a motor-powered lifeboat 90 miles off the Naze. He reported the position and circled for 20 minutes before he had to return to base. At 9.40 a.m. Stork and his Hudson crew were ordered to return to the last known position of the lifeboat and act as an escort. It took them 45 minutes to return to the spot but, despite searching, they could not find the lifeboat. Stork returned to base at 11.10 a.m. to report that the lifeboat had vanished.

A Sunderland flying boat from Invergordon was now sent into action with orders to find the lifeboat and rescue the men. Escorted by four Beaufighters, the Sunderland flew out into deteriorating weather. A storm was blowing up and by the time the flying boat was nearing the last known position of the men of the *Storsten* it had lost sight of all the Beaufighters. Decreasing visibility and heavy seas that would prevent the Sunderland landing and rescuing anyone, forced the aircraft to turn back and abandon the search.

There was no let-up in the storm during 5 April, and when the search resumed the following day there was little hope of finding the men. They had vanished into the vast ocean and official opinion was that they had perished during the storm, possibly before the Sunderland was even launched. Curiously, the belongings of one of the lost *Storsten* men, engineer Erling Bakke, were reported to have been found in a lifeboat off the coast of Denmark on 3 August. The motor lifeboat they were found in, however, was not the *Storsten* vessel that had vanished but a craft from the *Tindefjell*, a ship that had been captured by the Germans in April. While her former crew claimed the lifeboat had been aboard the *Tindefjell* when they left, the Germans insisted that the craft had already been lost. Whatever the case, there seems no obvious explanation as to how Bakke's belongings ended up in a completely different lifeboat off the Danish coast.

Reeve's fate after the two parties separated was similarly grim. His lifeboat drifted towards the Norwegian coast, but unable to land at Jøssingfjord, he headed instead to a nearby inlet at dawn on 4 April. Luck was not with the survivors. They were spotted by two fishing vessels which immediately took off and presumably reported them to the Germans, for not long after, soldiers arrived on the scene from a nearby battery and captured all but nine of the survivors.

Reeve was among the captives. He was exhausted from commanding the fraught escape attempt and did not have the strength to flee when the Germans descended. He spent the rest of the war in a concentration camp. Finn Bie abandoned his wife and disappeared into the night, eventually making it back to Sweden. Heavily pregnant Mary Bie managed to avoid being sent to Germany because of her condition and was admitted to hospital instead where she had her baby.

The handful that escaped found themselves in occupied territory. Carpenter Alfred Nymoen tried to cross a bridge, only to discover it guarded by Germans and had to retreat to a nearby farm. Fortunately the farmer was friendly and gave him clean clothes to replace his damp garments, food and a place to sleep.

In the meantime more escapees had stumbled across the farm, only just avoiding a German patrol that was looking for the missing men. The farmer hid Nymoen and five others in a large wardrobe upstairs while he spoke with the Germans. Bravely, he distracted the Germans and eventually they left without fully searching the property.

Nymoen and the others now tried to reach Oslo, having to cross a mountain on skis during the process. Once again the weather was against them and while three of the sailors pushed on, Nymoen and two friends turned back for the coast. They were trapped once more on Norwegian soil and in desperation they hitch-hiked to Kristiansand and boarded a bus. Germans were everywhere and, to Nymoen's despair, they stopped the bus to check the passengers. With more bravado than sense perhaps, Nymoen simply rose from his seat and left the bus, walking straight past the Germans who ignored him! He loitered in the shadows near a house and watched what was happening.

The Germans were inspecting the papers of everyone aboard. Whether this was a routine check or they were still looking for the escaped *Storsten* crew Nymoen had no idea. Miserably, he watched his two friends being bundled off the bus where they stood on the pavement surrounded by Germans while the other passengers were sent on their way. Nymoen had a vague hope of helping his friends; he left the security of the house and headed down the road, passing directly by the Germans but not stopping. He kept walking in the direction of town and eventually heard the Germans approaching behind him. He held his breath but the soldiers marched past him, escorting his friends. He followed them into town and saw his companions being led into a building swarming with Nazis. This was the last he saw of them.

Nymoen boarded another bus, this time headed for Arendal. He was lost, confused and frightened when he stepped into the town. It was late at night and curfew meant people should not be out walking the streets, but Nymoen had nowhere to go.

He wandered aimlessly for a while until he bumped into a German soldier on patrol. The German shone a torch into his face.

'What are you doing out at this time of night?'

Nymoen had to think fast for an excuse.

'I've just been paid off a ship and I can't find a hotel room.'

The German's expression changed from suspicion to sympathy.

'Come with me, I will help you find a room.'

Under German escort, Nymoen was led to a seamen's hotel and helped to find a room.

'I've left my papers at my friend's house in Kristiansand; I stayed there last night,' Nymoen explained when he was asked for his identification.

The hotel keeper was equally understanding and told him he must go to the police station the next day and get them replaced. That is exactly what Nymoen did. Again he stated that he had left his papers in Kristiansand and wondered if he could have a temporary pass to Oslo. To Nymoen's surprise it was issued on the spot and he left for the Norwegian capital which had so recently been the centre of Nazi occupation.

Oslo was far from safe. Nymoen could not relax until he was back in Sweden. Seeking out the police again, he offered his same sob story and said all he wanted was a pass to get back to his home town of Rendal. The police officer was uncertain; Oslo was under closer inspection by the Germans than its outlying neighbours and he did not feel comfortable issuing the pass.

'Call the police in Rendal; they know me and can tell you who I am,' Nymoen suggested. That was entirely the truth, as he was friendly with the police in Rendal. They had no idea that he had been taking part in a British operation, so the story that he had just come off a ship in Norway would sound plausible to them. After a brief phone call the Oslo police officer was satisfied and issued Nymoen with his border pass. From Rendal, he escaped to Sweden and eventually found himself on a plane to the UK where he joined the Norwegian forces. He was one of eight *Storsten* crew members who escaped. Later sources disagree on the number who made it to Sweden, but a letter received by Annie Reeve, wife of Captain James Reeve, stated that Finn Bie, Tor Jorfald (the valiant radio operator), Johannes Loken, B. Anderson, Gjertsen, Joar Krohn, Nymoen and Borchgrevink all made it to London.

Captain Reeve was not so lucky. Captured by the Germans, he was at first mistaken for George Binney and regularly threatened with being shot. Binney, of course, was safe back in Stockholm. In 1943, Reeve, along with his crew and other captives, was sentenced to 'nacht und nebel' (night and fog) detention – a directive designed by Hitler to root out political rebels and those who might assist the Resistance against the Nazi regime. It was aimed at anyone deemed to be a threat to 'German security', and those convicted were secretly shipped to Germany. Reeve ended up in Sonnenburg concentration camp, a former prison which was ironically referred to as a 'Convict's Paradise' in *The Times* of 1929. By 1930, it had been closed, only to be reopened and manned by the SA (Sturmabteilung) stormtroopers in 1933. It soon had strong ties with the Gestapo, and prisoner numbers rocketed. Another brief period of closure was followed by its darkest period, from 1939 to 1945, when it housed 'anti-Germans', and the usual atrocities associated with Nazi-run camps became an everyday part of the prisoners' lives. Overcrowding, starvation, brutality, disease – Reeve faced everything that the Nazis could throw at him for his failure to escape the Skagerrak. He was one of the lucky ones to survive and was eventually awarded the OBE by King George VI on 16 October 1945 'for gallantry and initiative in hazardous circumstances'.

THE SABOTEUR'S DREAM

On 8 December 1900, the White Star Line (later to become infamous for the *Titanic* tragedy) launched the last of its Jubilee quintet, the slender *Suevic*, into the Irish waters off Belfast.

Constructed by Harland & Wolff (as would be the unfortunate *Titanic*) the *Suevic* was designed to serve the newest White Star Line route between Liverpool, Cape Town and Sydney. Her arrival in the Mersey before her first voyage to Cape Town was recorded in *The Times*. At 12,531 tons she was the largest of the quintet and could carry 400 passengers – all steerage class. But the *Suevic*'s quiet life as a passenger and cargo ship was to be short.

With the ongoing Boer War raging in South Africa, the *Suevic* was commissioned to sail British troops across the ocean. She was neither fast (13½ knots at best) nor armed, but she returned unscathed from trip after trip. Her first accident occurred in safe waters when she slammed ashore at full speed near Plymouth. Her master had miscalculated his route by 16 miles and heavy fog sealed his ship's fate. The *Suevic* could only be returned to the ocean by using dynamite to blow off her bow. She limped to Southampton, to await a new bow already under construction at Harland & Wolff. Remarkably, by 1908, the *Suevic* was back in the water.

For six years all was settled for the liner as she plied back and forth between England, Africa and Australia; then the First World War broke out. Again the *Suevic* was drafted into war service, this time because of her capacity for carrying cargoes of frozen meat. She was also to be a troop transport. The Jubilee quintet all served during the war, journeying along the hazardous commercial routes, dodging German submarines during the increased German shipping campaigns of 1917 and the usual dangers of seafaring. During the Dardanelles campaign of 1915, the *Suevic* carried troops to the Mediterranean and served valiantly throughout the war years. When she was finally returned to the White Star Line it was decided that she deserved a well-earned refit before carrying on with her regular business.

From 1920, the *Suevic* served the White Star Line's Australian route. Her refit had included providing accommodation for 266 second-class passengers, and for the next eight years she made her peaceful way back and forth across the ocean. She had been in service for twenty-eight years when it was decided that she was showing her age and should be sold. Having carried troops during both the Boer War and Great War, and thousands of passengers to the new opportunities Australia presented, the *Suevic* was now sold to the Norwegians for the sum of £35,000 and converted into a whale factory ship. Renamed the *Skytteren*, her glory days were done and for the next decade she ploughed through the icy Arctic waters reeking of whale fat.

When Binney spotted the *Skytteren* trapped in Gothenburg like so many other Norwegian ships, he could not know that she had once been the glory of the White Star Line, one of a famous quintet that had filled the British with patriotic fervour as they proudly sailed to the outskirts of the Empire. Instead she looked like a tired whaling vessel, not very fast, but big.

Stepping aboard the *Skytteren*, British captain William Wilson thought that she looked a reasonable vessel for the attempt. However, he had a niggling doubt about her safety while in harbour. The Foreign Office had suggested that she offered 'exceptional opportunities' for saboteurs. Wilson was of a similar view; the ageing ship could be damaged in a number of ways. He was also not convinced about the scuttling charges Binney had installed. The *Skytteren* had so many tanks and bulkheads that the explosives might not do sufficient damage. Wilson came to the conclusion that he would have to set her alight if he could not elude the Germans.

Wilson's crew consisted of 111 people, three being women who came under the category of approved stowaways and fourteen being British crewmen. Carrying only a minimum cargo, the *Skytteren* followed her fellow ships out of Gothenburg and into the icy Swedish waters. She was yet another vessel that would never receive the message sent by Binney on the *Dicto*, so Wilson had no knowledge that his commander had quashed the mission. Besides, he had other problems to worry about. Something seemed to be wrong with the *Skytteren*'s steering and it was all too easy to wonder if a saboteur had managed to get aboard as feared.

As dawn approached, the *Skytteren* was making her attempt to escape the Skagerrak when the *Lind* and *Rigmor* came sailing past her at top speed. From the *Rigmor*'s deck her captain William Gilling called across to his colleague and informed him that they had a German patrol ship on their tail and Wilson should turn back. Wilson hardly needed telling, seeing his comrades fleeing as fast as they could and, knowing that he was no match for the heavily armed Germans, he ordered his ship to be turned around. It was at this moment that the *Skytteren*'s steering problems came to a head. She was not responding correctly and was turning far too slowly and awkwardly. Wilson had no choice but to halt his ship and send down men to see if they could fix the problem.

All the time the Germans were drawing closer. A lead German patrol boat spotted the *Skytteren* trying to turn and signalled furiously for her to stop. Even if Wilson had wanted to obey the Germans, his ship was unresponsive to commands and he was drifting. Thinking that the *Skytteren* was trying to evade them, the Germans fired a warning shot. It was probably meant to sail just over the *Skytteren*'s deck, but instead it went under the bridge and slammed into the boatswain's cabin. No one was hurt, but Wilson was rattled.

After the war, the Nortraship representative aboard the *Skytteren* would suggest that Wilson panicked when the Germans drew close. He made the decision to scuttle his vessel, the detonators for the charges being in his cabin. He hastened there, giving a brief warning to his crew of what was about to happen. There was not enough time for word to spread. As Wilson fired the charges, crewmen were still below. Stoker Thorfinn Johannessen never realised the danger and was killed instantly as a scuttling charge exploded in the engine room; another stoker was badly burned. British crewman Bill Hatchly was racing down to the boiler room as the charges went off, lifting the *Skytteren* out of the water and bringing her down heavily on her port side. He skidded along the corridors, hoping to be able to warn the men who were still below. Just inside the engine room he stumbled across Johannessen's body. Not far away was the badly burned stoker, who Hatchly helped to his feet and led out of the engine room.

Wilson ordered the lifeboats to be launched, thinking that he had at least removed the *Skytteren* from German hands, but she now began to straighten up. Confusion reigned: men were trying to climb into the lifeboats, some jumped overboard to reach those already launched, while others climbed down ropes hanging from the davits. At some point in the panic the *Skytteren* caught fire. It may have been Wilson's doing as he had stated that he would set his ship alight before the Germans got her. However, nearby Swedish vessels reported seeing a torpedo boat attacking the *Skytteren* along with a U-boat. In any case, the *Skytteren* was finally close to sinking.

Lifeboat No 1 was still alongside her, helping the stragglers to escape. Many of them were injured either from the attack or the disastrous early explosion of the scuttling charges. Two further lifeboats started to head for the coast, the men rowing furiously to try to escape the Germans. The boat Wilson had landed in was not so lucky; she was too close to the armed German patrol ship and was brought alongside.

No 1 boat tried to escape. She was a motorboat, but in the confusion of the evacuation none of the men who had boarded her happened to know how she worked, so they frantically tried to row her ashore hoping that they might also distract the Germans from the two other lifeboats. They were out of luck; the Germans caught up with them in 15 minutes and took No 1 boat in tow. The only targets now left were the men in the remaining two lifeboats. They had headed for shore, but thick ice blocked their route and no matter how they tried, they could not force the boats through. The Germans turned their attentions on them, despite protests that the survivors were in Swedish waters and could not be captured. The Germans were feeling vengeful; they threatened to shoot at the lifeboats if the men in them did not turn themselves over. Trapped between the pack ice and the heavily armed German trawler there was clearly no choice. Miserably, the remaining survivors threw a line across to the German vessel and were taken in tow.

The *Skytteren* now burned fiercely. The one-time glory of the White Star Line was enduring an ignoble end. She would take time to sink, but there was no hope of salvaging her. As Wilson watched his unfortunate vessel disintegrating, he couldn't help but wonder if he had been doomed from the start, if indeed sabotage had scuttled the *Skytteren* before she even left Gothenburg.

In the distance a Swedish vessel was approaching. Wilson's crew looked on eagerly. The ship must have seen them being hauled out of Swedish waters and would now demand that the men be handed over to them. At least that would spare them the wrath of the Gestapo. The Swedish ship came within 165 feet and signalled to the Germans; a flurry of signals were sent back. The *Skytteren*'s survivors glanced at one another, uncertain of what had been communicated. Tense minutes passed and then the Swedish ship turned away. Unable to believe their eyes, Wilson's crew realised that they had been abandoned to their fate.

The men and women of the *Skytteren* found themselves en route to Germany – the fate that they had dreaded from the instant they had volunteered for Operation Performance. At least seventeen of the crew and stowaways would eventually die at Sonnenburg, several being executed shortly before the Allies reached Germany to liberate the camps. Yet another black mark against Swedish neutrality.

BRAVE *BUCCANEER*

One of the smaller boats in the convoy, the *Buccaneer* was also one of the most valuable. She was carrying a sizeable cargo under the auspices of British captain Smail. Also among her crew was the valiant and ferocious James D. Lenox-Conyngham, originally from Ireland and one of the Finnish volunteers who had become trapped in Sweden. He had taken personal charge of the guns smuggled aboard the *Buccaneer* and had every intention of using them should the opportunity arise. He had formed two Lewis gun crews and was ready at a moment's notice to launch an offensive.

Despite being one of the faster ships to leave Gothenburg (she could manage between 12 and 13 knots) the *Buccaneer* soon encountered trouble. Not far from the burning remains of the *Skytteren* she ran into a German patrol. Lenox-Conyngham was quick to the guns, and the Germans would later complain to the Swedish about the casualties they sustained trying to intercept the *Buccaneer*. But even the efforts of Lenox-Conyngham were not likely to save the ship and her cargo now. The Germans had wedged themselves between her and the coast, preventing a retreat into Swedish waters. They wanted to capture the vessel intact – they had no knowledge of the worth of her cargo, but were tired of being outmanoeuvred by the British. Smail realised his options were limited; he ordered the lifeboats to be launched and prepared to detonate the scuttling charges.

Not wanting to be deprived of their prize, the Germans began strafing the *Buccaneer*'s deck with bullets to send the crew running for cover. Smail was unimpressed. He detonated the scuttling charges anyway and there was a tremendous explosion. The *Buccaneer* slowly began to sink. The Germans chose to be merciful and held fire while her crew made for the lifeboats. In the panic to launch the boats, the motorboat failed to release properly and hung uselessly from the aft tackle, causing the Third Mate to be injured. Desperate struggling with the ropes finally released her and she smashed down into the water.

Smail was one of the last to leave the *Buccaneer*, glaring at the Germans who had forced his hand. He started down the rope to the motorboat. The commotion around him and the knowledge that the *Buccaneer* would sink imminently made climbing difficult, but it was worsened by the thick rubber gloves he was wearing. Not far down the rope Smail lost his grip and fell into the ocean.

This in itself would not have been a calamity had he not struck his head on the edge of the lifeboat as he fell. His crew rescued him and dragged him aboard, but Smail was unconscious and clearly injured.

The *Buccaneer* suddenly started to sink fast. The survivors rowed away, watching their vessel vanish into the water stern first. The Germans rapidly rounded up the crew and took them aboard. But after a few minutes the *Buccaneer*'s progress into the icy depths halted. She settled in the water and after a while the Germans decided to brave a boarding party. Watched on by the *Buccaneer*'s crew, who entertained a hope that she might start sinking just as the Germans went aboard her, the Nazis stepped onto the vessel and started a search. Their loot was not spectacular, though they did come away with a copy of Binney's orders of the day and a large portrait of Churchill.

As the *Buccaneer* stubbornly refused to sink, the Germans loitered around her until midday wondering what to do. They could hardly tow her, but she was now a hazard to shipping and, potentially, her cargo could be salvaged by a daring British raid. Eventually the decision was made to sink her properly. It took ten or twelve German shells before she finally gave up her struggle and disappeared beneath the ocean. Her crew were taken to Frederikshavn as prisoners, to be interned in concentration camps. Smail was spared the ordeal of camp life. He died at Frederikshavn. It turned out that he had broken his neck when he fell.

POOR OLD *RIGMOR*

The legal trials that the *Rigmor* had endured since the first planning of Operation Performance had been tiresome and frustrating. To learn finally that she was free (though possibly only temporarily) and could sail with the rest of the convoy was a delight to those who intended to man her, and a snub to the Nazis who had tried to use Swedish law to trap her at Gothenburg. British captain William Gilling took charge of the controversial ship and her crew of forty. After being stuck in Sweden for so long he had every intention of making a good effort at the breakout and defying the Germans.

At 6 a.m. on 1 April, the *Rigmor* set forth from the Swedish coast, the weather looked promising, being foggy with occasional squalls, and Gilling was hopeful. As far as he was aware, Binney aboard the *Dicto* was making the same break for freedom, and he was optimistic that he would be in Scottish waters soon.

Gilling's good humour rapidly diminished along with the favourable weather. The skies cleared and almost immediately revealed a lurking German patrol boat. Gilling ordered that the *Rigmor* be turned about and retreat to Swedish waters. Unfortunately the German patrol had spotted her and proceeded to follow. The *Rigmor*'s retreat took her past the *Skytteren* and Gilling yelled across that they should turn about as the Germans were hot on her tail. After that they lost sight of the old White Star Liner and were unaware that their escape had led the Germans straight to the *Skytteren*.

The Swedish Navy had decided to be as obnoxious as possible to the British convoy, so when a destroyer spotted the *Rigmor* scurrying back into Swedish waters it rumbled over to her and demanded that she head back into the Skagerrak. Gilling was no fool; he knew that the Swedes would push him straight into the Germans if he let them. Instead he resolutely ignored them and loitered along the Swedish coast until 10 a.m. when it appeared the weather was deteriorating again. Gilling decided that it was time to take another chance at running the Skagerrak. He ordered the *Rigmor* out to sea.

Visibility was bad, much to Gilling's delight, as it would hamper any aerial observation. For most of the day the *Rigmor* sailed unchallenged. Intermittent clear spells in the heavy weather were troubling, but each one passed without incident until early evening when a lucky German aircraft spotted the

Rigmor. Immediately she was recognised as one of the escapees and the Luftwaffe pilot went on the attack. Raking her with his machine guns, he also dropped two incendiary bombs. One harmlessly fell in the ocean, the other fell onto a hatch, ripped open the centre tank and caused severe damage to the railing on the storm bridge. Fortunately the centre tank was used for ballast and was full of water.

Less fortunate was Gilling. Standing on the bridge trying to co-ordinate what frugal defences they had in the form of Lewis guns while keeping the *Rigmor* on course and praying for further bad weather, he did not anticipate becoming a target for the aircraft. The Luftwaffe pilot was trying to pick off anyone he could with his guns and swung around near the bridge, strafing the metal and wood with his bullets. By chance his bullets found a flesh and blood target, catching Gilling in the thighs. It was an almost identical episode to that suffered by First Officer Nils Rydberg aboard the *Ranja* over a year ago, except Gilling had no intention of dying or losing control of his ship.

The *Rigmor* suffered attack after attack from the lone aircraft until, at long last, darkness descended and the pilot had no option but to pull away. It was just after 8 p.m.; Gilling was badly injured and unable to stand, the wireless room was damaged and would take time to repair, and the centre tank had been ripped open, but, remarkably, most of the chaos was superficial and aside from the captain no one was hurt. The *Rigmor* stoically carried on; the darkness was promising cover and throughout the night mist and rain helped conceal her passage.

Around 9 a.m. the following day Gilling was informed that there was a plane overhead. Anxiously the crew watched the circling plane. It approached a little lower and everyone breathed a sigh of relief – it was British, a Beaufighter from Dyce. Moments later a second Beaufighter appeared, the planes flying about the *Rigmor* for 15 minutes before turning back to base. Meanwhile the British destroyers *Faulknor*, *Eskimo*, *Escapade*, *Wallace* and *Vanity* were heading east as fast as they could, trying to track the escaping Norwegian vessels. The *B.P. Newton* had already been found and was being escorted home. As yet the destroyers had no news of the location of the *Rigmor* or any other vessel.

At 9.20 a.m. two Blenheims also out patrolling for the convoy spotted the destroyers. They flew on and at around 10.10 a.m. spotted a ship alone in the waters. One flew so low that her pilot could read the name *Rigmor* on her side. Immediately the Blenheims split up; one would stay and guard the ship while the other hastened back to the destroyers to give them the exact position. Sitting on his bridge and in a great deal of pain, Gilling at least now knew that their saviours were in sight.

However, the story of the *Rigmor* was not to be so simple. The destroyers were around 50 miles away and the Blenheim was slowly running out of fuel, with no sight of any fresh British planes that could replace it. At the same time the Luftwaffe had been calculating the possible position of the elusive vessel after they had lost sight of her. Using her last position, her estimated heading and speed, they had compiled a rough search area to patrol; the *Rigmor* was not about to escape them after all the trouble she had caused.

By midday the Blenheim had reached the limits of its fuel and had to head for home; it was a woeful moment for the crew as they had become aware of increasing German activity near the *Rigmor*. Left alone once again, Gilling and his crew waited anxiously for the first sight of the British destroyers. It wasn't long before a crewman spotted a plane flying towards them, but he couldn't tell if it was British or German. He soon found out when the aircraft came in low and started firing its machine guns at the *Rigmor*'s deck, before dropping two bombs, both of which fortunately fell harmlessly into the sea off the port side.

A second German plane now appeared on the horizon. The crew rushed to their Lewis guns and tried to ward off the planes, but with two attackers the defence was woefully inadequate and the Luftwaffe machine-gunned the defenders and put their guns out of action. More bombs were dropped, two landing in the ocean off the stern and detonating, putting a diesel engine out of action and breaking an axle, preventing the ship from manoeuvring. Two further bombs ripped a large hole in the *Rigmor*'s starboard side and she developed a heavy list.

Down in the wireless room radio operator Ivar Thorleif Riise was desperately trying to send an SOS. With the noise of explosions and machine guns all around, and the occasional bullet penetrating the radio room and reminding him too much of the fate of Gilling, he sent out his first message with the incorrect position of the ship. As the *Rigmor*'s list increased, Riise sent another message. The time was around 1.15 p.m. and on deck the order had been given to abandon ship. Riise sent out his final SOS and then joined the evacuation.

Miles away, the destroyer *Faulknor* had picked up both messages. Realising that the first had them heading for the wrong position they altered course and ramped up the speed to 24 knots. Even so, they knew that they would be lucky to arrive and save the *Rigmor*; all they could hope for was that the crew had survived her demise.

A temporary reprieve was allowed the crew as they made for the lifeboats, including the injured Captain Gilling. The Luftwaffe watched over them menacingly, but refrained from firing at them – in later incidents they were not always so merciful. The *Rigmor* was doomed. From the east two further German planes appeared, loaded with torpedoes. No sooner had the crew abandoned the *Rigmor* than the Luftwaffe launched their torpedoes, one hitting her amidships though failing to sink her.

Unknown to the men in the lifeboats the fight was about to turn against the Germans. From their higher vantage point in the skies the German pilots could see the destroyers on the horizon which were rapidly coming into firing range. Briefly the Germans turned their attention to the destroyers, the two newest arrivals launching the last of their torpedoes at them and narrowly missing HMS *Eskimo* which was hauling the *Rigmor*'s crew from the water. In return the destroyers opened all their guns on the planes.

Aboard the *Eskimo* intense discussions were taking place. Captain Monsen, the Nortraship representative assigned to the *Rigmor*, was of the opinion that everything should be done to save the valuable cargo he had been helping to transport. The *Rigmor* was still disinclined to sink, and the commander of the *Eskimo* wondered if it might be possible to tow her. Immediately the suggestion was raised several of the *Rigmor*'s crew offered to row across to her and arrange a tow-line. After their eventful journey, no one wanted to see the old girl sink without at least trying to save her.

The endeavour was agreed upon and, still under German fire, a handful of British and Norwegians took a lifeboat and rowed to the *Rigmor*. She proved impossible to board, her starboard list and the heavy swell of the sea, not to mention the commotion of the battle, proving too much for the men. After trying their hardest they resigned themselves to defeat and started to return to the *Eskimo*. The lifeboat had remained attached to the destroyer via a rope, but a lucky bullet from one of the enemy planes severed the rope and left the boarding party stranded in the water.

Fortunately the air battle was drawing to a close. Against the destroyers and without further torpedoes, the German planes were outmatched and reluctantly turned tail and headed for base. They had no idea what would become of the *Rigmor*, but it was with chagrin that they realised they had failed to sink her when they had the opportunity.

The boarding party was at last rescued and Gilling and Monsen went into discussions with the commander of the *Eskimo* over the fate of their ship. It was decided the only option remaining was to sink her. The *Rigmor*'s crew could only watch on miserably as the British destroyers opened fire with their heavy guns and shelled the unfortunate craft. She finally sank to the deep with her cargo, and her crew were transported to England, arriving on 4 April. Gilling was given immediate medical care and made a full recovery.

GUDVANG AND *CHARENTE*

From the time they were spotted loitering near the Swedish coast before their attempted run of the Skagerrak, the *Lind*, *Gudvang*, *Rigmor* and *Charente* had been harassed by the Swedish naval patrols to leave neutral waters. Warning shots had been fired and signals flown, but the crews had held their ground waiting for the weather to turn in their favour.

Finally the *Gudvang* had had enough. Her captain was Henry Nicholson, formerly of the SS *Romanby*, and among the crew were five former *Romanby* sailors. Out of all the ship masters, Nicholson was the only one to retain a significant chunk of his former crew. The *Gudvang* was one of the smaller vessels attempting the passage with a crew of only twenty-five. Built in 1912 and previously known as the *Stalheim*, the *Gudvang* had already provided good war service, taking part in convoys from Norway to the UK prior to the Nazi invasion. Operation Performance, however, would prove to be her most dangerous.

Around 10 a.m. on 1 April, and after asking the opinion of his crew, Nicholson ordered the *Gudvang* out to sea. A promising fog had arisen and he was hoping for an easy passage. With her engines at their maximum 10 knots she made good progress, catching brief glimpses through the foul weather of her companion ships. The last time Nicholson spotted any of his fellow convoy was at 5 p.m. when he briefly caught sight of the *Lind* ahead of him. After that things began to go wrong.

It was just after 8 p.m. when two vessels were spotted approaching fast. Nicholson was not prepared to enter a firefight in his old ship and ordered that her course be altered to try to avoid the intruders. It was to no avail; the two approaching vessels were armed German trawlers and they sent up frantic signals for the *Gudvang* to stop. Nicholson initially ignored them, but when they sent a signal to say they were preparing to fire he knew that the game was up. The *Gudvang* would not last long in a sea battle and his priority now was to try to save his men.

He ordered the engines to stop, and the dark night went suddenly quiet as the *Gudvang* sat idle in the waters.

Nicholson quickly called for his crew to come on deck and to start lowering the lifeboat on the starboard side, opposite the side that the trawlers were approaching and thus out of sight. He barely had a chance to put his escape plan into action when there was a shrieking sound and three shells struck the helpless *Gudvang* – it had clearly been too late for the Germans to prevent their guns from firing. The *Gudvang* lurched in the water, her aft hatch and the motorboat strapped to it being completely destroyed.

The noise of the destruction and the fright of the attack sent the crew into a panic. Nicholson's authority just about held sway. He shouted for the lifeboat to be launched and kept his men under control, while his voice was almost drowned out by the piercing shrill of the steam whistle which had somehow become jammed and could not be stopped. Despite the darkness of the night and the dread of the approaching Germans, the men pulled together and launched the starboard lifeboat, but it was quickly apparent it would not be able to hold everyone.

Nicholson was busy preparing the scuttling charges while the remnants of his crew hurried to launch the port lifeboat. It was an awful task with only eight of them trying to pull together in the pitch black of a Scandinavian night. The two lifeboats were just in the water and Nicholson safely aboard as the scuttling charges blew and the *Gudvang* slowly sank. Desperately, the men tried to row for Norway, but there was little chance of outsailing the German trawlers. Ordered to a halt, the men were marshalled onto the trawlers and destined for a concentration camp.

The *Charente* had an equally abortive voyage. Her captain, James Donald, ordered her out last from the quartet of ships that had loitered near the Swedish coast. Despite his delay, his speed of 11 knots eventually took him past the *Rigmor* and *Lind*. For a time all seemed quiet, then at 1.30 p.m. a shot was heard nearby. Scanning the waters, Donald saw an armed German trawler fast approaching. Though it is difficult to be certain, it seems that most of the convoy had stumbled into a shrewdly laid out blockade of Nazi-commandeered vessels. Another trawler suddenly appeared flying a 'stop' signal. Trying to think on his feet, Donald pretended to have misunderstood the signal and asked for it to be repeated. Abruptly a warning shot sailed just in front of the *Charente*'s bow. It seemed that the Germans were in no mood to play games.

Donald called for his crew to launch the lifeboats and abandon ship. Bjorn Egge, the able seaman placed in charge of the illegal Lewis gun, was trying to surreptitiously throw it overboard while Donald primed the scuttling charges and the lifeboats were lowered. One of the armed trawlers had also lowered a boat and was sending over a boarding party led by a German officer. Donald hastened to set off the scuttling charges, but nothing happened. Egge was still struggling with his Lewis gun as the German officer came aboard. At the same moment, Donald tried the scuttling charges again and there was a massive explosion which felt to Egge as if the whole bottom of the ship had been blown off.

Everyone was shaken. A couple of men were injured in the blast and then someone noticed that fellow able seaman Kaspar Eklund was missing. Brave-hearted Egge had finally disposed of his gun and volunteered to seek out Eklund; he didn't particularly want to watch the Germans march aboard anyway. He went below and hunted around, eventually arriving in the crew quarters only to find Eklund sound asleep in his bunk. He woke him and told him bluntly they had been captured by the Germans.

Donald's scuttling charges had proved more destructive than he had bargained for. Not only was the *Charente* sinking fast but two of her lifeboats and been destroyed. The remaining two had been launched and the crew were all aboard while Donald was still standing miserably on the deck of his ship. The *Charente* was deep in the water and in moments the icy ocean would be flooding over her deck. Egge had the eerie feeling that Donald intended to go down with her. At the last moment he couldn't bear it and reached out for the British captain, hauling him into the lifeboat. The lifeboats were drawn up to the trawlers and the prisoners taken on board. As the *Charente* went to her icy berth, the crew anxiously wondered what the Germans intended to do with them.

AND THEN THERE WERE TWO

There was a light haze drifting across the water at dawn on 1 April as Captain John Nicol looked out to sea from the deck of the *Lind*. He consulted with Nortraship representative Hans Anton Trovik and they agreed they would attempt the crossing while visibility was low. The *Lind* was the smallest of Binney's fleet, and with a crew of fewer than twenty and a top speed of barely 9 knots she looked far from the most promising prospect for a successful crossing of the Skagerrak.

Less than an hour after leaving the coastal waters a German patrol ship was spotted ahead and Nicol decided it was prudent to turn back at this early stage of the venture and not risk interception. The weather was clearing and Nicol was well aware of his craft's limitations. No sooner were they back in Swedish coastal waters than three more boats approached them, all Swedish, consisting of a destroyer, a trawler and what appeared to be a minesweeper. The minesweeper immediately fired warning shots at the *Lind* and ordered her back out to sea. Nicol refused to budge. He clung to the fact that the Swedish were unlikely to take direct action and attack his ship.

Just after 8 a.m. two more destroyers appeared, along with a warship, and they gave the same signal to return to sea. Again Nicol ignored them. The skies were now blue and clear, and crossing the Skagerrak would be suicide. He was not alone in feeling bitter that the supposedly neutral Swedes were trying to send him and his crew to their deaths. As the situation became more desperate, Nicol spotted the *Rigmor* and *Lionel* heading towards him. Their captains had also decided against an immediate venture into the Skagerrak. The three conferred and reluctantly agreed that the best option seemed to be to head back for Gothenburg – they had no idea that their leader, Binney, was reaching the same conclusion.

Their Swedish escort accompanied them as they headed for harbour, keeping landward so that the convoy vessels were between themselves and the open water. In a later report it was sarcastically remarked, 'It is difficult to understand why the Swedish warships should have found it desirable to use the [Performance] ships as a shield within their own territorial waters, when it was their duty to protect them from attack.'

It was then that the weather turned again; thick fog had rolled in from the south and visibility had reduced to no more than 400 yards. It was perfect weather for attempting the Skagerrak. Nicol looked out to sea and made his decision. It was shortly before 10 a.m. when he turned the *Lind* for her second attempt at running the open waters.

Captain Gilling aboard the *Rigmor* had reached the same conclusion and turned too. Together the ships slipped their escort and made for the sea. The *Rigmor* rapidly outpaced the *Lind* and vanished, but that had been expected. All the captains were aware that they were to complete their passage alone. Nicol charted a course down the middle of the Skagerrak and sailed for most of the day without incident despite the fog clearing. During his voyage he briefly spotted the *Gudvang* and then the *Rigmor* before they vanished.

Nothing out of the ordinary happened until just after 6 p.m. when a crewman shouted that he had spotted an aircraft about 2 miles to port. Everyone watched anxiously as the plane came closer; it was flying at sea level and would easily spot the *Lind*. Abruptly the plane wobbled and then veered uncontrollably into the sea mist. Shortly after, a sheet of flame was seen and Nicol could only conclude that the plane had crashed. The night passed as peacefully as the day, with only brief glimpses of enemy patrol vessels that the *Lind* could avoid by altering course. It almost seemed as though the *Lind* was leading a charmed existence.

Luck, however, is often fleeting. Thursday 2 April dawned as a bright, sunny day with blue skies overhead and the promise of fine weather. At any other time, Nicol would have enjoyed such sailing weather, but at that moment he cursed it. Even so, the *Lind* managed to avoid detection until noon when a German plane spotted her and dropped flares in preparation for a torpedo attack.

For the first time the men were in action. Nicol headed for the Lewis gun mounted on the roof of the galley, while Trovik took over the helm and started zigzagging violently to prevent the enemy plane having an easy run-up. Nicol began firing, his tracer fire suggesting that he was making repeated successful hits on the enemy plane at a range of 300 yards, yet the plane showed no signs of damage. Fortunately the enemy was having similar problems thanks to Trovik's skilful manoeuvres which were hampering the aiming and launch of a torpedo. For half an hour the two opponents remained at a stalemate, Nicol not letting up his attack and the plane refusing to come any closer and risk damage. Eventually Nicol would have run out of ammunition and the *Lind* would have been helpless even to the most cautious German pilot, so it was with great relief that a British Beaufighter was spotted approaching and chased off the enemy aircraft with a short burst of fire.

Thanking the German pilot's strong sense of self-preservation, Nicol returned to his bridge as the *Lind* ploughed on for home. The Beaufighter did not loiter for long over the *Lind*. Having reached his operational limits, the pilot noted the position of the vessel and headed for home. Nicol watched him go heavy-hearted then turned his attention to scanning the skies for a renewed German attack. As expected, a German plane quickly appeared. It was an He 111, identical to the first attacker and very likely the same plane that had merely temporarily retreated in the face of British opposition. Nicol raced for his gun, but the Heinkel was faster and launched two torpedoes at 600 yards on a direct course for the *Lind*. The torpedoes skimmed into the water and sank below on an unerringly straight path. Everyone held their breath. There was a moment of silence as the torpedoes vanished from sight and they awaited the inevitable explosion.

The silence continued. Slowly, and much to the confusion of the Heinkel pilot who had assumed he made a direct hit, it became apparent that the torpedoes had missed. Nicol was ecstatic. It seemed that the *Lind*'s shallow draught, which could make her an awkward sea vessel, had in fact saved her. The torpedoes had sailed harmlessly underneath her. Nicol retaliated with the mounted Lewis gun and believed that once again he had struck the aircraft. In any case, the Heinkel was out of torpedoes and running at the limit of its range. It turned away and did not reappear. Nicol instructed a continuous SOS to be sent and with some relief heard that it was acknowledged by an English coastal station.

It was 3 a.m. when the *Lind* arrived at the pre-arranged rendezvous point. There were no destroyers in sight. Ahead was a dense minefield that Nicol would have appreciated being led through, but the lack of any British ships started to make him think that they had been forgotten. In fact several planes had been sent from Scotland to try to spot the *Lind*, but without success. The destroyers had also lost track of her after being directed to her last known location. Perhaps that isn't entirely surprising, considering the small size of the *Lind* and the vastness of the sea she was sailing in. Fortunately the Germans had also lost track of her.

Nicol loitered at the rendezvous point wondering what to do. The morning dragged on, it was Good Friday and families in Britain would be heading for church. By lunchtime Nicol was fed up and thinking that it was a jolly good job he had lost the Heinkel earlier and had not been banking on salvation from a squad of destroyers at the rendezvous point. Then someone spotted a plane. It was one of the Hudsons that had been scouring the seas for the *Lind*. From that moment on, the *Lind* received much-appreciated air cover, even if the main threat from the Germans appeared to have evaporated. A destroyer finally arrived to escort her through the minefields and the *Lind* was led into Methil Roads the following day, having spent around 80 hours at sea. Nicol was disappointed to learn that only the *B.P. Newton* had managed to join him in the successful crossing of the Skagerrak.

The *Newton* was commanded by Captain Calvert, but she had one significant figure aboard – 'Brian the Lion' Reynolds, Binney's second-in-command at sea. Reynolds could hardly have been more elated when he learned which vessel he was to sail aboard. The *Newton* was the fastest ship in the convoy, able to reach speeds of 16 knots. She was also the second largest and brand new, having been completed only the year before at Kockums' Works, Malmö. Since then she had been sitting idle and now was her first chance to prove herself.

With a cargo of 5,000 tons, the *Newton*'s importance in the fleet was second only to the *Dicto*, hence Reynolds being aboard her. On the morning of the adventure, Reynolds and Calvert were keen to be off, but yet again it was the weather that was holding them back. They were 3 miles north-west of Paternoster Point and heading north when they spotted the first of the Swedish destroyers sent to flush them from the coast. Calvert was far from impressed as the destroyers raised their ensign flags and flashed searchlights on the *Newton*. Rockets were fired into the water westward, which Calvert assumed meant that the *Newton* should head that way; not that he had any intention of following Swedish orders. Just then two armed trawlers were seen approaching them from the coast. As they drew closer, the captain of one shouted from his bridge in Swedish:

'*Newton* ahoy, proceed to sea. I have orders to force you out of territorial waters.'

'Ignore them,' Reynolds said.

'I intend to,' replied Calvert. When it came to the relative dangers of the Swedish or the Germans, he felt he was much safer with the Swedes.

He was soon proved right. Despite their bad mood over the whole operation, the Swedish Navy ships were not prepared to fire directly onto the *Newton* and they travelled with her, observing her movements, without firing a shot. As the morning drew on it began to snow and Reynolds' patience was at its end. Everyone agreed that it was time to run the Skagerrak and, leaving the Swedes behind, they set out to sea. They had not gone more than 4 or 5 miles when they passed the *Lionel* heading in the opposite direction. The *Lionel* signalled that she had been attacked by an armed German trawler and danger was just ahead.

'Ignore them too?' asked Reynolds.

'Absolutely,' Calvert replied. He had confidence in the *Newton* and he was a daredevil at heart, much like the red-headed man who stood beside him.

The *Lionel*'s fear for the *Newton* proved unfounded. There was no sign of a German trawler and by 10 a.m. a heavy sea fog had settled over the water and engulfed the *Newton*. For 2 hours she sailed completely invisible to all but the closest of ships. But the fog could not last forever and, a short time after it cleared, a spume of water was seen off the port beam. A moment later there was another spume, closer this time. In the distance an armed German trawler was heading for them and trying to shell them. Calvert turned away and, with his engines at full speed, rapidly outpaced the trawler. It was a close call, but nothing serious.

An hour later the situation was less light-hearted. The *Newton* was about 35 miles off Kristiansand when two more armed German trawlers appeared out of nowhere. They signalled furiously for her to stop, but Calvert had no intention of doing so. Abruptly the Germans began firing on them. Shells and machine-gun bullets flew at the *Newton*, the latter making several hits in her hull. The Germans were determined to sink her, letting off between fifteen and twenty large shells, each of which could have caused serious harm. Remarkably, not a single one either fell on her or close enough to cause damage. Over the course of half an hour the *Newton* remained under fire, the nerves of her crew strained, with every new explosion feared to be the one that would sink them. Several SOS signals were sent out and picked up by various stations, including the radio operator on the *Rigmor* and George Binney on the *Dicto*, who happened to be in the radio room at the time.

The *Newton* was now in serious peril and Calvert reluctantly gave the order to come to a full stop so that the scuttling charges could be set and fired. A remarkable act of bravery and disobedience then took place. Second Mate Gunnar Album refused to acknowledge the order and insisted that the engines remain running. Exactly what occurred in the next few moments, as Calvert realised his orders had been disobeyed, remains unclear, but Album's defiance saved the *Newton*, her cargo and, most importantly, her Norwegian crew from the clutches of the Gestapo. Album ordered full steam ahead and she finally moved clear of her attackers. Though he had caused a serious breach in the command chain and defied a direct order, Album was later recognised by Britain for his brave conduct.

For a little over an hour the *Newton* sailed on unmolested. As the late afternoon began to slip into evening a Junkers 88 appeared overhead. Reynolds acted quickly, heading for one of three Lewis guns mounted on the *Newton*. Because of her importance to the mission, the *Newton* had been given more than a solitary gun and Reynolds now commanded his gunner crews to man their stations. The Junkers 88 flew over and started firing its machine guns. Reynolds and his gunners managed to drive it back with their return fire before it could drop any bombs. The Junkers 88 eventually turned away, but now it had the *Newton*'s position it was bound to send other planes in their direction.

At 5.30 p.m. a second German plane appeared, followed barely 10 minutes later by a third. Two bombs were dropped and landed 150 feet behind the ship, their explosions so powerful that they briefly lifted her out of the water. The gunner crews held tight to their Lewis guns and began firing again. It was only the dense hail of bullets they created that kept the planes back and prevented them from dropping bombs onto the *Newton*'s deck.

Calvert was worried that the explosions had damaged the *Newton*'s engines, as she suddenly seemed sluggish and less responsive. He ordered a full stop so that the damage could be assessed. That was exactly what Reynolds did not want. His gunner teams were working flat out to keep the planes at bay, but at least while moving they were pulling out the distance between them. Now that they were stationary, the planes could attack at any angle they wanted. As hasty repairs were being made to the engines, a German pilot grew daring and came close enough to drop a bomb just off the *Newton*'s stern. Reynolds and Calvert held their breath; the bomb was bound to take a chunk out of the ship's hull and leave them dead in the water. As the minutes drew out and nothing happened, both men wondered at their luck – the bomb had failed to detonate. Meanwhile Reynolds' gunners had scored a hit on one of the aircraft which was now leaving a filthy, black smoke trail in the sky.

With dusk drawing on and their bombs used up, the planes lingered over the *Newton*, trying to find a target for their machine guns, but failing to get through the hail of bullets Reynolds was sending their way. Finally it was too dark for them to operate successfully any more and they turned back.

Calvert's engines had only required a little tinkering to get them back to full speed and now the *Newton* sped through the night, making good progress and encountering nothing more than the German minefield scattered across the Skagerrak. Dawn brought the welcome sight of a British destroyer off the port bow and soon afterwards friendly aircraft. HMS *Valorous* acted as an escort for the *Newton* while a Beaufighter flew overhead and kept a keen eye open for the Luftwaffe. By the next morning, the *Newton* was safely docked at Leith and her crew were learning the dreadful fate that had befallen most of her fellow ships.

10

AFTERMATH

From any perspective, it was impossible to see Operation Performance as anything but a near complete disaster. Six of the ten ships in the convoy had been sunk, while two (including the *Dicto*, which had one of the most valuable cargoes in the consignment) had been unceremoniously chased back to Gothenburg. Of the survivors who had made it to Britain, the *Newton* was the most significant as she carried 27 per cent of the overall cargo in terms of value. (In terms of weight she carried 20 per cent.) However, 45 per cent of the cargo was still stuck at Gothenburg and 34 per cent (in terms of weight) had been sunk to the bottom of the ocean. The *Dicto* had been carrying the vital heavy machinery that Britain was desperate for to be able to begin production of its own ball bearings. It looked very unlikely that this would reach Britain until the following winter, if at all.

In human terms, Performance had a high cost. Of 471 volunteers taking part in the mission, 234 were taken prisoner, three people were killed during the course of the operation including the *Buccaneer*'s captain, and then there was the tragedy of the people in the *Storsten*'s lifeboat who simply vanished.

The Germans were eager to brand the operation a British failure. Binney was called a coward for turning back to

Gothenburg and leaving his convoy to face the Skagerrak alone. Germany remained silent on the messages that Binney had tried to send out to his convoy but had never arrived. It played up the nobility and honour of the German naval crews that had intercepted the ships, and remarked on their 'self-sacrificing readiness' to save the unfortunate men they had just sunk! As the icing on the cake, they implied that the Norwegians they had 'rescued' had revealed that they had been enlisted into the operation by threats.

Stoking the German ire, a Reuters telegram arrived purporting to quote one of the Norwegian survivors of Performance, who said that enemy aircraft were kept at bay by means of Lewis guns. This was a horrendous slip-up. The British had been making quiet assurances that the convoy would have no armaments of any kind aboard; Binney had even kept Mallet in the dark about his smuggled guns and the minister had been happily assuring his Swedish colleagues that the ships were unarmed. It was a nasty matter. By arming the ships, the British had breached Swedish neutrality and given the Germans another reason to up their threats against the country. However, little sympathy could be felt for the beleaguered Swedes, considering the outrageous behaviour of their Navy which had effectively sent many men to their deaths in a German concentration camp.

The Germans complained bitterly. They had been attacked by those annoying Performance vessels and had sustained damage, (possibly even a death if the Luftwaffe plane seen crashing into the sea by the *Lind* was hit by fire from the Lewis guns of one of the convoy) while only carrying out their perfectly legitimate duty of intercepting the ships.

By mid-April, the German Legation had sent a new memorandum to the Swedish Ministry of Foreign Affairs reiterating German expectations for Swedish co-operation. The Swedish press now jumped on the bandwagon, siding with the Germans to divert attention from the miserable actions of their own Navy. Britain, in contrast, played up the angle of heroic self-defence.

In an article in the *Daily Express* one Performance seaman was reported as saying:

> We were spotted by a lone German plane. He swooped down over the top of us, raking our deck with his guns. We gave him a surprise when we opened at him with our two Lewis guns – the only guns we had – and gave him a lot of lead.

The seaman must have been on the *Newton*, the only ship to have more than one gun (though it is stated that it actually had three).

Further discord came from the Norwegians, who were distressed at the number of their people who had been captured in the operation. They complained to Britain that the Royal Navy and RAF had not done enough to cover and protect the ships. Britain responded that it was not feasible to send forces (seaborne or airborne) into the Skagerrak and it had always been known that the ships would have to cross that perilous piece of water alone and rendezvous with British destroyers just past the German minefield. Planes had flown over the North Sea in continuous sorties during the day; they were at the extreme of their operational limitations and could not remain out long before having to head back. Seven sorties were flown with no ships sighted. On the eighth sortie, the *Storsten* was spotted but appeared empty. During the course of the flying on 1 April, the 'aircraft destroyed one enemy aircraft, damaged three and drove off six other enemy aircraft at various times'. In any case, many of the ships were intercepted long before they came close to the rendezvous point.

BINNEY'S BLUNDER

George Binney was stuck in Stockholm watching the fall-out from an operation that he had pushed forward and had had such high hopes for. His mind was nagging at the failed wireless message. Had it been sabotaged and had this sealed the fate of the Performance vessels? While sitting in Gothenburg it had been obvious to all that the ships were easy targets for German agents. Aside from damaging engines – which appears to have happened – the saboteurs would have been focusing their attentions on radio equipment to hamper communications. Binney had ensured that all the ships' wireless gear was sealed up by the authorities, and none of the wireless operators had been allowed to access it until they were out at sea. Prior to sailing, the sets had been tested by a Marconi inspector, who was Danish and believed to be completely reliable. He certified that the sets were in proper working order.

Despite this, not only did the *Dicto*'s message fail to be received by anyone, but no SOS message was ever received from the *Skytteren, Buccaneer, Charente, Gudvang* or *Storsten*, though attempts were made to send them. However, messages were received from the *B.P. Newton* and *Rigmor*. The former had not been inspected by the Marconi man, while the latter had.

The radio operator on the *Dicto* was a rating from HMS *Hunter* and believed his set to be operating correctly and was fully convinced he had successfully sent his message. It seemed that he could have been correct, as on 1 April, a Swedish steam trawler fishing around 3 or 4 miles from the last position of the *Dicto* was intercepted and searched by the Germans on no fewer than three occasions for being suspected of carrying wireless equipment or having Norwegians or English sailors among her crew. It seems that the Germans, at least, were able to pick up the *Dicto*'s message and plot her position from it. The only solution to the conundrum that the Foreign Office could see when they made an official report on the matter was that 'it is not beyond the lengths of possibility that an expert could contrive by readjusting the mechanism and dials to delude an operator into supposing that he was transmitting on 600-metre wavelengths when, in fact, he was transmitting on another pre-arranged wavelength on which the Germans were tuned'. Had the Marconi inspector considered so reliable been, in fact, a German agent? Binney had no idea, but it was either that or some extremely clever act of sabotage. In any case, the result was many Norwegians and British falling into the clutches of the Germans. More than ever, Binney realised the treachery all around him.

The Swedish backlash first fell on Victor Mallet who had been made a fool of by Binney (not for the first time). He was deeply embarrassed and mortified when he had to come before the Secretary-General of the Swedish Foreign Office, Erik Boheman. Mallet and Boheman were good friends and Boheman was known to favour the Allies in the war, even if he was rigid about policy concerning Swedish neutrality. He had impressed Churchill, who had invited him to his country house, Chequers, and was able to charm the Germans into thinking that they were gaining more from the Swedes than they actually were. But Operation Performance had strained even his good nature.

Binney was summoned to the same meeting with every intention of admitting fully his role in the smuggling of guns and scuttling charges onto the vessels. He was far from remorseful over the matter. He had firmly believed (and still did) that he was protecting his men's lives by installing guns on the ships. Both Boheman and Mallet were impressed by Binney's candour. Mallet later remarked, 'I must say I admired the honesty with which Binney admitted what he had done but I felt uncomfortable at having unwittingly had to make an earlier statement to Boheman which I had indeed made in all innocence.' Boheman, in confidence, told Binney that he also admired his honesty and in his position would have probably done the same. But his hands were tied. Complaints had been lodged with the Foreign Office and Binney was officially unwelcome in Sweden. It was really no more than Binney had expected; there was only so long you could pull faces at the Germans before they finally had enough. Binney packed his bags and returned to England on 18 April.

Bill Waring and Peter Coleridge also came under fire for their part in the plan. The Swedish authorities demanded that they be recalled to England. In this instance the Foreign Office refused to budge and Waring remained at the Legation, hoping to become an even bigger thorn in Sweden's side. Coleridge, however, went home. The blockade-busting team had been severely dismantled, and Waring had the unwelcome task of re-establishing contacts alone. Then he heard that Brian Reynolds, survivor of the *B.P. Newton* was on his way back to Sweden and keen for further action. Even better, Binney was far from being out of the picture and was already contemplating his next operation.

Erik Boheman was too savvy a diplomat to believe for one moment that the British had given up. The *Dicto* and *Lionel* were still sitting in Gothenburg harbour. Officially they were not to be let out ever again, or at least until the war ended, but unofficially Boheman knew that Binney still had his eye on them and would do whatever he could to steal their cargo. The two ships rapidly drew all of Boheman's attention and obsessed his every moment. He told his wife that if they ever had twins they would have to be named Dicto and Lionel. He knew the British were up to something; the question was *what*, and could he avoid having to interfere?

MEANWHILE, DEEP IN GERMANY

The story of those brave Norwegians, British and other nationalities who had volunteered for Performance and then been captured is often overlooked. A total of 204 had been captured, the vast majority Norwegian, but also two Dutch and one Polish. There were six women and one little girl among the captives. Aside from two crewmen from the *Skytteren* who had been caught in the explosion when the scuttling charges of their vessel had gone off, all were in good health as they boarded a train for Tarmstedt from Bremen. They had been shuffled from one German town to another over the course of the few days they had been in Nazi custody. Now it was 6 April, and it seemed to them that not only had Operation Performance completely failed but their own futures were precariously balanced.

Peter Jebsen, mess boy on the *Skytteren*, was not prepared to meet whatever fate the Germans had in store for him. During the train journey he asked to use the toilet and then slipped out of a window. He eventually made it to Sweden and then England.

For the rest, a life of captivity and hardship was about to begin. First stop was the prison camp Milag Nord. Milag had been adopted as the main camp for holding merchant seaman and naval prisoners. Merchant seamen had a hazy status as captives, since by the regulations of the 1907 Hague Convention they should technically be treated as civilians and allowed to remain free as long as they vowed not to take part in any military operations or enemy action. Both Germany and Britain were well aware that such vows were worthless and treated captured merchant seamen from their respective enemies as prisoners of war.

Life in Milag was complicated. On the one hand, it was barren and miserable. Milag was desolate, set in a large, open, sandy area where the wind always blew. Rommel had likened its conditions to a desert and had even trained some of his troops destined for Africa at the camp. The prisoners referred to it as 'Siberia', though its conditions were not nearly as severe as that in Siberian camps. The camp contained thirty-six huts, mainly barracks. Barrack No 24 was used to house the Performance prisoners, while the women were placed in the guardhouse, actually just outside the camp. The prisoners had no clothes other than those they arrived in. There was little water and the only toilet was a bucket. Lice infested the walls and rapidly the men, food was minimal and life quickly became hard.

However, aside from the isolation, the camp was not always unremitting horror. There was a sports field and library, supplied by the Red Cross and YMCA. Courses were run on various subjects to keep the prisoners occupied, and Milag even had its own 'jockey' club that met every Saturday evening and held pretend horse races using wooden horses and dice. There was no limit on the number of letters a prisoner could write, even if they were heavily censored, though for the time being the Performance prisoners were forbidden such privileges.

Transports were regularly arranged for groups of twenty-five to thirty prisoners to be taken to Wilhelmshaven for interrogation. On one such trip, Einar Sorensen of the *Buccaneer* slipped away from his guard and disappeared into the crowd on the platform of the train station, but he failed to get far and eventually had to give himself up in Hamburg. He was returned to Milag and made another escape attempt when he was loaded onto a train destined for a more secure camp. This time he succeeded and eventually made it to Sweden.

Life in Milag improved slowly, in large part due to the efforts of the Red Cross, which sent in food parcels and other supplies. Unfortunately for around 150 of the Performance men, matters were about to worsen. In 1943, they were sentenced to 'nacht und nebel' detention in the horrendous Sonnenburg camp, which was especially bleak with little prospect but execution.

Sonnenburg was already known for its horrors, though today it is one of the lesser-known concentration camps. Opened in 1933 to house political prisoners, it later included prisoners of war accused of 'war crimes'. Sonnenburg was a hellish enough-place in which to reside without the Nazi brutality and cruelty that infected everyday life. The water naturally occurring in the camp was undrinkable and the whole place was damp with dripping water that resulted in regular epidemics of dysentery and influenza. Inmates were often beaten and tortured. Political prisoner Erich Mühsam had all the hairs on his head and in his beard plucked out. Other inmates had to pass the time digging their own graves under the watch of camp guards who were quick to strike out with a club, iron bar or rifle butt at anyone they deemed to be slacking.

Thirty-six of the brave Performance men died in the first winter at Sonnenburg. When the camp was liberated, only a handful had survived the conditions unscathed. British sources state that forty-three died, leaving over 100 survivors; however, Norwegian sources give a bleaker estimate: that only fifty-four lived until the end of the war and many of them were so weakened that they died shortly after liberation. Whichever is the case, it was a horrendous end for the brave souls who had striven to bring ball bearings to England.

There were some who escaped from transportation to Sonnenburg. The six women and young girl were sent to a camp in Württemberg, from which it is said only 180 Jewish prisoners out of the thousands sent there survived the war. It is not known if the women survived. Two men from the *Skytteren* avoided Sonnenburg by hiding out in the Milag camp hospital. Initially they were genuinely ill, but when their health improved, the hospital doctor, a British major who was also a prisoner, claimed that they were still too sick to leave his care. On several occasions the Gestapo arrived to claim the two men only to be turned away. Eventually they gave up and the two men stayed at Milag for the rest of the war.

In November 1944, the Russians were pressing the Germans hard, and it was decided to remove 800 men from Sonnenburg to make room for evacuated prisoners from the east. Among this group were the Performance men who could hardly know at the time that this transfer was their lucky escape. Just before the Russians overran Sonnenburg, the SS moved in and executed all the prisoners. The 800 were first moved to Sachsenhausen, which seemed like paradise in comparison with Sonnenburg, and were then gradually divided up and split between various camps. The last few months of the war, awaiting the arrival of the Allies, was perhaps the hardest, with constant transfers between camps, sometimes on foot with sick prisoners dragging themselves along.

For those Performance men who survived, the ordeal was to leave lasting marks and neither Binney nor the British authorities could quite adjust to the torment inflicted on these men because of their plan. The last push across the Skagerrak had been desperate and reckless; Binney had realised it too late. If only his radio had worked, the crews of the captured vessels would never have experienced the full horrors of the Nazi regime. The saboteur – if there was one – had a great deal to answer for.

II

BRING ON THE CABARET

B ritish eyes were on the *Dicto* and *Lionel* as the war took a new turn with the arrival of the Americans. Sweden suddenly found the Allies less accommodating of its suspect neutrality. A tougher attitude was taken, particularly after the actions of the Swedish Navy during Performance, and the American President Roosevelt was far from impressed with the Swedes' lack of co-operation. The Swedish Foreign Minister had promised the Germans that the *Dicto* and *Lionel* would never leave Gothenburg, yet already he was realising that he would have to eat his words. Britain wanted the steel those ships contained and now America was backing Britain.

Erik Boheman travelled to the US via the UK in the autumn of 1941, convinced that he would be received with as warm a welcome as Churchill had offered him. Indeed the British Prime Minister had promised to send a personal introduction to the American President to smooth the way. Boheman felt confident and calm as he arrived in the US to discuss safe conduct traffic. War had only just started to touch the American people and the Nazis seemed a long way away as Boheman stepped onto American soil. He had yet to realise that this would prove to be a disadvantage to him.

President Roosevelt had other matters on his mind as Boheman was introduced to him. He already had little patience for the Swedes and their tainted neutrality. America had finally taken the plunge into war and his attention was focused on the landings in Africa due to take place the day after his meeting with Boheman. The Swedish Secretary-General found himself bumped from minister to minister – no friendly lunch at the president's home awaited him as it had with Churchill. Eventually he stood before a committee of seven politicians who voted six to one to allow Sweden to continue imports from America and to uphold the safe conduct traffic policy.

Then Roosevelt finally turned his attention away from the sands of Africa and took a glance at the decision of his ministers. He knew how badly Sweden needed its imports and he was also well aware of the steel shortages in Britain. He approved the recommendation of his politicians but with one significant condition – Sweden had to allow the *Dicto* and *Lionel* to leave Gothenburg. Torn between two equally tough masters, but with the threat of suspended imports hanging over his head, Boheman agreed. On American soil, Nazi wrath seemed less potent and he was prepared to defy them this once.

A few weeks later, Sweden slipped two tankers through the German blockade and was preparing the *Dicto* and *Lionel* to follow. As usual there was no way of keeping Operation Cabaret secret, and the Germans quickly became aware of the situation. With alarming speed they tightened their patrols and put a stop to any ships leaving Sweden, declaring the Swedish breach of faith as their legitimate reason. The *Dicto* and *Lionel* were herded into a corner of Gothenburg harbour and their exit prevented by a 20,000-ton ship that was placed alongside and chains stretched across their bows.

George Binney, stuck in England, was needless to say frustrated at the action. However, the war situation was changing and Sweden was starting to realise that ingratiating itself with the Germans might no longer be in its best interest. The British and Americans began to pile on the pressure; weeks of exhaustive messages, interviews and debates slowly wore the Swedes down. The successes that the Allies were beginning to win and the downturn in German fortunes could only help. On 11 January 1943, Sweden agreed to release the *Dicto* and *Lionel*, and by 17 January they were sailing downriver, making a break for it before the Swedes changed their minds yet again. A safe berth was found out of sight of land but still in neutral Swedish waters and then it was just a case of waiting for orders from the Admiralty.

Binney was beside himself at the turn of events. The plan was to send out fast motor gun boats (MGBs) to rendezvous with the two tankers and transfer guns and gun crews to them in order to aid their safe crossing of the Skagerrak. Binney insisted on being on one of the MGBs, and it finally seemed that the last of the cargo – particularly the significant load held on the *Dicto* – was to fall into British hands.

But it was not to be. As feared, the Swedes got cold feet and sent out an order that the *Dicto* and *Lionel* must return to harbour. Reluctantly, the two vessels turned around. Yet another escape had been foiled. For two weeks they sat in port while Sweden decided on yet another course of action. Finally they were allowed to leave on 2 February, but under a familiar Swedish tactic, being forced to sail out in full view of eager German agents who instantly reported their departure. Sweden was still playing it safe, but the Allies were fast running out of patience.

The *Dicto* and *Lionel* hovered out at sea, dreading German attack, waiting for the arrival of the valiant MGBs in vain. The bad weather that Binney had once so much craved now forced his smaller vessels to abort their mission after a day and a half of trying to negotiate a North Sea gale. The *Dicto* and *Lionel* continued to loiter, hoping the weather would break and allow the MGBs through, but after several hours it was apparent the mission would not succeed. Binney's only consolation was that the endeavour had tied up no fewer than thirty-four German ships and aircraft ordered to prevent escape should it be attempted.

Operation Cabaret was a disaster, but at least it had not involved the human cost of Performance. Bill Waring and George Binney were still determined to rescue their ball bearings and needed to confer in order to plan the next operation. Waring was under threat of expulsion from Sweden, but tactful negotiations had ensured that he would not be forbidden from returning to Sweden if he made a brief journey to England.

Air travel between Sweden and Britain had increased with little opposition from the Nazis. It had begun in 1941, concentrating on transferring passengers, often ministers, but also refugees and the odd load of essential cargo. Over the next three years, 1,200 flights were performed, 490 of which were in 1944. Hudsons and Whitleys were first sent to pick up small loads of ball bearings and steel. They were a mere fraction of what Britain really needed, but at least it was something. They were eventually replaced by faster planes – Lockheed Lodestars, Dakotas, Liberators and ultimately Mosquitos – which could do the journey in 2–3 hours, as opposed to the 6, 8 or even 12 hour trips required by the bigger, heavier planes. Between November 1943 and March 1944, the planes carried 88 tons of invaluable steel under difficult and risky conditions. In monetary terms the value was £1.8 million, but it was a drop in the ocean compared with what was actually needed. Something more had to be done.

In the middle of May, Bill Waring donned a flying suit, a parachute pack with oxygen mask, a Mae West life-jacket (so termed because when inflated it resembled the busty appearance of the actress), an emergency whistle and a red light to attract attention should the worst happen and his plane ditch in the sea. Travelling by military aircraft was neither glamorous nor particularly comfortable. Passengers crouched in the bomb bay, icy cold and with no means of looking out. Those who suffered from airsickness had to endure it in silence. There was only one means of communication with the pilot, which was by an intercom. Bundled up in a rug and with feet wedged against the bomb hatch, Waring made himself as comfortable as possible, ignored the cold and noise, and kept one eye on the bomb doors which were prone to flying open in the slipstream.

THE BRIDFORD GANG

Binney was convinced that running the Skagerrak with big tankers was no longer an option. Operation Performance had cowed him and he no longer had the stomach for such a risky endeavour. There was no word on the men who had been captured, and their sacrifice sat uneasy with him. The *Dicto* and *Lionel* remained the key since they contained vital cargo that the British had already paid for. Binney and Waring came to the conclusion that an operation similar to the abortive Cabaret would be their best option. SOE would provide finance and Binney's new fleet would consist of five 149-ton MGBs.

The MGB had come into existence at the start of the war when it became apparent that the Royal Navy was desperately short of small boats for protecting coastal convoys and attacking enemy shipping. The Navy had a handful of motor torpedo boats (MTBs), sometimes described as the bombers of the shipping world, which could fly across the waves and attack enemy shipping. Not only were more MTBs needed, but a secondary craft that could act much like the fighter planes in the RAF was desired.

Prior to the war, British engineers had been working on highspeed powerboats that could survive an ocean sailing. Many were used simply for sailing competitions, but the growing tensions of war turned attention elsewhere. By 1935, there were worries that Germany and Italy were both developing high-speed motorboats and Britain was determined to keep pace. The prototype MTB was thus created and the Admiralty ordered six in 1937. Various versions of the MTB were produced, ranging in size from 60 to 70 feet, and were sold not just to the Admiralty but to navies across the world. Converted MTBs without torpedoes, but carrying depth charges and sonar, were operating off the east coast in

1939. They were underpowered, able to achieve only 25 knots, but they served their purpose as submarine hunters.

As the war progressed, various British-built MTBs were acquired from (or simply never delivered to) other navies and converted into MGBs. In 1940, luxury yacht company Camper & Nicholsons turned their hand to a variety of motorboats for the war effort, including the MGBs 502–509. Each of these vessels was 117ft long, with a beam of 20ft 3in, a draught of just over 4ft and displaced 95 tons in the water. Powered by three Davey Paxman diesel engines (except for MGB 509), they could reach a speed of 28 knots. Their initial design included a two-pounder pom-pom gun at the aft, two twin .5in machine guns mounted in powered turrets either side the bridge, two twin .303in Lewis machine guns, also either side of the bridge, one Holman Projector (an anti-aircraft weapon), two 21in torpedo tubes and twelve depth charges. Camper & Nicholsons were building them for the Turkish Navy, but they were acquired by the Royal Navy in February 1941 before they were finished. MGB 502, 503 and 509 were completed as normal MGBs, while 504–508 were transformed into blockade-runners for Binney.

Binney's little fleet had its armaments reduced to suit blockade-running. Now they carried only one twin 20mm Oerlikon gun amidships and two twin Lewis machine guns; the remainder of their space was to be taken up with their cargo. Binney could not resist naming the members of his fleet. Like any good admiral, he would rather a vessel under his command had a name and thus a personality, rather than an anonymous number. MGB 504 became HMS *Hopewell*, MGB 505 became HMS *Nonsuch*, MGB 506 became HMS *Gay Viking*, MGB 507 became HMS *Gay Corsair* and MGB 508 became HMS *Master Standfast*. Binney thought of his fleet as his 'little grey ladies' and gave them names that had some meaning to him. *Nonsuch* was the name of the ship he had first sailed in to the Hudson's Bay Company, all of the other names represented traditions, aspirations and a certain light-heartedness on the part of their 'admiral'.

The 'grey ladies' were fine little ships, but they had their foibles and were not renowned for their reliability. Charles Hambro at SOE spent a great deal of time finding spares for them, on occasion borrowing parts from the diesel engines that ran the air-conditioning system at the Bank of England – there were some advantages to being director of the institution.

Binney gathered his team around him. Bill Waring was over from Sweden, but his former second-in-command at sea, Brian Reynolds, had joined a commando unit after his safe arrival from Performance. Reynolds' adventures had made him unpopular in Sweden and he was not welcome back, so an element of subterfuge was required. Reynolds grew a beard (the famous red one which gave him the nickname 'Brian the Lion') and changed his name to Brian Bingham. He also acquired a naval uniform and decorated it with the medals he had won in his commando unit. A British security officer spotted the subterfuge and was very displeased with a man wearing naval uniform under an assumed name and with medals he wasn't entitled to (though Reynolds *was* entitled to them).

Commodore of the new flotilla, Binney was proud once more to be in command of a fleet and Reynolds became his vice-commodore. Waring was to return to Gothenburg as deputy head of the operation dealing with the Swedish side. Binney had acquired his own naval uniform and, in full regalia, set foot on Swedish soil with the defiance only he could muster. There was no reaction, nor was there a murmur raised about the appearance of 'Brian the Lion', now also decked out as a naval officer.

Waring returned without disguise. His job was to secure ball bearings for the operation. Intelligence had confirmed that the Germans were planning to buy up the Swedish stock and so prevent the British from having it. Waring had to move fast to get his orders in first. Erik Boheman was another problem. He may have been on friendly terms with Churchill, but it stuck in his throat to ignore the fact that several heavily armed motorboats were going to invade Swedish waters. He told Waring as much.

Waring countered with the argument that a 117ft vessel carrying an assortment of guns was really only *defensively* armed, as long as the weapons were kept out of sight while in Swedish waters. Boheman was unhappy at the arrangement, but he knew there was little he could do. Waring travelled along the coast to pick a suitable spot for rendezvous with the MGBs, eventually settling on the little port of Lysekil. Along the way he enjoyed spreading rumours that the British were planning their invasion of Europe with landings in Sweden.

Lysekil was perfect for the operation, but it had become feasible only because the Swedish Navy was at last realising that it had more to lose by supporting the Nazis than it had to gain. It would forever tarnish the Swedes' reputation that they had so doggedly supported Hitler and cost many of the Performance men their lives. Only now were they recognising their error.

The port was set up with cranes, accommodation, storage and, of course, the all-important cargo. Operation Bridford was now all set to go. The MGBs would travel to Lysekil, load with ball bearings and other steel and then head back for Britain. The voyage would not be without risks. Though German attention was slowly turning elsewhere, they would still mount patrols to try to prevent the little craft from getting through.

Careful negotiations and promises that the *Dicto* and *Lionel* would not leave Swedish waters eventually enabled the tankers with their important loads to be transferred to the Bro Fjord, the starting point for the successful Rubble operation. From there, their contents could be transferred discreetly to MGBs without contravening promises to Sweden. At long last, everything was in place and Britain's ball bearings could finally come home.

BRIDFORD BEGINS

On 27 October 1943, the five 'grey ladies' set sail from Hull. It was daylight and the North Sea was choppy, but the plan was to head at full speed for Sweden and not let up until dawn. It was an unpromising start; of the five MGBs, only one (the *Gay Viking*) arrived at Lysekil the next day, having failed to hear the message sent by the others that they were turning back due to the breakdown of one of the craft. But engine trouble was par for the course during the war and Binney was not unduly perturbed.

Three days later, Captain G.W. Holdsworth was standing on the *Master Standfast* with news of favourable weather in his mind. The *Gay Viking* was just returning from Lysekil, the first 'grey lady' to have made the full trip. Holdsworth was eager to be off. The wind was light and the grey sea looked relatively calm even as October rapidly faded to November. There would be many unpleasant crossings ahead as the winter came on, so a first voyage in relative calm was appealing. Nearby, Captain D. Stokes was preparing the *Hopewell* and Captain W. Jackson was aboard the *Gay Corsair*. They were all awaiting nightfall and the cover of darkness.

Dusk came quickly on that Halloween. At 4.30 p.m. Holdsworth, Stokes and Jackson were sailing down the lock at Immingham when a cry came from the *Gay Corsair*.

'Our engines are gone,' Jackson called to his colleagues. The MGBs' engines had been a nightmare since they had been hastily finished for Operation Bridford. They were constantly breaking down and in need of maintenance.

'I'll have to go back,' groaned Jackson. 'Sorry chaps.'

As the *Gay Corsair* limped back down the lock, Holdsworth and Stokes thought of their own engines. A quick check was made and after a few adjustments delayed further progress for 2 hours. Finally at 6.30 p.m. they were proceeding down the inner channel to Spurn Head.

The first obstacle was a British minefield, but the captains had instructions on the safe route to take through the mines and sailed harmlessly onwards. They set a north-easterly course, hoping to avoid contact with the Danish fishing fleet which might report their movements to the Nazis. Both vessels were lightly loaded with a cargo of around 20 tons of fuel oil in drums, intended for the *Dicto*, so it was possible to sail reasonably fast throughout the voyage and the MGBs maintained an average speed of 16 knots, slightly under their maximum.

The going was soon rough as the wind began to increase and the sea became choppier, but Holdsworth and Stokes had experience with the MGBs and knew that as long as they kept them clear of a 'head sea' they could make good progress despite the weather. Travelling in the MGBs, which bounced over waves, was not the most pleasant of experiences. Seasickness could affect the hardiest of crewmen as the light vessels dived and rose with the waves and danced about on the water. As they cut through the ocean, sheets of icy salt water shot back over the deck and soaked anyone around. The passage could be miserable and the crew had to learn to endure it.

At about 2.20 p.m. a strange sight was spotted to one side. It appeared, at first glance, to be the upturned hull of a small boat with a 5ft pole stuck in the centre. On moving closer, it was recognised as an unusual buoy device made of mahogany. Holdsworth checked his location readings. The buoy was not familiar and it might mean that they had drifted from their target line into the Skagerrak. He had plans to confirm their position using a series of Direction Finding fixes from the intersections of the RAF coastal beacons which his wireless operator could pick up clearly enough. But there was a problem: of the three beacons he had been told the positions of, only one was set to a frequency that could be picked up by his radio equipment.

Holdsworth was far from pleased. Navigating the sea at the best of times was difficult, but in the small MGBs and with a rough sea knocking them off course it was well-nigh impossible without assistance from stationary landmarks. For all Holdsworth knew, he was now lying to the far side of the Skagerrak instead of near the centre where he had intended to enter. Too far to the side and he ran the risk of entering close to the coast and in range of enemy radar stations. Stokes was equally unimpressed.

'I'll complain in my report about this,' he assured Holdsworth.

The two captains conferred and used dead reckoning to make their way to what they believed was their pre-arranged dusk-time position. Only later would they realise that they were around 15 miles off course.

Stokes took the lead through the Skagerrak, maintaining a position approximately 25 miles off the Danish coast and 35 miles off the Norwegian coast. The autumnal night had sunk to its darkest point and Stokes struggled to keep in contact with his companion. Fortunately the sea was highly phosphorescent that night, so it was easy enough to spot the water sweeping over the *Master Standfast*'s bow, 'in spite of the fact that she maintained poor station throughout the night ...' Stokes later complained.

A radar sweep was made every 5 minutes, producing negative contacts every time. The two MGBs slunk past the Danish fishing fleet and several lone Swedish and Danish vessels unnoticed. They were almost at their destination when the *Hopewell* developed a problem. There was an airlock somewhere in her fuel system and Stokes was forced to slow down while his engineers tried to fix it. This finally enabled Holdsworth to close the gap between them and draw close. It was the first time in several hours that Stokes had clearly seen the other ship.

'Try and keep pace!' he called to Holdsworth, but there was little response.

The airlock was dispersed and the *Hopewell* speeded up her engines, reaching 18 knots as the last lap of their journey approached. Stokes looked back and was disappointed to see the *Master Standfast* failing to keep up yet again. She had slipped back to two cable lengths and it was impossible to see her clearly. Stokes was concerned that she might lose them altogether, but there was nothing he could do. Shining a signal would almost certainly draw the attention of the enemy.

At about 1 a.m. a radar sweep was conducted and an object was discerned 600 yards dead astern.

'That will be *Master Standfast*,' Stokes said with some relief. Her bow wave was still visible just behind them.

At around 2.30 a.m. Swedish coastal lights were spotted and a course was set to bring the *Hopewell* into Swedish waters while avoiding the known watch-zones of the Nazi patrols. Stokes took his boat towards one of the many rocky passages that led to the various ports and harbours of Sweden. The route was narrow and intricate, though it didn't worry him. He called for their speed to be reduced and once more the *Master Standfast* could be seen catching up. Abruptly Holdsworth turned aside.

'What the devil is he doing?' Stokes muttered. It seemed to him that Holdsworth was uncomfortable attempting the route Stokes had chosen, though it would take them safely past the German patrols. Instead Holdsworth turned away and appeared to be heading towards the Vaderobad islands, which he could round and use as a short cut to the Hallo light.

Stokes was flabbergasted by the dangerous manoeuvre.

'It can't be her,' he said in disbelief. 'Holdsworth would not be fool enough to completely disregard flotilla practice.'

'It is her,' observed a deck officer, and several other seamen joined the debate and agreed that the silhouette so clearly visible astern had to be that of the *Master Standfast*.

'It could be a German patrol vessel,' Stokes said, though he didn't really believe his own words.

'They would have engaged us, sir.'

The crew of the *Hopewell* watched in astonishment as the *Master Standfast* slowly disappeared into the darkness.

'Damn it!' Stokes snorted. 'What would Captain Goodman say to this? He goes sick and his first mate Holdsworth is promoted and the first thing the fool does is send his MGB straight into the hands of the Germans.'

'He was warned about German patrol ships masquerading as Swedish pilot vessels. He knows not to try the direct route,' a deck officer answered.

At a loss as to what else to say, Stokes had his own mission to attend to and could worry no more about the foolishness of Holdsworth.

Stokes pulled into the quayside at Lysekil (berthing opposite the German Consulate for good measure) at 6.15 a.m. There was no sign of the *Master Standfast*. Stokes set about making some discreet enquiries as to the location of Holdsworth and his MGB, and he eventually learned from a Swedish government official that the *Master Standfast* had been spotted and signalled to come into port. All had seemed well; there were patches of fog that might delay her, but the official thought that she would arrive in the next 25 minutes. It was a weight off Stokes's mind and he could concentrate on his own mission while waiting for the errant Holdsworth. He would certainly have a few choice words to say about Holdsworth's recklessness in his report. However, 25 minutes passed with no sign of the *Master Standfast*. Stokes kept an eye open for her, but as time ticked by it was clear that she was not about to arrive.

Information on the fate of the *Master Standfast* trickled in slowly over the next few days. The Swedes reluctantly confirmed that she had been boarded by a vessel flying the Swedish colours and purporting to be a pilot ship. Almost immediately, Holdsworth would have realised his mistake as armed Germans invaded his ship and hijacked her under the very noses of the genuine Swedish patrol vessels. It seemed that she was then sailed to Frederikshavn, her crew under arrest.

Later, a Danish pilot who worked at Frederikshavn arrived at Lysekil and told the local pilots that the *Master Standfast* had indeed arrived at the harbour. Ominously, German ambulances appeared as she berthed and went to both the MGB and the German patrol vessel, indicating that there had been a struggle during the attack and more than one person was injured. Word came through the Swedish shipping agent they were using that a Swedish naval officer commanding the west coast had been rebuked for a 'serious incident' that had occurred on the same

day as the *Master Standfast* was captured. Was he being repri-
manded for allowing the Germans to hijack a boat on his watch?

Of course, Sweden was always universal with its anger and
Stokes's crew were made to feel its wrath when various petty
naval restrictions were imposed on them. The Swedish authorities told them the new regulations were their own fault, for all
'the trouble they had caused'.

Life in Lysekil for the British was testing. The locals proved
sympathetic and did all they could to help, but there were a
number that were working for the Germans. The Gestapo in
particular had spies in the area and were keeping a close watch
on Stokes's activities. The port was a restricted naval area and
Stokes and his crew were allowed onto dry land only with a
police escort. They stayed overnight in a local hotel which the
police raised a picket line around, as much for their own protection as to keep them inside.

Swedish sentiment was changing with the waning of German
power and the rise of Allied might. Most Lysekil residents did
everything they could to ensure that the British were welcome,
and the authorities at last started to put a bit of weight behind
their pro-British sympathies. A Swedish Nazi who worked in the
local Co-operative and showed an unnatural curiosity towards
the activities of the *Hopewell* was arrested, while another man
– the Gothenburg agent for the Gulf Oil Company, who had a
knack for turning up in the hotel where Stokes and his crew were
staying – was kept under surveillance. But they were only the
obvious suspects; other agents were managing to avoid attention
and report back to their masters.

The heavy surveillance put the possibility of a secret getaway
out of the question. As soon as the *Hopewell* made any move, the
German patrols would be informed. The Swedes were as aware
of this as Stokes himself and made the remarkable offer to allow
the *Hopewell* to berth in one of the nearby fjords for a time and
then sneak out when she felt the coast was clear. Exactly the
procedure the Performance crews had been desperate for and

had been denied. Stokes wasn't about to point out this irony; not when he needed to get home safely.

There had been talk among the crew of them berthing near the *Dicto* and *Lionel* in Bro Fjord, but Stokes rejected the idea. Asking permission to sit beside the two contested vessels might fuel debate that they were attempting to smuggle arms aboard the ships. Instead he sought permission to berth in Gulmars Fjord and make his escape attempt when the going looked good. To his surprise, the response from the Swedes was that he could not use Gulmars Fjord, but that he was quite welcome to berth in Bro Fjord. It was a remarkable about-face, and perfect for Stokes. Aboard the *Dicto* was an RNVR meteorologist who could provide Stokes with precise information on the best date to sail the very place the crew wanted to wait but hadn't dared ask for. It seemed hardly possible that the previously intractable Swedes would now offer him the ideal place for escape.

Without further ado, Stokes made plans to sail to Bro Fjord. On 7 November the *Hopewell* left Lysekil, much to the consternation and confusion of the German agents watching. Stokes hoped that they would report the manoeuvre and have German patrol vessels scrambling for the Skagerrak to try to catch the errant MGB, while instead she was safely berthed in Bro Fjord.

Stokes had not set eyes on the *Dicto* and *Lionel* for many months and when he found them in Bro Fjord it was difficult to tell if they were under guard for their own protection or to ensure that they did not escape. The Swedish had placed a boom across the narrows leading into the fjord, preventing tall ships from entering, and the guard ship *Odin* was constantly patrolling and watching the waters for trouble. (She was later replaced by the auxiliary gunboat *Skagerrak*.) The *Odin*'s crew were most welcoming to Stokes, especially when he offered what little remained of the *Hopewell*'s alcohol supplies from their time in Lysekil. The Swedes apologised heartily for the childish manner in which their commodore in Gothenburg imposed restrictions on the British crews who were already in a very difficult position.

These included refusing to allow the crew of the *Hopewell* to visit the *Dicto* or *Lionel* for baths, insisting on 3 hours' notice before the *Hopewell* opened her boom in preparation to go to sea, and banning Swedish naval officers from inviting the British onto their ships. Bill Waring was informed of the petty restrictions and through his contacts managed to get the authorities in Stockholm to cancel them, except the boom order, which was only reduced to an hour's notice.

Despite this, the time spent in Bro Fjord was pleasant enough. The Swedish naval crews were generous and friendly; they gave Stokes fresh water and bread and even offered their own weather reports to help him decide when best to leave. When the *Hopewell* did finally leave on 15 November, she was cheered by the Swedes who waved her a fond farewell – quite a change from the Swedish naval encounters that had blighted Performance!

But the excitement for their departure was premature. The sea was rougher than expected and the *Hopewell* was now loaded with 41 tons of ball bearings that increased her draught in the water. She lumbered through the waves, her engines struggling to keep her on course and her crew all feeling mightily seasick. Among them were six Norwegian seamen who had come aboard as refugees and now gagged and groaned with each swell and bounce of the *Hopewell*.

It was not long before Stokes realised that they could not continue. As ever, the MGB's engines proved the main issue: a gearbox seized and nothing the crew could do would get it working again. Floundering 30 miles off the coast, Stokes conceded defeat and gave the command to turn back.

A bedraggled *Hopewell* reappeared in Bro Fjord. Stokes's first concern was to get a message to Britain to prevent Coastal Command sending out planes to look for them in the morning. Meanwhile the crew were particularly miserable at the failure; the faulty gearbox was completely ruined and while they waited for a replacement, they tried to dispel the last dregs of seasickness and remind themselves that they would soon be making the attempt again.

The gearbox proved particularly problematic. It had to come from England and that involved filing a request, having the gearbox carried from Nuneaton by lorry and then loaded onto a Dakota aircraft, which then flew to Gothenburg. This was all done through the Inter Services Research Bureau, an officer of which was dispatched to guard the 1-ton gearbox on its journey. The part arrived four days after the request had been sent, a remarkable turn-around considering the war that was raging.

The *Hopewell* had not been to Gothenburg in four years and Stokes felt brave enough to sail her there under the Red Ensign. The new attitude of the Swedish Navy encouraged him, but his confidence was misplaced. Even with a Swedish escort and a Swedish officer on board, a coastal fort fired on them as they were headed to the naval base where they had to leave their guns and ammunition before heading into Gothenburg. Stokes noted that this caused the Swedish officer on board a great deal of discomfort.

The reaction of Swedish civilians to the *Hopewell*'s arrival was completely different. Stokes deemed their journey up the narrow passage to Gothenburg a triumphal parade, with workers in the shipyards and docks lining the water, abandoning their tasks to cheer on the crew. Several gave the victory sign to the British and for the next six days the crew were treated almost like returning heroes, welcomed and spoiled at every turn. Stokes was rather impressed that after nearly a week of this, only one man missed their departure for the more austere confines of Bro Fjord. As usual this swell of goodwill was quickly dampened by the Swedish Navy, on this occasion rather literally. The guns and ammunition Stokes had left with them for safe-keeping had been allowed to stand in the pouring rain for 4 hours and some were naturally ruined, while the rest would need to be cleaned and oiled. Stokes lodged a complaint with the British Legation and received the response that the Swedish Navy regretted the error. Once again, Stokes felt that the Navy was playing its own game and making life as impossible as it could for the British.

Bro Fjord was grim after the liveliness of Gothenburg. The crew's morale dropped, especially when they were put on restricted rations due to shortages and their cigarettes and tobacco ran out. Stokes was more relieved than ever to have their loyalty and appreciated that they had given up the comforts of Gothenburg for a miserable wait in cold weather for the signal to leave and cross the Skagerrak. For seven days the weather was unpromising and the trip could not be attempted. Finally, on 30 November, the meteorologist aboard the *Dicto* informed Stokes that, if he was prepared to chance it, there was due a break in the weather which he could use to his advantage. It would not hold for long and it was possible that the bad weather would catch up on the *Hopewell*, but by now the men were so fed up that they were ready to try anything. The boom across Bro Fjord was raised at 4.15 p.m. and the *Hopewell* slipped out towards the ocean. She had forgone a pilot as this would have meant alerting Lysekil, and thus the German agents, to her planned departure.

The night proved uneventful. The *Hopewell* maintained 17 knots, though it was always on Stokes's mind that they were low on fuel since their abortive first attempt to reach home. The radar was used regularly through the night and indicated ships nearby. On two occasions Stokes spotted lit ships sailing close, apparently headed for Oslofjord. Neither appeared to see them. Just after midnight Stokes reckoned their position to be close to Kristiansand and at the same time the radar registered a substantial echo one mile from their port bow. There was nothing to be seen, and Stokes was in no mood to investigate. They continued on their course, making adjustments to avoid the large object that created repeated contacts on the radar screen. Only later did Stokes learn that he had come within a mile of German destroyers stationed at Kristiansand.

Everything appeared to be going smoothly until there was a sudden change in the *Hopewell*'s running speed. One of the big end bearings in the central engine had broken and consequently the main engine was out of action. The lack of reliability in the

MGBs was infuriating – even on a simple run they seemed unable to cope. The vessel limped on. When first light approached, everyone watched the horizon anxiously for a sign of any enemy ships, except for the engineers who were below and trying their hardest to fix the central engine.

The sea had grown choppy, and the *Hopewell* lunged and dived in the waves. Below decks, the engine room reeked of diesel fumes and oil, sickening the men who worked in the constant miasma, often forcing them to leave and retch up what little they had in their stomachs. The turmoil of the sea did not improve matters. The rise and fall of the *Hopewell* seemed exaggerated below, and the men slipped and slid as they worked in the dark confines. It was not unusual for MGB engine crews to fail to eat during a voyage because they were so nauseated by their working environment.

It was not until late afternoon that two Beaufighters were spotted and signalled. The planes escorted the *Hopewell* for an hour and a half before they had to head for home. Shortly after they left, the port engine failed. Despite the best efforts of the engineering crews, the central engine would not work and Stokes had no choice but to rely on his one remaining engine to get him safely to the Humber. With only 120 gallons of fuel left, and having endured a further delay of over an hour because the Humber radio station had not recognised the *Hopewell*'s cypher signal, Stokes finally berthed his ship in the Albert Dock at Hull. It was 9 a.m. on 3 December.

BINNEY'S PRIDE

George Binney was understandably ecstatic at the success of the *Hopewell*. Though the *Master Standfast* had vanished, this first adventure by the MGBs had proved it was not only possible but highly profitable to use the light and small MGBs as blockade-runners. Binney was quickly planning new voyages and ensuring that he would participate.

Forever the keen sailor since his time on Arctic explorations, Binney was an eager adventurer and it would have been impossible to prevent him participating in Bridford. By January he was already on his second mission with the MGBs and all too ready to relay the events that had occurred during his travels. He had arrived in Lysekil to a warm welcome and a message from the mayor congratulating him on his success and hoping that he would come again soon.

As usual, relations with the naval authorities were less cordial. Binney's MGB had arrived and he had briefly gone ashore for a few moments to speak to people. When he returned, his first lieutenant was looking flustered. During Binney's absence the Swedish naval authorities had appeared and insisted on removing the MGB's radar equipment. Binney was furious. Not only was this an imposition on the British but the Swedes had taken one of the most secret pieces of equipment the British had aboard. Radar was still quite new and there was no knowing what useful information the Swedish, or more likely the Germans, could gain from inspecting the British equipment.

Binney set out in haste to recover the device. He immediately went straight to the head of the local naval authorities and confronted him on the matter. As Victor Mallet had discovered, it was never easy to argue with Binney, and he seemed to have a way of always winning his case. Within 20 minutes, Binney was walking away with his radar equipment and an apology.

The trouble was that some of the Swedish naval officers were following different rules and were not inclined to let the British have things their own way. Whether with German encouragement or not, a Swedish naval officer boarded Binney's MGB and insisted that the radar equipment be handed over. Binney blankly refused. To ask for it in the first place was akin to espionage, he informed the Swede, seeing as there was no reason for its confiscation otherwise. They argued, but Binney was firm; the Swedes could not have his radar and the more they protested, the more he believed they were trying to steal British secrets.

Finally the Swedish officer discovered what his superiors had – that it was impossible to argue with Binney. The Swede backed down and left. No more attempts were made to take the radar.

However, that didn't mean that life ran smoothly for Binney's fleet. The Swedish Navy was starting to cause problems about where the MGBs could anchor in Bro Fjord. It was insisting that they moor alongside a Swedish corvette, suitably positioned to keep a watch on them. Binney was outraged. The rough weather in the fjord was making the water choppy and the corvette rolled heavily with each swell. If the MGBs were anchored next to it they were liable to suffer damage. Binney insisted that he be allowed to moor the MGBs near the *Dicto* and *Lionel* where they would be protected from the bad weather. At first this was agreed, but someone was devious enough to send word to the Swedish Admiralty in Stockholm, which immediately sent the order back that Binney *must* moor alongside the corvette.

Binney was furious and not prepared to back down. He asked to phone the British Legation to lodge a complaint. He was only allowed to use a telephone with an open line, as he had expected. The open line could be intercepted by the Swedes and the conversation overheard. Binney told the Legation in no uncertain terms that he wanted to lodge a strongly worded protest against the Swedish naval authorities. He dictated exactly how the protest should be worded and then put down the phone. A short time later the Stockholm officials rang and cancelled the order to force Binney to moor by the corvette – the British Legation hadn't even had time to file their complaint.

Otherwise the trip was uneventful and Binney came home with 40 tons of ball bearings and other steel.

In many regards Bridford was the quietest of the operations, with little incident, and, aside from the capture of the *Master Standfast*, no loss of men. This result was as much a case of a greater understanding of blockade-running, as of the Germans becoming preoccupied with other war matters and the changing political climate. Had Bridford happened a year sooner, there would have been more efforts to negate its results and more danger, but it had happened at a time when the Allies were pushing Germany back and when Hitler's concerns were as much turned to the East and Russia as to the West and the UK and US.

On 15 March 1944, Peter Tennant paid a visit to his old friend Binney while he was briefly in Lysekil loading more ball bearings in his MGBs. George was there with Bill Waring, enjoying the triumph of his plan. He was on his fourth trip with his fleet and loving every moment. Even the inevitable seasickness endured by the most hardy on an MGB did not detract from his pleasure. Tennant had his mind on post-operation publicity. There were a number of things he wanted to clear up by releasing a carefully worded statement to the press, not least the rumours circulating in certain Swedish and German quarters that the operation was purely piratical and that the British were operating some form of modern-day privateer ships. He also hoped any publicity would help the captured men of the *Master Standfast* by making it clear that this was a merchant navy operation and they should be treated accordingly. As mentioned earlier, this should have meant releasing them from custody as they were not technically POWs. A press release might even make it harder for the Swedes to withdraw their reluctant support for the operation the following winter, and it would have no end of benefit for the morale of the MGB crews.

Binney was all for the idea; he believed publicity was the key to ensuring that the operation could continue the following winter. He left Tennant in Lysekil tasked with writing the first draft, which Binney would need to approve.

Tennant watched Binney board one of the MGBs and waved as he headed out to sea. A snowstorm had descended and almost obscured them, but Tennant managed to take a photograph, even if it did turn out rather 'foggy'. A keen amateur artist, Tennant sketched the scene with shaking fingers as the cold numbed him. It was the last sailing of the season and seemed an occasion to be marked. Little did anyone realise that it was also to be Binney's last sailing with the MGBs altogether.

Not long after returning from his latest voyage, Binney suffered a serious heart attack. Always a large man who enjoyed life to the full, the tolls of his adventures and pleasures had hit him hard. He would take many weeks to recover and SOE had no option but to invalid him out of Operation Bridford. Binney was beside himself with fury. He had always been a part of the missions, and to be retired now, just when things were going well, was painful. The only consolation was that he was awarded a DSO in recognition of his work and involvement with the various blockade-busting operations.

He was not the only casualty. It later became known that Captain Holdsworth and nineteen of the crewmen aboard the *Master Standfast* had perished, and all because Holdsworth had not dared risk the narrow fjords and chose to sail through open waters.

THE END RESULT

Binney's fleet of MGBs had proved their value (if not their reliability) during the long winter of 1943–44. Seven missions had been run; the *Hopewell* had participated in two, the *Gay Corsair* and *Gay Viking* had both participated in three and the *Nonsuch* had made a single voyage. On every occasion bar one they had managed to bring home between 38 and 40 tons of ball bearings and steel (the exception being the *Gay Corsair*'s March mission when she carried only 27 tons due to engine failure making it impossible to carry more). The total was almost 348 tons, all vital and invaluable to the war effort. In terms of cost, the cargoes were worth 2,826,627 Swedish Kronor. Aside from materials, the vessels had also rescued and brought sixty-seven refugees to Britain. On outgoing missions the MGBs had also carried cargo, but not in the same league as on their return voyages and mainly with the aim of setting up stashes of engine spares, fuel and cigarettes in Sweden.

The operation had a special place in the hearts of the residents of Hull. The majority of the crews of the MGB were local, including the unfortunate Holdsworth who died from wounds he received during the boarding of his vessel in November 1943. Tennant and Binney both thought it important to celebrate this link and the heavy sacrifice that Hull would have suffered had the MGB operation proved as disastrous as Performance.

Binney had travelled on four of the MGB missions. First with the *Hopewell* on the fateful occasion when Holdsworth had chosen to risk German attention and suffered the costs; secondly in December when he went out with the *Hopewell* and returned on the *Gay Viking* in January; thirdly in February aboard the *Nonsuch*; and finally on the *Gay Corsair* in March, his final mission.

The success of Bridford was unprecedented. The Ministry of Aircraft Production estimated that 100 tons of ball bearings would cover 75 per cent of the airframe work for 1,200 Lancasters and 60 per cent of the airframe work for 1,600 Mosquitos – the combined efforts of the MGBs and airlifts had brought to Britain more than 400 tons. By any estimate, Bridford had proved invaluable.

Binney had finally succeeded as a blockade-buster, but because of the timing of the runs (late in the war), the uneventful nature of the voyages and, aside from the *Master Standfast*, the lack of human cost, Bridford is largely ignored in contemporary history books.

The question of publicising Bridford gave Tennant, Binney and Mallet more than one headache. Mallet acted the typical diplomat when he said that he had no strong opinions either way on the matter of issuing a press release, but that it might be prudent to confer with the Swedes since there had been a great deal of pressure on them to keep Operation Bridford out of their press. Mallet failed to account for the fact that Bridford would have been a disaster had it been publicised in Swedish papers.

As for British security risks, there was little to worry about. The capture of the *Master Standfast* had already provided the

Germans with all they needed to assess the capabilities, build quality and nature of the MGBs used in the runs, except for possibly knowing the speed of the vessels. Binney therefore opined that it would be a good plan to exaggerate the speed of the MGBs, stating in the press release a top speed of 30 knots (almost double!). This would cause the Germans consternation, as only their destroyers could match such a speed. It might even cause them to reconsider their patrols of the Skagerrak. If their vessels could not match the MGBs for speed then they were almost pointless except for reporting movements of ships to air bases. The Germans would not want to tie up their destroyers in the Skagerrak, even if they were the only vessels fast enough to catch the MGBs. The result, mused Binney, might be a relaxation in the patrolling of Scandinavian waters, giving the blockade-runners an even clearer passage the following winter. The pleasure of winding up the Germans rather appealed to him.

As ever, the press release was a complicated matter of internal politics. Draft after draft was devised and sent to various people for assessment and corrections, the censors adding their blue pencil marks to anything deemed secret, too controversial or damaging to Britain's position. When the article finally did appear, on Tuesday 18 July 1944, it was headlined in *The Times* 'British Blockade Runners' and credited as 'from our Naval Correspondent':

> When blockade-running has been mentioned in the last few years, it has generally referred to Axis attempts to run the British blockade of German-occupied Europe; but it is a game that two can play. Germany has held practically full control of the entrance to the Baltic ever since the rape of Denmark, and has thus been in a position to cut off British access by sea to Sweden, and did so entirely up to last autumn. But since this country was in need of certain Swedish products in greater quantity than it was practicable to transport by air, and also of a passenger service of

greater volume, early in 1943 it was decided to organize a shipping line for those purposes. How that was accomplished is now made public for the first time.

The ships, of course, had to be merchant vessels, so as not to compromise Swedish neutrality, and they were operated by the Ellerman Wilson Line …

The crews, about 20 in each ship, were specially selected and trained for their arduous task. Blockade-running is a young man's job and their average age was about 25; none of the masters was over 40 …

It was careful planning and preparation, courage, and good seamanship that carried them through. All the officers and men were made abundantly welcome in the Swedish ports they visited, where the inhabitants were well pleased to see British merchant ships in their ports once more.

Only one of the Ellerman Wilson fleet failed to get through, the *Master Standfast*, which was captured by German warships. Her master, Captain C.R.W. Holdsworth, was killed.

Tennant noted that the original press release contained the following final paragraph not mentioned in *The Times*:

It is perhaps worth adding the *Hopewell* took her name from a Hull whaler which was famous in the early whaling history of that port. The name was conferred on the present *Hopewell* as a compliment to Hull which was the home of the majority of the crew.

Binney's influence is apparent. The press release was short on details of actual voyages and some of its details were mildly exaggerated (it was not a warship that took the *Master Standfast* but an armed trawler and many of the crew were in their 30s, and of course Commander Binney was well over 40). Yet it did what it needed to: dispel the myths circulating around Bridford, give a boost to the morale of the MGB crews and give a nod to the heroics of Hull and its men.

For the time being, the approach of summer had put blockade-running on the back burner, but all the main parties were still absorbed with the problem of ball bearings, in more ways than one.

A WHOLE LOAD OF MOONSHINE

Bill Waring had his hands full with the irate American before him. He was lunching with Peter Tennant at a Stockholm men's club in Sällskapet, surrounded by civil servants, politicians and newspaper editors when Stanton Griffis, representative of the US Foreign Trade Administrator, finally exploded.

'I'll have the air force bomb that damned SKF works in Gothenburg if these damned Swedes don't stop trading with the enemy!'

A heavy silence fell over the lunch as the many Swedish Government employees within the room took stock of Griffis's words. They should have come as no surprise. Griffis had arrived in Stockholm in May 1944 with one purpose on his mind: to discuss the cessation of ball bearing exports to Germany. Waring had been tentatively hopeful about the Boston-born Democrat's arrival. Griffis was tough, level-headed and above all not used to having his requests refused. He was a president of Paramount Films and a relatively well-known name among the American people, having just before the war bought interests in the newly emerging phenomenon of television.

Not far off his 60th birthday, Griffis was a hard-boiled politician, used to dealing with big business deals and tricky negotiations. Sweden had not seemed such a hard challenge. There had been a slight suspicion that Britain had been a little too soft on Sweden and, with increased American pressure, the country would crack and give in to Allied demands.

Griffis came across as the typical American businessman. Dressed in a pin-stripe suit, his round, full face ornamented with a pair of equally round and large glasses, he could look at one moment an easy-going gentleman, but displease him and his full, wide mouth would twist into outrage and he would bellow out his anger. The outburst in Sällskapet was not entirely unexpected. His indignation was fuelled as much by patriotism as the horror of losses that the American Air Force had incurred in recent raids on ball bearing factories in Germany.

On 17 August 1943, the USAAF had launched a strategic bombing attack on German heavy industries, rather unimaginatively called Mission No 84. A total of 376 Flying Fortress bombers from the Eighth Air Force, subdivided into sixteen bomber squads, flew into Germany. They had an escort party including 191 RAF Spitfires, but the distance to the targets prevented the escorts from following the bombers all the way. The last leg of the journey was flown by bombers alone. The Flying Fortresses were to divide into two parties and separately attack the factories at Regensburg and Schweinfurt, to cause maximum confusion and distraction to opposing Luftwaffe forces. Almost as soon as they lost their escort, barely 15 minutes into Germany, the bombers were attacked by German fighter planes and AA guns. Despite the heavy opposition, Regensburg was successfully bombed. The attack on Schweinfurt was more chaotic. The first bombs dropped had caused thick smoke that prevented accurate drops from subsequent bombers. Schweinfurt survived relatively unscathed, but the Eighth Air Force had suffered a loss of sixty bombers, and between fifty-eight and ninety-five B-17 Flying Fortresses (sources disagree on exact numbers) suffered severe battle damage and were forced to land in French Algeria. Many were so far beyond repair that they never returned to active service.

Intelligence reports suggested that ball bearing production at Schweinfurt had been reduced by the disappointing figure of 34 per cent. An immediate follow-up raid was needed, but too many planes were out of action and it was two months before the USAAF was ready to try again. On 14 October 1943, a force of 291 B-17s was sent to attack the factories. This time the group would not separate but concentrate on Schweinfurt, and an effort was made to provide a better escort, but still the bombers would have to fly mostly alone.

The attack was a failure. Sixty bombers were destroyed outright, another seventeen were so badly damaged they could not be salvaged, and a further 121 suffered battle damage. Losses totalled 26 per cent of the attacking force and 22 per cent of the air crews. The damage to the factories had actually proved quite significant: of 598 bombs dropped, 286 were later identified to have fallen within the factory area and 35 made direct hits on buildings. But the cost was high – too high – and to the outrage of the Americans it was rumoured that the SKF works in Sweden had helped repair the damage to the German factories and production was almost back to normal within a fortnight.

Griffis was furious at the loss. He had many theories about how the war could have been ended sooner, including a belief that if the raids had continued in Germany the war would have been over by the time he met Bill Waring. He failed to account for the horrendous loss of life and machinery that had almost crippled the Eighth Air Force. Unfortunately Griffis had a lot of strong opinions, many of which were inaccurate or too simplistic. Along with many Americans, fuelled by the US press, he believed that Sweden was deliberately helping Germany in its war effort by maintaining exports. Britain knew that the situation was far more complicated; Sweden had agreed to continue exports to Germany not out of consideration for the Nazis but because it needed certain vital imports from Germany that it could not obtain elsewhere. If the Swedes blocked exports they could, potentially, cripple their own country. Thus Britain had been lenient on the matter, even if it would have preferred the cessation of all exports.

The situation had changed in late 1943 when Germany had done everything in its power to intensify imports of Swedish iron ore, depriving Britain of the same resources. This had gone down badly with the Allies, especially with Americans like Griffis working on foreign trade agreements. Now the Allies were pushing for a complete ending of exports, but Sweden was understandably reluctant. Officials requested that Griffis clarify exactly how much of the country's ball bearing exports were being used by Germany in its war effort. (Previous figures had estimated that only 3 per cent went to the German war machine.) Though the raids on Schweinfurt had naturally increased this, the Swedes were still not convinced. They felt the Allies were overestimating the success of their raids.

On 9 May, Waring and Griffis were exerting pressure on SKF to immediately cease exports to Germany. Griffis had calmed down slightly, telling the British press, 'I will try to settle the ball bearings question on a purely business basis, negotiating directly with the firms concerned.'

The German trade negotiator, Karl Schnurre, was staying in the same hotel as Griffis in Stockholm, but he refused to be drawn on the matter of ball bearings. He walked around in a fog of gloom, no longer the proud German who had handed a list of demands to the Swedish Government in 1941 as Hitler sent his troops to Russia. One of those old concessions he had demanded was that Sweden allow German military courier traffic to fly between Norway and Finland. At the time it had been accepted after great debate. Now Sweden was demanding that the courier traffic cease and Schnurre, feeling the effects of German defeats, had no option but to accept.

The question of ball bearings was another matter, but that too would soon be dealt with. An interim agreement with SKF was reached on 27 May, but was instantly rejected by both the American and British governments. On the eve of D-Day, a new agreement was reached, helped not least by leaked rumours of imminent action by the Allies against Germany. SKF agreed to reduce their exports to Germany by 60 per cent for the next four months. What happened after that would depend on the progress of the Allied invasion.

THE LAST OF THE BLOCKADE RUNNERS

Binney was recuperating from his heart attack with little patience. The seasons were turning yet again, and with winter looming, blockade-running was once more on his mind. On 6 June, Allied troops had launched the Normandy landings, with suitable distraction operations simultaneously performed to confuse the Nazis as to Britain and America's true intentions. D-Day is legendary as the waymarker for the changing tides of the war. The Allies went from defensive operations to offensive, and though it would still be many months before peace would be reached, the end of war was in sight. France had been liberated on 25 August and General Charles de Gaulle had marched proudly back into Paris and given a victory speech. He had stood before the tomb of the unknown soldier from the First World War and saluted. There had been victory parades and celebrations in the street.

A similar liberation of Norway was still a long way off. The Nazis were heavily embedded in the country and even Swedish demands to stop courier traffic would not have them running for cover yet. They were, after all, still allowed one plane a day to travel to Norway.

For the time being, Binney saw no reason to believe that the German blockade of the Skagerrak would be lifted before the long nights of winter took hold and gave optimum opportunities for blockade-runners.

'Brian the Lion' Reynolds was to run the next blockade operation, codenamed Moonshine. He would use three of the MGBs to run regular cargo convoys between Sweden and Britain.

Reynolds was still *persona non grata* in Sweden for the hand he had played in Operation Performance. The Swedes had never forgiven the British for the outrage that the operation had caused and the backlash from the Germans. Reynolds kept his pseudonym of 'Bingham' for Moonshine. He shaved off his glorious red beard and was given the temporary rank of Commander RNR, to help him slip past Swedish eyes and to give him some form of protection should he be captured by the Germans.

Reynolds was more than ready for a new adventure. Together with Binney he had chosen the *Hopewell*, *Nonsuch* and *Gay Viking* for the operation. With Moonshine there was less concern with ball bearings and more emphasis on loading cargoes of arms and various war equipment (with the full co-operation of Sweden, which now saw the way the tide was turning) for the Danish resistance.

In October 1944, Lieutenant Choyce, a meteorologist, was sent to Sweden to provide up-to-the-minute weather reports. Having a meteorologist to hand had proved essential to the previous missions and Binney's advice was taken to have one ready for Moonshine. However, Choyce would remain in Sweden for only two months, before he was needed elsewhere. Reynolds, therefore, had a short window of time to do as much as he could.

Yet almost immediately there were problems. The winter of 1944–45 proved particularly bad for seafaring. Between September 1944 and January 1945, Choyce's reports of bad weather conditions prevented any attempt being made. That winter has become known as one of the coldest in modern European history, the temperature regularly dropping below zero on the Fahrenheit scale. Reynolds could only wait ashore for news to go ahead.

At home, the British were welcoming the respite from German air raids as Hitler was kept busy with attacks on his home turf. For the troops abroad the bad weather was abysmal. For centuries warfare had always taken a break during winter for practical reasons. The two World Wars had changed that. American soldiers in the Hürtgen Forest had fought day after day in freezing temperatures. They slept out in icy mud and snow, with no shelter, ate their rations freezing cold, and fire was banned in case smoke alerted the Germans to their location.

Less fortunate American troops would be caught up in the Battle of the Bulge, fighting through the Ardennes region in icy temperatures, under-equipped for the conditions. The Germans had learned to their cost during winters in Russia how dangerous bad weather could be to their troops and had supplied their men accordingly. The Americans were less ready, and suffered greatly from the freezing temperatures. In other areas the winter took its toll on civilians. In the Netherlands the appalling winter became known as the Hunger Winter, as the plummeting temperatures coupled with German blockades of food and fuel produced a famine in Nazi-occupied territory. That winter, 22,000 people died from starvation.

For Reynolds it looked like the 1944–45 blockade-running season was to be a complete failure. Every morning the reports were bleak from Choyce and other meteorologists, and the MGBs remained in their berths. In desperation it was suggested that the base for the blockade-runners be shifted from Hull to Aberdeen. This provided a slightly shorter route should the weather break, even temporarily. The break occurred on 13 January, a Saturday. While Reynolds was preparing his crews, the operations over Germany were in full flow, despite the terrible weather. Nineteen American aircrews were setting off on a bombing raid to Kaiserslautern, a city in western Germany, that morning. While the US Marine bombing squadron was sending out eight planes to search for a lost aircraft at sea, across in Belgium the 506th Parachute Infantry were launching an attack to clear out the remaining Germans from Foy and the 5th Black Watch were preparing for an assault against the Germans in the Ardennes. The RAF was sending eleven Mosquitos to Bochum and nine Mosquitos to Recklinghausen to bomb synthetic-benzol plants, thirty-one Halifaxes to lay mines off Flensburg and Kiel, and a mission to bomb Saarbrücken involving 274 aircraft. A solitary Hudson flew out on a resistance operation. It was going to be a busy night!

Reynolds' mission proved successful. The MGBs transferred camouflaged cargo to lighters, including the armaments for the Danish Resistance, then they headed south. They arrived at Gothenburg with a full moon shining down on them, flying the 'Red Duster' – the symbol of British merchant seamen used since the seventeenth century – and entered the port to a warm welcome. Greetings were showered upon them as they had been the year before, and Reynolds and his crews were treated to Swedish hospitality while they serviced their MGBs. As usual, the boats were their own worst enemy and needed constant tinkering to keep them working. They were a nightmare, yet most of their crews thought of them fondly and treated them with the same regard as if they were a massive Navy destroyer.

On 5 February, the MGBs sailed from Hunnebostrand, a departure point they had not used before. The outlook seemed hopeful and with their cargo off-loaded and the Germans occupied, Reynolds was not concerned about any disasters befalling them as they sailed home. Little did he know that the 13 January mission was to be the one and only successful operation that season.

The *Nonsuch* quickly drew ahead of the others. Bad weather was creeping in and soon she had disappeared from sight. Navigation started to become difficult, visibility was at a minimum and the crew peered helplessly over the sides of the boat trying to catch sight of anything. Suddenly a silhouette loomed before the *Hopewell*. There was no time to avoid it and to her crew's horror their MGB rammed into the side of the poor *Gay Viking*. The collision at nearly full speed was catastrophic. The *Gay Viking* was stricken; her crew were told to abandon ship while her Chief Officer reluctantly set demolition charges to sink her. Nothing wanted to go right that night. The Chief Officer had barely primed the charges and set them to detonate when he discovered his life-jacket was snared on some of the wreckage. He twisted and turned, trying to pull the jacket loose, all too aware that at any moment a hefty explosion was due. Finally panic overwhelmed him. He tore off the jacket and threw himself into the freezing sea without it. There was no sign of the *Gay Viking*'s dinghy and the rest of her crew, and the miserable Chief Officer had to swim for 200 yards in icy water that weighed down on his limbs and pushed him into an almost catatonic state before he miraculously stumbled upon the *Hopewell*. He was helped aboard, shivering and very lucky to be alive.

The *Hopewell* went in search of the dinghy. It was found not far away, splashing about in the water. The panic-stricken crew had launched the craft minus its oars and were now trying to direct her with two frying pans that they had found in the stores they had rescued and a large Swedish sausage. Somehow, even in disaster, the MGBs and their crews managed to be comical. The *Gay Viking*'s men were saved and brought aboard the *Hopewell*, which was damaged herself. There was no prospect of making it across the Skagerrak and home. Reynolds had no option but to turn the *Hopewell* back to Gothenburg for repair. She limped into harbour with her shamefaced crew; it was one thing to be attacked and damaged by Germans, quite another to ram into your fellow ship due to carelessness. Reynolds' thoughts were occupied with saving the *Hopewell* and the rather surprising news that the Chief of Staff of the Swedish Navy had promised every assistance. It never crossed his mind that it had failed to hear the *Gay Viking*'s scuttling charges go off.

As the shipyards were out of action due to workers' strikes, the *Hopewell* was repaired in a yacht-builders' yard. Swedish enterprise had stumbled and no one was certain what the future would be. On 12 March, Reynolds returned to England on his valiant MGB. Blockade-running was at an end. Moonshine had been a poor endeavour and had cost Binney the *Gay Viking*, but the culmination of the war swept aside the failings. The adventure was over. Allied troops were sweeping into Germany and releasing prisoners, including the survivors of the unfortunate Operation Performance. The world had changed yet again and life was returning to something like normal. Binney and his blockade-runners were due a well-earned retirement.

AFTER THE WAR

War in Europe officially ended on 8 May 1945 with the German surrender. For the survivors of Operation Performance who had been imprisoned in Germany this signalled the welcome opportunity to make their way home. When the Russians had entered Germany from the east, towards the end of 1944, there had been a general panic among the guards and commanders of the concentration camps. Some 800 men, including the Performance captives were evacuated to Sachsenhausen. As mentioned earlier, this was a lucky escape as the remaining prisoners in Sonnenburg were brutally murdered before the Russians arrived. When the Red Army finally marched into the abandoned concentration camp it found only three prisoners who had somehow survived the death squads.

For those in Sachsenhausen, life took an unexpected turn for the better. The Swedish Red Cross, with its vice-president Count Folke Bernadotte, was taking an interest in the camps now that the German barriers that had once refused them entry were dropping. It was possible to have food smuggled into Sachsenhausen, and for those prisoners who had been nearly starved to death in Sonnenburg this was a life-saver. Slowly the Performance men regained their strength, unaware that Bernadotte was busy negotiating with Heinrich Himmler for the release of Danish and Norwegian prisoners.

Himmler was perhaps the only Nazi chief now aware of how badly Hitler's regime had fallen, that defeat was imminent and that he had barely a chance to save himself from complete condemnation and trial by the Allies. He had to try to appear merciful. Bernadotte had spent considerable time talking to Himmler, who had wanted to discuss things like an armistice. Himmler wanted Bernadotte to convey to Churchill and the American President Truman (who had taken over the presidency after Roosevelt's death in April 1945) that he was willing to talk about peace with the Allies, and to surrender to them as long as they would allow Germany to keep resisting Russia. Bernadotte told him bluntly that he doubted that the Allies would be impressed, and needless to say they weren't. Himmler was plotting all this behind Hitler's back, trying to save face, perhaps preserve an element of German honour, and save his own neck. It wouldn't work, but while he retained hope that it would, it at least left him open to suggestions to release prisoners from concentration camps.

For the Performance men there was a noticeable increase in benevolence and kindness from their guards. Some were allowed to write short messages home, the first notes they had been able to send to say they were alive since 1943. They were allowed to mingle with other Norwegians and in January rumour ran among the men that the Germans were trying to have them moved to Austria. As it happened, this transfer was forestalled by Bernadotte's efforts. In March, Bernadotte's famous White Buses were sent to collect Norwegians and Danes from Sachsenhausen. The buses were painted completely white apart from a large red cross to show clearly that they were not military vehicles.

All but nine of the Performance men were picked up by the buses to be taken to freedom. Those that remained were among 1,000 sick prisoners deemed either too weak or too infectious to be taken by the Red Cross. These left-behind men were shipped to Bergen-Belsen, yet another camp that has gone down in history for the horrors that took place there. Bergen-Belsen had housed large numbers of Russian POWs, as well as Jewish men, women and children. Anne Frank died there.

For the 1,000 individuals sent from Sachsenhausen it came as a complete shock. Not only were conditions terrible, with inmates starving to death and dying in their hundreds, but there was a typhus epidemic circulating about the camp. When the Allies finally liberated the camp, the BBC's correspondent Richard Dimbleby was with them. He reported what he saw:

> ... here over an acre of ground lay dead and dying people. You could not see which was which ... The living lay with their heads against the corpses and around them moved the awful, ghostly procession of emaciated, aimless people, with nothing to do and with no hope of life, unable to move out of your way, unable to look at the terrible sights around them ... Babies had been born here, tiny wizened things that could not live ... This day at Belsen was the most horrible of my life.

Sick and terrified, the nine remaining Performance men found themselves among corpses and disease. They were too ill to move far or protest. When an order came two weeks later that all Norwegians and Danes should be moved to a separate part of the camp, away from the misery and despair, they did not know whether to be glad or whether this was a veiled instruction to have them killed. Thirty-two were moved to another area of the camp, while a further thirty-two were awaiting another transport which hopeful rumours held were to be 'White Buses'. Yet Bergen-Belsen already had a grip on them. Typhus started to strike down the unfortunate prisoners. When the miraculous White Buses did arrive, twenty-three of those waiting for them were sick with typhus and could not be taken. Within two weeks, twelve of these men were dead. Over the course of the next few days, the sixty-four Norwegians and Danes watched as one by one they were taken ill with the disease. One minute a man was healthy and talking; the next he was feverish and dying. The horror of not knowing who might or might not be next was appalling. As the days dragged on, the number of men whittled down further and further, until when the Red Cross at last returned on 8 April, only ten Norwegians and one Dane remained alive. These eleven men were rescued and were some of the first freed prisoners to cross the Danish border later that day.

That same day a handful of Performance men were milling about Wolfenbüttel, a barely remembered prison camp. Thirteen of them had been transferred there in 1944. Nine men remained there in 1945, and on the same day that their comrades were rescued from Bergen-Belsen, they, among 200 men, climbed aboard an old ammunition train heading for Elben. They had no idea where they were headed or what awaited them. Perhaps execution? Perhaps an even worse camp? Weak and tired, they huddled on the train, pressed against its wooden walls, trying to block out whatever fears they had. Some slept. No one realised that just on their tail were American troops and that *they* were the reason for the mass evacuation.

They arrived in the historic German medieval city Magdeburg, once home to the Holy Roman Emperor Otto I, the next day. Magdeburg was a ruined place. Heavy bombing by the RAF had left few buildings intact. The target had been a synthetic-oil factory, but the collateral damage had been high. The impressive suburbs north of the city, containing many old and fine houses, had been flattened along with the Baroque buildings lining the main street. The Germans were bitter over the loss of such an ancient and grand city and complained of 16,000 civilians killed in the raids – a more realistic figure was 2,000 to 4,000 citizens.

The Performance men stood in a city reduced to rubble, kicking their feet among brick dust and debris, hardly alert to the grandeur that had once been as they awaited the Germans' next move. There was little room to house prisoners, so the ruins of a jail were taken over temporarily. Had they been fit, the prisoners might have contemplated escape, but they were worn and weary. They huddled in rooms without ceilings and with broken-down walls. At least it was not winter, so they would not freeze to death, but there was little food or water and the desperation on their guards' faces was troubling. Word was spreading among the Nazi guards that the Americans had reached Wolfenbüttel and that it would take only two days of marching to reach Magdeburg. No one wanted to be discovered with a group of emaciated and sick prisoners; no one wanted to be held responsible.

A last stand was planned for Magdeburg, but to be on the safe side the Nazis evacuated their prisoners yet again. Some 200 weary men were forced from their temporary prison and ordered to march on. It was night, but even with little light the SS men at their posts could be spotted, and soldiers were manning defensive positions. The prisoners marched all night before finally being allowed to collapse into a train carriage. They were taken to Brandenburg-Görden and housed in yet another jail. Ominously, it was Friday the thirteenth.

The jail had an unpleasant history. Built between 1927 and 1935, it was the usual style of Nazi construction – a home for the criminal and also the political prisoner. Though initially lauded (by the Nazis) as the most modern and secure prison in Europe, it quickly became a site for execution and was used to exterminate around 10,000 physically and mentally disabled people. After the 20 July plot to kill Hitler, many of the conspirators were housed in the jail and eventually executed in a converted garage where a gallows and guillotine resided. The Performance men found the prison overcrowded and filthy. It housed more than double the capacity of prisoners it was designed for, and many were sick and starving. But if the Nazis now had plans to dispose of these prisoners – witnesses to countless atrocities – they were no longer able to implement them for the Soviet Red Army was scratching at their door. Working their way from the east, the Soviets were out to take Berlin and work their way towards Elben, while the Americans were approaching from the west. There would be no more evacuations; the prisoners were abandoned to fend for themselves as best they could, while the Germans tried to counter the attack of the Red Army.

Two long weeks brought the fighting of the war closer to the Performance men than it had ever been before. They heard the sounds of gunfire, smelled the smoke of smouldering explosives and listened to the rumble of tanks. Before long the jail was at the hub of the fighting – a last stand for the Nazis – while their prisoners watched cautiously from the windows. A bloody gunfight ensued in the streets surrounding the prison. Everyone held their breath, no one knew quite what was going to happen and hope was interlaced with fear. The hands on the clock in the jail slowly turned to 4 p.m. There had been silence for a time outside and it seemed that the fierce fighting had died down. Huddled together, those nine remaining Performance men waited and wondered.

A mumbling sound of voices came from cells on the far side of the jail; the noise grew louder; suddenly there was a scream of joy – the Russians had arrived! French prisoners flung open cell doors. The Performance men stepped out into an atmosphere of ecstasy and disbelief. Prisoners were running back and forth, hardly able to believe it. Russians were hugged and kissed, and thousands of dry, hoarse voices started to sing triumphantly the Marseillaise and any other song they could think of. After two weeks of being confined in the prison and countless months in various concentration camps, the Performance men ran out into the daylight, just nine among 3,600 prisoners who had been set free, some of whom had been hours away from execution. The relief was palpable; the moment was immense. But their saviours were the Russians, not the British or Americans, and the Soviets had no plans for dealing with such a large number of prisoners. They had done their duty and freed them; now they saw no reason to do anything more, and moved on to continue their fight against Hitler.

The Performance men filtered out into the streets, uncertain what to do. They were joined by hundreds of thousands of similar prisoners all across the area between Berlin and Elben who had been freed then abandoned. The first priority was food, and the prisoners swarmed on anything they could find, be it raw potatoes from a field or bread looted from a shop. But pickings were surprisingly slim. The mighty German war machine had consumed a large chunk of the country's economy and resources. Food was scarce for ordinary Germans and heavily rationed. In some parts the prisoners encountered conditions of starvation little better than in the camps.

For the last nine from Operation Performance this final episode was the hardest. After the exhilaration of freedom, they limped along hungry, forced to steal what they could and take from those little better off than themselves. Three weeks of this strange pilgrimage ensued before they finally stumbled upon some Americans and were taken on a transport back to Magdeburg, now part of the American zone. From there it was just a matter of time before they found their way home.

SYLVANUS'S STORY

'Brian the Lion' Reynolds was in fact born Sylvanus Brian John Reynolds in Gloucestershire in 1908. He rarely went by Sylvanus, his father's name, and by 1911 the red-haired 3-year-old was simply Brian, though he had had Bingham added to his middle names. Reynolds came from a well-to-do family. His father was a gentleman with a houseful of servants; his mother was 10 years junior to her husband.

Reynolds craved adventure, and the lure of the sea was great. He was a good sailor and overflowing with patriotism and bravery, and by 1945 he had earned a DSC and an MBE for his services. Probably peacetime would not have suited him. He lived for action and returning to a quiet post-war existence would have been hard. He never found out if he could cope with peace as well as he could cope with war.

Two days after VE Day, Reynolds boarded a naval MGB with a crew of thirty-two on a mission to retrieve the *Dicto* and *Lionel*. The tankers that had caused contention for the last five years were about to be brought to England, even if their contents were now of little importance. It was the tail-end of the operations begun with Rubble, and once the two tankers were unloaded they would be returned to Norway and the last loose end would be wound up.

Reynolds was enthusiastic as always. He loved going to sea in the MGBs, despite their ability to make the hardiest sailor seasick. He left Aberdeen on a clear day and was never seen again.

Four days later, a search party came across a raft with two survivors clinging to it. The men were incoherent and uncertain of what had happened, but it was assumed that the MGB had been unfortunate enough to sail into a floating mine. Throughout Bridford and Moonshine, Reynolds had avoided such perils in foul weather and darkness. Now, in peacetime with the best of conditions, he had struck a mine and perished. So that was the end of Sylvanus Brian John (Bingham) Reynolds.

While Reynolds was disappearing into Scottish waters, the formal organisations that had appeared as a direct result of war were being slowly discontinued and wrapped up. SOE, so fundamentally helpful to Binney, was closing down, disposing of many of its files and keeping only a skeleton crew to address any outstanding problems. By 1946, there would be no SOE, and Charles Hambro would happily return to the world of banking.

Bill Waring earned a CMG for his administrative efforts during the various blockade-running operations. Though the least glamorous part of the missions, his role was vitally important and effectively ensured that they happened. He had negotiated tirelessly with ministers, dealt with the purchasing of the contraband materials, and seen to all the other dull but necessary administrative tasks that kept Binney's crews and their adventures afloat. By the end of the war he had amassed a mountain of detailed records.

Aside from helping Binney, he had been responsible for negotiating with the governments of the various dominions, and with the Russians once they switched sides – by far the most taxing of tasks, as the Soviets had no appreciation for the difficulties faced by the British shipping goods from Sweden past the aggressive Nazis. They complained about water damage to tubes left on the *Dicto* and *Lionel* and begrudged not being able to insure their cargoes when they sailed in British ships. They never took into account that secret dangerous operations are naturally uninsurable!

Waring took a new and rather ironic role after VE Day – he became head of Steel Control in Germany. Over the next few years he moved from job to job, spending time at the British steelworks firm GKN, before becoming head of the steel division of the Economic Commission for Europe in Geneva and then returning to GKN. He parted from Anne Waring and later married Sue Jacob, but it was a short-lived union as he died in a plane crash at Luxembourg in 1962 while on his way to a meeting.

Victor Mallet left Sweden and went first to Spain to be an ambassador and then to Italy in 1947, where he remained until 1953. The quietness of post-war life enabled him to indulge an interest in writing, and he wrote the book *Life with Queen Victoria*, which was based on letters written by his mother, who had been maid of honour to the queen. The book was published a year before he died in 1969.

Even a heart attack could not keep George Binney still for long. Irritated that his recovery had not been fast enough to enable him to go on the last Moonshine operation, he didn't consider peace an excuse to slow down. After the war he returned to United Steel, which had so kindly 'loaned' him to Sweden in those early days of conflict. Binney returned to a life of travel, good dinners and endless meetings. He travelled widely until his retirement, always busy and always active.

Peter Tennant stayed in touch with him and persistently told him to write a memoir about his operations. Binney liked the idea, but the literary spirit was one he couldn't quite muster. He fussed over sentences and was never satisfied with what he had written. Considering his lengthy efforts over memos, this is unsurprising. He ended up with an extensive pile of papers and drafts, out of which he was certain he could make at least three books and a film. But it never happened. Somehow, despite all the material, a final book eluded Binney. Still, he was content to write and rewrite his adventures and to tell the stories of Rubble and Performance over dinner with guests.

Binney married Sonia Simms, widow of Lieutenant Colonel Simms, who had been a prisoner of war in Italy, in 1955. Sonia had played her own part in the war as a code-breaker. She had an 11-year-old son, Marcus, who would go on to become an architectural historian and author, notably writing about his stepfather's experiences during Operation Performance in *Secret War Heroes*.

George Binney finally settled down to a quiet life, retiring to a peaceful old house at La Domaine des Vaux, Jersey, where he spent considerable time redesigning the large garden. His pleasures now revolved around antiques, which had always held a fascination for him, and digging, weeding and planting in his garden. Tennant paid him a visit just before his death. 'The last I saw of him was with a hoe in his hand, his white hair and blue eyes glinting in the sun.'

The mastermind of Operation Rubble, Performance, Bridford and Moonshine died on 27 September 1972. He had requested that the flag he had flown when greeting the British destroyers after he had successfully crossed the Skagerrak during Operation Rubble be draped over his coffin, and this was done. George Binney – Arctic explorer, adventurer, steel trade expert and wartime hero – was laid to rest with the memory of his greatest achievement lingering in the air.

AS SHIPS WE SAIL

The last survivors of the blockade operations were the ships that had sailed from Sweden to England. For those which had not sunk to the bottom of the ocean, their war work had just begun, and of course their crews were with them every step of the way.

The *Elisabeth Bakke* took part in various convoy operations after Rubble. She travelled to Bombay and New York, crossing German-patrolled waters without serious incident. During the invasion of north Africa (Torch operations) she became a troop transport and carried men to Gibraltar. The *Elisabeth Bakke* led a charmed life. In 1943, she was headed for New York again when the convoy she was part of was attacked. However, she had sailed ahead and missed the drama. In the same year, on another voyage across the Atlantic, her crew witnessed a fierce U-boat attack on a different convoy, during which the Germans used newly developed 'Gnat' torpedoes with hydrophone technology that enabled them to track targets by their propeller movements. Two ships were sunk, but the Gnat torpedoes were not as effective as the Germans had hoped and the U-boats suffered heavier losses in subsequent attacks. The *Elisabeth Bakke* completed her voyage unharmed yet again.

Surviving the war with barely a scratch, she returned to Norway and to a peaceful life in transport. In August 1970, she was sold and her name shortened to *Elisabeth*. She went on various short trading voyages around Norway and was sold twice more, eventually being renamed *Bigra*. In 1974, she made her last voyage, towed to a Spanish breakers' yard.

The *John Bakke* also became part of important trade convoys for the British, but her time at sea was less charmed. In late 1942 (there is some query over the exact date, but probably at the end of November or beginning of December) the *John Bakke* collided with a British ship in the same convoy as herself and caused serious damage. The British ship had to be abandoned by its crew. The *John Bakke* received only minor damage that did not prevent her sailing, but her crew's chagrin at hitting a fellow ship was palpable.

She was now more heavily armed and crewed by a sizeable force of gunners – and she needed to be. She was regularly attacked, even when off-loading cargo in contested ports. Though she was never seriously damaged, she did suffer one crew loss, a mechanic, ironically due to an accident rather than enemy action. She was still at sea when peace was declared and her crew celebrated VE Day afloat.

After the war, the *John Bakke* returned to Norway and her regular trade routes. During the course of one of these voyages she had an unfortunate accident and ran aground. It was possible to refloat her, but a closer examination of the damage sealed her fate. She was old, and the damage extensive and not worth repairing. In October 1964, the *John Bakke* was condemned and towed to a breakers' yard.

The *Tai Shan* found convoy work dangerous. Not long after her successful escape from Sweden she made a voyage to New York. On returning, she was attacked by a lone Focke-Wulf that came at her with bombs and machine guns blazing. Now away from Sweden, there were no restrictions on armaments aboard civilian vessels and the *Tai Shan* was well armed to take on a lone plane. Her gunners jumped to their places and were able to return fire and damage the aircraft. It limped away, but it was not clear if it crashed. The *Tai Shan* was probably damaged on this venture, as she stayed in port at Liverpool for over a month before setting out on her next voyage, implying that she had been undergoing repairs. This was a pattern for the *Tai Shan*, which would often spend extended periods in harbour after a voyage. There is an unconfirmed story that she sank in Liverpool harbour on one occasion, indicating that she was not in the best condition. She eventually returned to Norway and for fifteen years served in peaceful waters, but war had apparently taken its toll. In 1960, it was considered that she was no longer fit for sailing and she was sent to Japan to be scrapped.

The story of the *Taurus* is even sadder. She had joined the convoys like her comrades shortly after Operation Rubble and for several months had led an uneventful existence. Then, on 6 June 1941, she had just reached Scottish waters, carrying a cargo of around 7,000 tons of groundnuts, palm kernels and cocoa, when she was attacked by a German aircraft. Her guns had been manned throughout the voyage, and though it was just after midnight, her gunners were alert and started firing at the plane as it came into view. The strategy had worked before, but on this occasion the plane made a daring dive close to the ship and dropped three bombs. Bombs were a highly inaccurate means of hitting floating targets, but on this occasion the *Taurus*'s luck failed her. The bombs exploded in the water just off her stern and port, the blast damaging the hull and allowing water to leak into the engine room. The *Taurus* began to list badly to port with her stern sinking as well. The rising water in the engine room shorted the electrics and within minutes it was clear that she was doomed. Orders were given to stop her engine, seal the engine room and shackle her steering, giving the crew enough time to find help.

The rising water had also shorted out the emergency radio transmitter, making it impossible to radio a distress. Instead the crew had to resort to old-fashioned methods and used a Morse lamp to signal to another ship in their convoy that they needed a tow. HMS *Tarantella*, one of the escort vessels, came to her aid. It was now around 2.15 a.m. and the *Tarantella* attempted to tow the *Taurus* to the nearest sandy beach north of Montrose Bay, hoping to ground her. They had not gone far when another enemy aircraft appeared to harass them. The plane came in low and dropped another three bombs, these landing once more on the *Taurus*'s port side. Fortunately they were further away and did not add to her damage.

Towing recommenced at 3 a.m., but the delay had enabled the stricken ship to take on a lot more water and sink lower. The *Tarantella* changed course to a nearer bay at Johnshaven when it became apparent that the *Taurus* was perilously close to being lost, but her efforts were in vain. By 5.30 a.m., with the weather deteriorating, her aft deck was level with the water and all but those crew essential to helping with the towing operation were evacuated onto life-rafts. The *Taurus* slipped further into the water and by 6.15 a.m. it was apparent that she could not be saved. The remaining crew abandoned ship and watched one of the heroes of Operation Rubble sink to the bottom of the ocean at 6.22 a.m. The last that was seen of the *Taurus* were a few bubbles caused by escaping air, and then she was gone.

The *Ranja* suffered a similar fate. She had been serving in convoys since Operation Rubble and was making a voyage as part of a convoy in early 1942 to Galveston, Texas. After dropping off her cargo, the *Ranja* headed out of Galveston alone to join another convoy, now loaded with a cargo of oil. She was spotted by a U-boat just before 6 p.m. on 17 March. It trailed her for an hour, her crew of thirty-four men completely unaware of the danger to them lurking below the water. It was almost 7 p.m. when the U-boat fired two torpedoes. Both hit the bridge just forward of the funnel and a huge plume of flame soared into the air. The oil cargo was apparently hit and within seconds the *Ranja*'s front half was engulfed in fire. She limped on valiantly, listing to port and sinking, her speed having dropped to a fraction of what it normally was.

The crew of the U-boat watched her struggle for almost an hour, until they finally grew bored and fired another torpedo just before 8 p.m. This was a surface torpedo aimed at the forward masts. It hit with a gigantic explosion and the ship disappeared into a ball of flame. The smoke from the burning ship obscured almost everything, but the U-boat crew saw the mast and the bridge collapse and the foredeck vanish below the water. Though they did not see her sink, it was clear that she had and by 8.06 p.m. they were satisfied with their work and left the scene. Of the thirty Norwegians, one Swede, one Dane and two British gunners aboard, not a single man survived.

All were either consumed by the oil-fuelled flames or drowned. The *Ranja*'s end was one of the most hideous endured by any of the blockade-runners.

Only four of the Performance vessels survived the operation. Of those four, the *B.P. Newton* was the newest, having been built only in 1940, and she was the best known among the sailors for the lengthy legal wrangles that had surrounded her attempt to leave Swedish waters. When she was finally able to sail, it was to the great relief of her crew. After her successful crossing of the Skagerrak, the *Newton* became a regular convoy ship for the next year. In July 1943, she was heading to London from Trinidad with a cargo of aviation fuel and oil. As the *Ranja*'s crew had fatally discovered, that was one of the worst cargoes to be carrying when in danger of attack. The *Newton* was part of a convoy of twenty vessels escorted by American ships and one Brazilian when at 1.25 a.m. a torpedo came out of nowhere and struck her between No 3 and No 4 tanks. Her cargo of oil was immediately ignited and splashed flaming fuel across her deck and bridge. Within moments she was completely ablaze. The fire was so bright that men on nearby ships could read papers without any other light.

In the engine room every man was dead. They had either been killed in the explosion or burned to death in the choking flames and smoke. This meant that the engine could not be stopped. The lifeboats were all ablaze and desperate men jumped overboard; in the panic many jumped over the wrong side and were caught in the flaming oil that had leaked onto the surface of the water. Others ran to the front of the ship, which was not yet ablaze, and tried to seek refuge there, while the captain and gunnery officer stayed on the bridge to see if anything could be done. They managed to extinguish the flames burning on the midships lifeboat, but it was badly damaged and full of water. They launched it anyway, as their only salvation, and four men jumped from the fo'c'sle to reach the lifeboat. Another twelve were fished from the water, all badly burned, with a mechanic in particular suffering extensively from his wounds. He was treated as best he could be in the lifeboat, before one of the American escorts picked up the men and took him to their doctor.

Another seven *Newton* men had had a fraught time. They were first rescued from the water by a lifeboat from the American ship *Eldena*, which had also been sunk by the U-boat, and were then transferred to another ship and finally reunited with their crewmates. Twenty-five men had been rescued from the *Newton*, but twenty-two had perished. The mechanic joined the dead later that day, dying from his burns and being buried at sea.

It had never been expected that the tiny *Lind* would make the Skagerrak crossing when other bigger, faster and better armed ships had failed. But survive she did. She lived out the rest of the war making journeys around Britain and avoiding the dangerous convoy routes – though by no means was coastal shipping a safe occupation during the war years. She was sold to France in 1947, but lasted only a year before she was badly damaged running aground. She did not go back into service and the valiant *Lind* ended her days as a shipwreck.

The *Dicto* and *Lionel* had never experienced the conflict of convoy-running and the war was merely an interruption in their usual voyages. They returned to work in Norway shortly after relieving themselves of their British cargo. The *Dicto* was sold to Greece in 1964 and became the *Onisolos*. She was eventually broken up in 1970. The *Lionel* was sold to Switzerland in 1955 and renamed the *Aguante*. In 1964, she made one last voyage to Britain, to be broken up at the Grays shipyard.

The blockade-runners were valiant, brave and heroic men. Because their mission was to save steel and ball bearings from the clutches of the Nazis rather than people or strategic locations, their story is often forgotten. Their sacrifice is also largely consigned to the archives. Even books on the subject gloss over a great deal of the suffering experienced by the men who took part in the operations.

George Binney, Bill Waring and the many men and women who helped get steel to Britain during the war years saved our country from defeat. Without those loads, supplemented by scant resources from America, we could not have continued to build planes, guns and tanks. We could not have equipped our troops. The Nazis knew this and that is why they tried so hard to prevent us bringing our cargoes from Sweden. If they had succeeded, history would have told a very different story about the war.

It is remarkable to think that a tiny ball bearing could be the key to success or defeat; that men gave their lives for a small lump of steel, conspired over it, plotted for it; and risked torture and retribution for something as minor as a ball bearing. Utterly remarkable, and yet it happened, and that is why this book has charted the story of an adventure that began with a tiny ball bearing.

SELECT BIBLIOGRAPHY

Andersson, Dr Ingvar, *A History of Sweden*, Anglo-Saxon Literary Foundation, 1956.

Binney, Marcus, *Secret War Heroes: Men of the Special Operations Executive*, Hodder & Stoughton, 2005.

Burn, Alan, *The Fighting Commodores: Convoy Commanders in the Second World War*, Pen & Sword, 1999.

Burt, R.A., *British Destroyers in World War Two*, Arms and Armour Press, 1985.

Churchill, Winston, *The Second World War: The Twilight War*, Cassell, 1964.

Davies, Peter, *Dangerous Liaisons: Collaboration and World War Two*, Pearson Education Ltd, 2004.

Derry, T.K., *The Campaign in Norway*, HMSO, 1952.

Haarr, Geirr H., *The German Invasion of Norway: April 1940*, Seaforth, 2009.

Harriman, Florence Jaffray, *Mission to the North*, J.B. Lippincott, 1941.

Harrison, W.A., *Fairey Swordfish and Albacore*, The Crowood Press, 2002.

Harvey, Maurice, *Scandinavian Misadventure: The Campaign in Norway 1940*, Spellmount Ltd, 1990.

Konstam, Angus, *British Motor Gun Boat 1939–45*, Osprey Publishing Ltd, 2010.

Oakley, Stewart, *The Story of Sweden*, Faber & Faber, 1966.

Rhys-Jones, Graham, *Churchill and the Norway Campaign*, Pen & Sword, 2008.

Roskill, Stephen, *The Navy at War 1939–1945*, Wordsworth Editions Ltd, 1998.

Tennant, Peter, *Touchlines of War*, The University of Hull Press, 1992.

The London Gazette (Supplement), 16 October 1945.

'The Sonnenburg Torture Camp' by an Escaped Prisoner (pamphlet published in 1934).

The Times Archives.

SOE Operation Files, The National Archives, Kew.

INDEX